Xenophon and the
Art of Command

THE PRINCIPLES OF WAR

Selection and maintenance of the Aim
Maintenance of Morale
Offensive Action
Surprise
Concentration of Force
Economy of Effort
Security
Flexibility
Co-operation
Administration

'The principles given . . . have been evolved by experience as generally applicable to the leading of troops. They are to be regarded by all ranks as authoritative, for their violation, in the past, has often been followed by mishap, if not disaster. They should be so thoroughly impressed on the mind of every commander, that whenever he has to come to a decision in the field, he instinctively gives them full weight.

The fundamental principles of war are neither very numerous nor in themselves very abstruse, but the application of them is difficult and cannot be made subject to rules. The correct application of principles to circumstances is the outcome of sound military knowledge, built up by study and practice until it has become an instinct.'

From Field Service Regulations, Part 1: *Operations* (1909) and reprinted in 0229, Army Doctrine Publication, Vol. 1: *Operations* (June 1994).

XENOPHON AND THE ART OF COMMAND

Godfrey Hutchinson

Greenhill Books, London
Stackpole Books, Pennsylvania

Xenophon and the Art of Command
first published 2000 by Greenhill Books,
Lionel Leventhal Limited, Park House, 1 Russell Gardens,
London NW11 9NN
and
Stackpole Books, 5067 Ritter Road, Mechanicsburg, PA 17055, USA

British Library Cataloguing in Publication Data
Hutchinson, Godfrey
Xenophon: and the art of command
1. Xenophon 2. Military art and science – History – To 500
3. Greece – History – Spartan and Theban Supremacies, 404–362 B.C.
I. Title
355'.00938

ISBN 1–85367–417–6

Library of Congress Cataloging-in-Publication Data
Hutchinson, Godfrey.
Xenophon: and the art of command/Godfrey Hutchinson.
p. cm.
Includes bibliographical references and index.
ISBN 1-85367-417-6
1. Xenophon – Military leadership.   2. Generals – Greece – Biography.
3. Historians – Greece – Biography.   4. Military art and science – Greece.
I. Title.

DF232.X4 H88 2000
938'.105'092 – dc21
[B]   00-038077

Typeset by DP Photosetting, Aylesbury, Bucks
Printed and bound in Great Britain by Creative Print and Design (Wales), Ebbw Vale

CONTENTS

LIST OF ILLUSTRATIONS

Maps

Plates

Battle Plans

Acknowledgements

In the production of this study I am greatly indebted to two people. To my wife, who firmly suggested that I do something a little more positive with my life-long passion for Ancient History other than read other people's work eulogising at one moment and muttering disagreement at another; and to John Lazenby, Professor of Ancient History at the University of Newcastle upon Tyne. It was he who lured me away from my main area of interest, that of Alexander's Successors, to the subject of this present study. His guidance and positive criticisms as my work progressed have been stimulating and invaluable and any shortcomings are entirely my own.

My thanks must also go to G.B. Watson who created the maps and plans, to the cartographer, John Richards, and to the photographers, A. Tatham and N. Overton.

Godfrey Hutchinson
Staindrop, 2000

PREFACE

We owe a significant debt to Xenophon in terms of recording military detail for a period which would otherwise be bereft of contemporary evidence. The period he writes of was one of transition both militarily and politically. Important to many of his contemporaries and to those thereafter who read him would be the clear evaluations which he gives in terms of qualitative command. The details we gather in terms of tactical development, the changes in the uses of ancillary forces and the information which he passed on concerning Persia go a long way to prepare us for the exploits of Phillip II and Alexander. However, he reminds us that much more is to be expected of a good commander than mere knowledge of tactics.

Brief Biography of Xenophon

Born in the last third of the fifth century, possibly around 430 BC, the young Xenophon experienced the tribulations of Athens which led to her defeat in the Peloponnesian War. As a member of a wealthy family he probably saw cavalry action in that war. Certainly the detailed account of actions in Lydia in 410 BC on the Asian littoral indicate that of a participant (*Hell.* I.ii.1–13). His formative years under the tutelage of Socrates and his social position led him to condemn many of the actions of the democrats, e.g., the illegality of the death sentence passed on the victorious generals at Arginusae in 406 BC and the lost opportunity for peace after the Athenian naval success at Kyzicos in 410 BC.

The short-lived brutal rule of the Thirty, a tyrannical oligarchy set up by the Spartans in Athens immediately following the end of the war, led to further political uncertainties. As an active young man of his class, Xenophon decided to leave. In the spring of 401 BC he accepted the invitation of his Boeotian friend Proxenos to join the expedition of Kyros the Younger. Kyros' attempt to topple his brother from the Persian throne failed with his death at the battle of Kounaxa, leaving the Greek forces within his army stranded at the heart of the Persian empire. With the loss of a significant part of its command structure through treachery the Greeks voted Xenophon as one of their new generals. In the course of the hard fought withdrawal through Asia Minor Xenophon eventually became commander-in-chief. His compelling account of this in the *Anabasis* describes one of the most astonishing military experiences in history.

Initially, the approach to Europe of this large mercenary force provoked trepidation. However, when it arrived in the Hellespontine region its strategic position was eventually recognised by the Spartans as an extremely useful resource in their war against the Persians. Xenophon continued to command the surviving portion of his mercenary army first under Thibron and then under Derkylidas from 399 BC. In 396 BC, when Agesilaos, one of the kings of Sparta, was given command of an expedition against the Persians Xenophon served under him until the time when Persian money given to Sparta's enemies resulted in the Corinthian War (395–386 BC) and the consequent recall of Agesilaos from Asia Minor by Sparta in 394 BC. Xenophon along with many of the mercenaries accompanied the returning army and saw action at the battle of Koroneia, fighting against his fellow Athenians who were allied to the Boeotians. Thereafter, he lived as an exile from his homeland in Spartan held territories where, because of his service to the Spartans, he was granted an estate at Skillous just south of Olympia. After the Battle of Leuktra in 371 BC, with the successive invasions of the Peloponnese by the Theban led forces, he lost his estate to the enemy and lived for a time in Corinth. At this point, however, Athens allied herself with Sparta and Xenophon's exile was repealed. In 362BC, just prior to Second Mantineia, one of his two sons, Gryllus, serving with the Athenian cavalry, was killed. This is the year in which Xenophon concluded his history.

It is likely that he returned to Athens soon after where he wrote his work on the finances of the city. The year of his death is not known.

The Main Locations in the Text

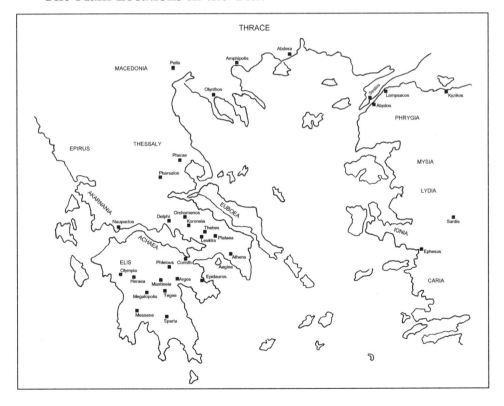

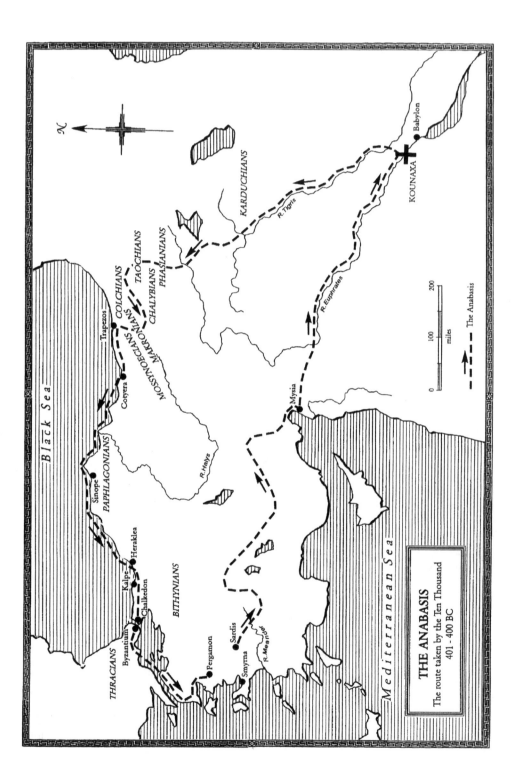

Black Sea

Mediterranean Sea

Babylon

KOUNAXA

R. Tigris

R. Euphrates

KARDUCHIANS

COLCHIANS
TAÓCHIANS
PHASIANIANS
CHALYBIANS
MOSYNOECIANS
MAKRONIANS

Trapezos

Cotyora

Mysia

R. Halys

Sinope

PAPHLAGONIANS

Heraklea

Kalpe

Chalkedon

Byzantium

THRACIANS

BITHYNIANS

Pergamon

Sardis

Smyrna

R. Meander

0   100   200
miles

The Anabasis

THE ANABASIS

The route taken by the Ten Thousand
401 - 400 BC

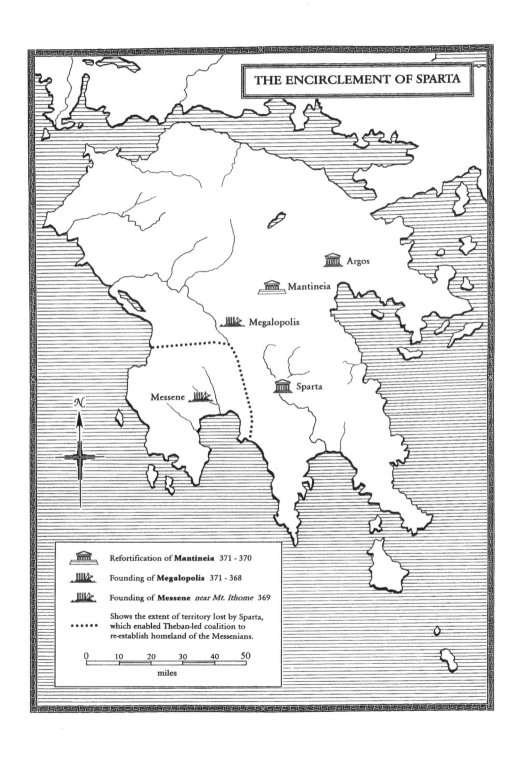

THE ENCIRCLEMENT OF SPARTA

Argos

Mantineia

Megalopolis

Sparta

Messene

N

Refortification of **Mantineia** 371 - 370

Founding of **Megalopolis** 371 - 368

Founding of **Messene** *near Mt. Ithome* 369

Shows the extent of territory lost by Sparta,
which enabled Theban-led coalition to
re-establish homeland of the Messenians.

0   10   20   30   40   50

miles

INTRODUCTION

There is none better to look to than Xenophon for an insight into the roles fulfilled by a commander in the first half of the fourth century BC. His background of personal command, close relationships with other commanders of note such as Agesilaos, Teleutias, Sphodrias, Thibron, Archidamos, etc., make his writings a rich vein to mine.

His corpus can be divided into three sections: his own life and interests, the historical and political writings and historical fiction. Each in turn forms the basis of the three main parts of this book.

The purpose of this study is to examine those aspects of command which are recurrent in his writings and reflect those which he and obviously his contemporaries thought important for anyone undertaking the role of a commander. Examples of good and bad practice abound and Xenophon's evaluations of them are highlighted. The approach is thematic rather than chronological so that comparisons between sections of the text and themes can more easily be made. As a result, differing aspects of the same action are often explored across a range of themes so that the fourth century benchmark for good command is clarified.

Direct scrutiny of contemporaneous source material is essential so that a valid picture emerges. To the modern reader some of the themes under which the examination of source material is carried out may come as a surprise. Piety, for example, can often be overlooked as a major day-to-day concern of the Ancient World.

In addition frequent reference is made to another early writer Sun Tzu, a near contemporary of Xenophon and a Chinese general whose views bear remarkable similarity to those investigated here. This may appear strange in a text which is dealing with a fifty-year period of Greek warfare but both are important as early writers on military theory. To compare similar viewpoints a half a world apart reinforces the notion that fundamental principles have a universality whatever the context.

The reader should be aware that the Kyros the Younger referred to in Parts

One and Two of the main text should not be confused with the Kyros who is the subject of the third part, The Ideal Commander. In references to the former, Xenophon is dealing with historical fact. With the Kyros of the *Kyropaideia* (The Education of Kyros), Xenophon is giving a fictional account of the life and virtues of Kyros the Great and in so doing theorises on the minutiae of good command.

Nothing is new in the principles of warfare or in the decisions facing a commander engaged in operations. It is only their applications which differ. Throughout historic times parallels can be made between actions which took place many centuries apart, the only differences being the technology and the differing weapon systems employed, and the skills of the commander. Whether an action is one of offence or defence or simply one of delay, the same considerations are addressed in the pursuit of a successful outcome.

However, these considerations are coloured by the prevailing viewpoint of the times in which they are undertaken. On occasion those involved were slow to appreciate the prevailing conditions, resulting in the misapplication of the very principles they sought to follow. Prime examples can be found in the annals of the First World War where old practices were applied to new conditions. The work of Fuller and Liddel Hart did much to address the need for constant reappraisal of practices within changing conditions. Thus it is no surprise that, following the Gulf War and the collapse of the Warsaw Pact, the recognition by the armed services that the concept of deterrence was now inappropriate to the new conditions led to a reappraisal of British Military Doctrine. The resulting publications were issued in June 1994 showing modified applications to unchanged principles. At this time they remain restricted under the Official Secrets Acts of 1911–1989 but readers who are, or have been recently, members of the armed forces will be familiar with their content. Such references from them within the end notes to each part of the main text are given in the knowledge that, for the foreseeable future, there will be limited access to these publications. However, it is hoped that in their limited use the underlying message will be clear to the reader.

At no time, however, during the last forty years were the western allies and the British Army, in particular, unmindful of the differing traditions, strategies and tactics of their possible opponents. The disasters of the Russian campaigns of Napoleon and Hitler had proved that there were other routes to success in warfare and that a blinkered adherence to Clausewitz was not enough, for in ignoring the role of the Cossacks had he not sacrificed factual example to preserve his theories untrammelled? Yet behind such Russian successes with a mode of warfare which took cognisance of eastern as well as western practice, lie the same principles stretching back in time to the writings of Sun Tzu some two and a half thousand years ago, those principles which he, as a commander, had to take into account and which Xenophon some hundred years later had to address.

The historical writings of Xenophon (*Hellenika*) which are the subject of the second part of this book cover the period from the closing years of the Peloponnesian War to the events of 362 BC and catalogue the decline of Sparta as a significant power and its failure to convert its hegemony to enduring purpose. The Persian Empire, stretching as it did from the Aegean to Sogdiana, Bactria, Ferghana and the fringes of northern India, led its rulers also to appreciate differences between the methodology employed by eastern and western styles of warfare. This gave rise to their application occasionally of 'eastern' methodology to their western neighbours during the Peloponnesian War and, in particular, during the first half of the fourth century, so as to ensure their own secure defence by keeping possible opponents divided (Sun Tzu III.2; III.3; III.6; VIII.10). Living through, but writing after many of the events described, Xenophon can be seen taking an analytical view of military matters when engaged in such essays as the 'Cavalry Commander', e.g., his suggestion that cavalry should have units of infantry attached (*Hipp*. V.13) and a tactical example of their use (*Hipp*. VIII.19). More importantly, he was aware of the purpose behind Persian machinations throughout the period of which he writes: the policy of setting Greek against Greek. Moreover, he makes it clear that Agesilaos understood this 'eastern' stratagem (Xen. *Ages*. VII.5–7). It is to be regretted that the city states were so easily manipulated.

The Greek and Persian modes of warfare differed mainly in the traditions in which they were formulated. The former relying on brief but decisive encounters of massed forces of heavy infantry at close quarters, the latter on more protracted encounters in which the use of missiles at long range was an important component. The Greeks had overcome the horror of death at close quarters whereas the Persians preferred death to be a distant occurrence. Both were the products of their topography. Greece being a mountainous region wherein major engagements took place on the flat plains surrounded by ranges led to slowly developing formulaic practice. Persia by contrast, adopted military arms best suited for the conditions in which they were to be used and, more importantly, against whom they were to be used, leading to the inclusion in their forces of mercenaries mirroring those of their adversary. Hence the inclusion of a Greek mercenary phalanx in many of their engagements in

Anatolia and the Aegean littoral. Persia's greatest strength lay in its calvary arm. To avoid any misunderstanding it is as well, at this juncture, to stress that while Greek warfare can be termed 'western', that of the Persians cannot be termed 'eastern'. Persia lay between the two and, being affected by both, like later Russian practice, developed its own individual style in dealing with neighbours.

Xenophon is of particular interest in that his personal experience led him to have knowledge of both Greek and Persian traditions. The information to be derived from his writings is invaluable on a wide variety of topics. The criticisms of inaccuracy and bias levelled against him relate only to the *Hellenika* and are sometimes not without bias in themselves. Therein much is based on first hand knowledge or obviously from reports from persons he knew and respected, not least his hero, Agesilaos. What is surprising is that his account is not more imbalanced. A highly competent soldier himself, his descriptions are in the main clear on strategy and tactics even if the reader is sometimes denied the component layout of a battle line. If he sins it is by omission and this seems to be striking in the case of Agesilaos' Persian campaign, his lack of comment on Tegyra, and as a reflection of his dislike of the Thebans. Xenophon's studied avoidance of any reference to Epameinondas at Leuktra is significant. It can only be presumed that grudging acknowledgement of the Theban commander's skills led him to give an even handed account of the second battle of Mantineia. However, Xenophon's writings prove to be a veritable treasure-house for examples of good and bad practice in terms of the exercise of military command. Our knowledge of the military history of the fourth century BC would be massively poorer without his output. The *Anabasis* (see Glossary), the greater part of which concerns the first part of this book, describes an astonishing feat by any standards. Yet more surprising is the rise of the young Xenophon himself from the position of an untried private person accompanying his friend Proxenos on the expedition, to that of general and eventually, by virtue of his skills, to that of supreme commander of the Greek forces.

The Historical Context

As a continuation of Thucydides history the period covered by Xenophon's writings is between the years 411 to 362 BC.

The closing years of the Peloponnesian War were fought almost entirely at sea. As a result of the Treaty of Miletus (412 BC) Sparta acknowledged the right of Darius the Persian king to exercise control over the Greek cities of Ionia in return for funding the building and manning of a navy. This done, the ending of the war was long in coming with oligarchic and democratic revolutions in Athens following hard upon each other between 411–410 BC, and with vascillating Persian Satraps siding in part with Athens in the hope that both Athens and Sparta would exhaust themselves and leave Greece at the mercy of Persia. It was only in 408 BC that the Persian king, tired of his Satraps modifying his agreed policy with Sparta, decided to give his young son Kyros overall control of Asia Minor. This proved to be the turning point of the war. With the unremitting support of Persia, Sparta, with few setbacks, gained the ascendancy. Lysander defeated the Athenian fleet off Notium (406 BC) and this resulted in the dismissal of Alkibiades, the Athenian commander-in-chief, who had left his lieutenant in charge of the fleet. Fearing his political enemies in Athens Alkibiades did not return to the city but went instead to his castle in Thrace. Thus was removed the one man who might have warded off Athen's eventual downfall.

A temporary respite was won for the Athenians later in the year at Arginusae where the Spartans lost approximately seventy ships and over thirteen thousand men. However, in the storm which accompanied the action the seas proved too rough for the Athenians to rescue the crews of their sunken vessels. In a gross miscarriage of justice six of the Athenian commanders were brought to trial and executed on a charge of negligence, the two remaining having gone into exile rather than return to their city. So, within the course of one year, Athens had lost the services of a large number of its generals.

Despite a Spartan offer of peace, the Athenians foolishly decided to carry on hostilities and from this point on, with continued Persian support against an increasingly destitute and desperate Athens, Sparta effected a stranglehold on her enemy's corn supply through the Hellespont. Following Lysander's crushing victory in 405 BC at Aegospotami, where the Athenians lost 160 ships, a naval blockade of Athens by the Spartan fleet and the presence of the Spartan army to the landward side of the city led to the inevitable surrender of Athens.

From this point on (404 BC) Sparta appeared to be the strongest power in Greece for the next thirty years. Initially, Lysander set up military governors in each of the Greek cities in Asia Minor supported by garrisons and a government of thirty pro-Spartan oligarchs in Athens. This last arrangement did not last long and democracy was restored in Athens in 403 BC and, thereafter, Lysander's political power base declined in Sparta largely on suspicion that he was conspiring to change the Spartan constitution for personal advantage.

The ending of the war produced its own problems. Large numbers of men for whom soldiering had become the only skill they possessed were now without immediate employment. Many came from the more impoverished areas of the northern Peloponnese and these proved a ready pool from which the Younger Kyros could build a secret army to make his attempt to unseat his newly crowned brother Artaxerxes II. Moral and clandestine support from Sparta was assured in gratitude for Kyros' sustained help in the last stages of the Peloponnesian War. Thus from the autumn of 401 BC to the summer of 400 BC the 'Ten Thousand' fought their way back from the heart of Persia after Kyros' death at Kounaxa.

Initially the Spartans at the Hellespont were wary of this force but eventually found employment for them from 399 BC in their war against the Persians in support of the Aegean Greek cities. In 396 BC King Agesilaos of Sparta campaigned in Asia Minor and in retaliation Persia, through the agency of Timokrates, disbursed gold to those Greek states which had been disaffected by the harshness and volatile nature of Sparta's authority. Those states such as Thebes and Corinth, which as allies of Sparta during the Peloponnesian War and which had called at its end for the destruction of Athens, now joined with Argos and Athens in a protracted and inconclusive struggle against Sparta and her remaining allies (Corinthian War 395–386 BC).

With the death of Lysander in an attack on Thebes early in the conflict Sparta recalled Agesilaos from Asia Minor. Just prior to his arrival at the prospective theatre of operations Sparta and her allies defeated the dissidents at Nemea. Konon defeated the Spartan fleet at Knidos in 394 BC, but with the suppression of this adverse piece of news Agesilaos defeated the land forces of the opposing alliance at Koroneia. With Konon's return to Athens in 393 BC Persian money helped rebuild the Long walls and refortify the Piraeus while the Persians saw that all Spartan garrisons within the Aegean were eliminated.

In 389 BC Sparta approached Persia through the agency of Antalkidas in search of a cessation of hostilities. Persia at that time was concerned at the growing revival of Athenian power in the Aegean and summoned all Greek states to Sardis in 386 BC to sign the 'King's Peace'. Its terms stated that all Greek states were to be autonomous and Sparta was to be the guarantor, by force if necessary. Athens was to retain Skyros, Lemnos and Imbros, and Persia was to control all cities in Asia. This meant that Thebes lost its control of the Boeotian League and was regarded as a separate state along with the rest of the

Boeotian cities. Thus Spartan supremacy on the mainland was sustained and her ultra-conservatism and interference in the political structures of the so-called liberated Greek states did little to enamour those she claimed to defend. This can be said to be the start of the period of true Spartan hegemony which lasted until 371 BC.

Sparta's actions against other states displayed an increasing arrogance. In 382 BC Thebes was taken directly under Spartan control by an act of deception on the part of Phoibidas. Three years earlier Sparta had destroyed the fortifications of Mantineia and by 379 BC had effected the dissolution of the Chalkidian League. The failed attempt of Sphodrias to capture the Piraeus by an overnight march one year later indicates some of the high handed actions the Spartans undertook. The recovery of independence by Thebes led to the prolonged ravaging of Theban territories by Agesilaos. The Theban victory at Tegyra (375 BC) by Pelopidas should have given Sparta pause for thought in terms of the tactics used. The defeat of the Spartan fleet by the Athenian admiral Chabrias (376 BC) near Naxos did not deter the Spartans from sending a force under Mnasippos to inculcate revolution at Kerkyra (374 BC) thus leading to an Athenian response which left Sparta with a bloodied nose.

The Peace of Kallias (371 BC), which sought to reimpose similar conditions to those of the King's peace, led to the refusal of Thebes to break up its revived federation. Sparta, without waiting for support from other signatories such as Athens ordered their army stationed to the north of Thebes to attack that city state. The Battle of Leuktra resulted in the death of one of their kings and such a significant loss of life that the myth of Sparta's unrivalled superiority on land was shattered.

Throughout the period under review increasing evidence appears showing a dramatic decline in the numbers of Spartiates. These were the full Spartan citizens who lived and trained together in military messes supported by the produce from their estates. If not able to meet the full financial commitment required of a citizen, an individual lost his rights and was demoted to a lower position in society. No clear and satisfactory answer has as yet been formulated to explain the rapid decline in citizen numbers but within the course of some sixty years it had moved from a figure of several thousand men to around fifteen hundred. Indeed, Herodotos at VII.234.2 quotes the exiled Spartan king Demaratos reporting to Xerxes at the time of the Persian invasion that Sparta had approximately eight thousand men. Greater reliance on mercenaries and emancipated *helots* (slaves) is to be seen as a consequence together with a growing paranoia concerning the possibility of revolution from the disenfranchised or of a slave revolt. As early as 396 BC Agesilaos had only been accompanied on his Persian campaign by thirty Spartiates.

Leuktra laid bare the truth. The number of Sparta's crack troops was exceedingly limited. This is not to say that the *neodamodeis* (new citizens but not full citizens, probably freed helots), the semi-independent *perioikoi* or mercenaries in particular were not effective soldiers. What Sparta needed desperately was an overhaul of its constitution.

With Thebes in the ascendant Sparta went on the defensive. Four invasions of the Peloponnese were undertaken in the years after Leuktra with Epameinondas as the architect of Theban policy. To the north, Pelopidas extended Theban Hegemony to Thessaly and Macedonia.

Sparta lost Messenia to the Theban led coalition and with it the basis of its economy. Epameinondas refortified Mantineia, founded a new capital for the Arkadians at Megalopolis and built the freed and hitherto exiled Messenians a new city at Messene. Sparta itself was threatened and only narrowly avoided being taken by Theban-led forces. The whole of Spartan held territory was subject to the ravages of the invader. The newly founded cities together with Argos saw the strategic encirclement of Sparta which, with the Arkadian league of states, neutralised Sparta's efforts to revive.

In 368 BC Sparta had recovered sufficiently to go on to the offensive for a brief period and during this time won the 'Tearless Battle' against Arkadians and Argives. 'Tearless' because not a single Spartiate was killed.

Thebes proved little better than Sparta in exercising hegemony over Greece and the killing of all male inhabitants in the city of Orchomenos alienated some of the Arkadian states. In 362 BC Epameinondas made his final incursion into the Peloponnese. On this occasion, however, he faced an alliance between disaffected Arkadians, Athens, Sparta, Elis and Achaeia. The second battle of Mantineia saw an initial Theban victory neutralised by the death of Epameinondas and the successful action of the Athenians in the later phase of the battle.

No Greek state had proved itself strong enough in terms of military power or moral rectitude to exercise hegemony. It was left to Phillip II, who had been a hostage in Thebes for much of the time of Theban ascendancy and who must have learned a great deal from both Pelopidas and Epameinondas, to force a form of unity on Greece.

Greek Armies at the Mid-Point of the Peloponnesian War

During the Peloponnesian War and the period which is under direct scrutiny in this book, considerable changes took place in the organisation and practices of Greek armies. Up to this time large parts of Greece had moved from monarchy, through aristocratic rule, to more democratic forms of government. Urbanisation was the fellow traveller of this political trend. What had hitherto been the power centre of the ruling groups became the citadel of the city state, defensible against attack and a refuge for those inhabitants of the area in which the city was situated. Further defences were added in some instances by circumvallation of those areas: businesses, and domestic housing, in close proximity to the acropolis.

Thebes, Athens and Corinth are good examples of this development. Sparta, despite the fact that it remained a monarchy under two hereditary kings, had a constitution under which the powers of those kings were severely limited. Other less developed areas such as Aetolia, Phokis, parts of Lokris and Archarnania remained largely as villages and did not develop heavy infantry to the same extent as the stronger city states but relied on the light infantry akin to the *peltast* more suited to mountainous regions.

Oscillations occurred from time to time wherein the governing bodies of city states moved from forms of democratic rule to oligarchies only to revert back. Evidence is limited and more, but not enough, is known about Athens and Sparta than elsewhere. As the area controlled and given protection by the city state grew, successive border wars were inevitable. The way to harm an opponent was to cause economic hardship by destroying his crops and the way to avoid this was to defend those growing areas. Thus, to put it simply, a formulaic practice evolved whereby differences between city states could be settled by a short, sharp engagement by a phalanx of heavy infantry on both sides. The battles took place on a plain which was sometimes to be the subject of depredation or defence. Up to the time of the Peloponnesian War hostilities were usually restricted to the summer.

The phalanx was a rectangular close formation of heavy infantry (*hoplites*) usually eight deep (but see later for the much deeper Theban formations). The men of the phalanx were full citizens often taking their place within the formation alongside friends. The name hoplite comes from *hoplon* – the name for the circular concave shield which was approximately three feet in diameter and covered much of the carrier's own body as well as the unshielded spear carrying side of the neighbour to his left in formation. Much of the weight of the shield could be taken by the left shoulder because of its concave shape. The left shoulder came into play because the shield was held by thrusting the greater part of the arm through a centrally placed band (*porpax*), with the left hand grasping a thong (*antilabe*) placed at the very rim. Occasionally, to protect the lower legs, a piece of leather was attached to hang from the bottom of the shield. The principle weapon was the spear used at close quarters. It was bigger than the height of the average man, up to six feet six inches, and was initially used by the front ranks in an overarm downward thrusting manner against the opposition. Successive ranks behind either levelled their spears against the enemy or pointed them skywards as a protective shield for the formation against missiles. The spear also had a spike at its butt which could be used should the spear head be lost, or to despatch those of the fallen enemy over whom they moved in an advance. A short sword was a secondary weapon rarely more than two feet in length. A bronze corslet was for both front and rear protection, and helmet and greaves completed the panoply. The helmet, usually of Corinthian style, cleverly protected nose and cheeks as well as the whole cranium but gave a restricted range of vision. This would suit the hoplite within the close formation of the phalanx but would not be helpful in terms of any open order fighting.

Such equipment did not come cheaply. The hoplite was therefore a land-owner, or man of some substance. The equation between full citizenship and the duty to fight for one's city is behind the establishment of phalanx warfare. The common good replaces the heroic single combat ethic. The integrity of the formation depended entirely on the suppression of personal feelings and the need to do one's duty in relation to one's companions in the line for the honour of the city and its deities.

Should neither phalanx break and run prior to contact, an inevitable clash of shields ensued. The outcome then depended on how well the front rank conducted its spear work and how much impetus was derived from those ranks behind acting almost like a rugby scrum forcing a forward movement by their very weight.

Such encounters were short and sharp. When one side finally broke and ran, possibly throwing away their cumbersome armament, pursuit by the victorious hoplites was short. It is at this point that other units within the army came into play, such as the light armed troops, *peltasts* or cavalry if they were present in reasonable numbers.

Non-hoplite footsoldiers included missile men, slingers, archers, javelineers and a corps of mobile open order light infantry which was intermediate between the javelineer and the hoplite. This was the *peltast* named after the shield used (pelte), a shallow crescent shaped fabrication of wicker covered in leather and as an aid to mobility, much lighter than the hoplon. The 'bite' of the crescent was at the top of the shield. The weaponry employed was slightly variable. Although a pair of javelins seems to be reasonably common, a long thrusting spear was sometimes used together with a short sword similar to that of the hoplite, or a machaira, a slashing weapon of similar length. Excellent in pursuit of a broken phalanx or on broken or high ground but they could not stand up to heavy infantry in formation. They were predominantly Thracian in origin and probably first used by the Athenians who encountered them initially at their coastal colonies in the northern Aegean.

The composition of a Greek army therefore reflected the social strata of its inhabitants and cavalry which, in later times, was considered as an elite force, but was not recognised as such at this point except in Athens and Thessaly. It may well be that horses were used earlier to bring some hoplites to a convenient point where they could dismount to fight. Athens had a cavalry force before the start of the Peloponnesian War and the Spartans were forced to establish one in the mid-420s to contend with the coastal incursions of the Athenians on Lakonia. Other states such as Corinth, Argos and those where pasturage was minimal did not establish cavalry until significantly later. In the north Thessaly, blessed with abundant fodder on its vast plain, was the major exception with Boeotia probably possessing a creditable force at this time. In Athens, unlike Sparta, membership of the cavalry arm soon became a prestigious appointment. The cost of supporting a horse was not cheap in those days either. The importance of the cavalry arm and its tactical uses will be traced throughout this book.

Non-hoplite forces were used for screening and protecting the flank and rear of their own heavy infantry, foraging, ambushes, harassing the flanks of enemy formations, reconnaissance, raiding and in the pursuit of broken formations. Specific actions of these forces within the period under scrutiny are given throughout the text and more information concerning changes and developments is given in the concluding part. Many of those changes were as a consequence of the extension of the warring period to an all year activity in the Peloponnesian War, the scarcity of major battles during its duration and the reliance on small scale engagements employing combinations of these ancillary forces, sometimes in conjunction with hoplites. It is in just these forms of small engagement that the virtues of these ancillary forces can be seen. Subsequent developments in their use are given in the main text and in the Concluding Comments.

In the recruitment of an army, city states relied on the moral obligation of the citizen to serve as a soldier. As has already been stated the position of a hoplite was a reflection of his standing within the polis. Within the fourth century Athens required a form of national service from its youth between the age of eighteen and twenty, in which training was given and guard duties at the Piraeus in the first year and frontier duties in the second were obligatory. At that time the state provided spear and shield but the remainder of the panoply was to be provided by the individual. It may well be that the Ephebate existed much earlier but, if it did, the total armament of the individual would most likely have been his responsibility. Athletics would be the basis of fitness training with exercises in marching, countermarching, etc., being the drill for those who would make up the phalanx. Athens was predominantly a naval power and averaged 350 or more triremes in her fleet. These were manned by rowers from the lower orders of the citizenry (*thetes*), foreigners resident in the state (*metics*) and those oarsmen supplied by their allies. Hoplites provided the necessary marines under the command of the trierarch.

Servants accompanied hoplites to battle and were responsible for carrying spare weapons and supplies. They fetched and carried while in camp and sometimes were responsible for the preparation of their master's food. After an engagement their duty included retrieving the dead.

As a consequence of the reforms of Lykourgos, Sparta, unlike other states, already had a state army whose sole activity was to pursue military training supported as it was by a serf population. In Sparta a boy stayed in his home until his seventh year. From that point on he lived communally under the supervision of a *paidonomos* who oversaw his training and education. From twelve to eighteen the rigour of the training increased and the ability to withstand physical hardship improved. One garment sufficed for all seasons, exercises were often conducted barefoot, even climbing cliffs. Food was supplied in limited quantities which could be supplemented by theft. This was permissible and punishment was only meted out as a reprimand for failing in his enterprise, if the thief was caught. In such ways self-sufficiency was the product of this training. During adolescence boys were kept too busy under tight discipline to be diverted. Any full citizen could administer punishment for misdemeanors if the *paidonomos* was not present. Respect for elders was essential and youths were expected to remain silent in public and keep their gaze towards the ground when walking the streets. The cadetship over, the young man was at the stage where he could be called upon to fight in battle but not in the front line. For two years, from eighteen to twenty, he undertook drills captained by those of between twenty and thirty years of age. From twenty-four years old a front line position became his responsibility which he held until the age of thirty, when he was recognised as a full citizen with its attendant voting rights in the Assembly. At that point, provided they ate in the mess each night, they could live at home with their wives and children. Each mess was made up of fifteen men each being required to provide a monthly amount of wine, and agricultural produce. Failure to maintain these contributions could lead to the loss of citizen status. His responsibility to serve in the army only ceased at the age of sixty. As a result Sparta was pre-eminent in arms skills and manoeuvre and was regarded as unbeatable on land. Admittedly, the 'mess system' which operated led to greater reliance and understanding of the skills of individuals thereby benefiting the cohesiveness of the phalanx.

Basically it did not require much training to take one's place within the phalanx for city states other than Sparta, however several of the ancillary forces were more specialist in their requirements. It soon became obvious that it was cheaper to hire a specialist such as an archer, slinger or peltast than to train citizens at State expense. The number of mercenaries employed therefore rose as the Peloponnesian War progressed, with slingers being hired from Rhodes, archers from Crete and peltasts from Thrace. With all year warfare becoming the norm the average citizen could not afford to neglect his business or crops. Athens in particular required a large number of oarsmen for its fleet and it proved easier to give payment for their services. For land operations specialist troops could thereafter be hired for a fee. Both sides during the war made use of available mercenaries and far from decreasing at the cessation of hostilities, the fourth century shows a further sharp increase in their employment as will be seen in the main text. Far from being expensive, the employment of con-siderable numbers of mercenaries kept the hiring price at a reasonable level.

The organisational structure of armies is known in only sketchy terms. The *strategoi* or generals were elected annually in such states as Athens and in the Boeotian federation under the leadership of Thebes. In Sparta the kings were in turn the commanders-in-chief, but by the late fifth century men of talent from the royal houses and their intimates were regularly given posts of command, their appointments being made by the *ephors*. These last, five in number and elected annually from the full Spartan citizen body of men over thirty years of age, held extraordinary powers. Even the kings were answerable to them and two of their number accompanied a king on any campaign to monitor his conduct. They were in charge of foreign policy, decided which year groups to mobilise in time of war and oversaw the training of the young. As representatives of the people they could propose censure of a king and even depose him. This appears to have given them greater powers than the kings. However, their election for one year only and the fact that they were accountable for their actions to the Assembly (*eklesia*) at the end of their tenure, provided a necessary curb. Another important function of the kings should be noted: their responsibility for all religious functions of the state including those concerned with warfare.

Athens enlisted by year groups from the tribes, each tribe being commanded by an annually elected *taxiarch*. There would therefore be ten *taxiarchs* whose responsibility was to appoint sub-commanders, *lochagoi*. Early in the war Perikles was said to have been told that Athens could produce 13,000 hoplites with an additional 18,000 being available from the under twenty and over forty-two year groups. Athenian cavalry was commanded by two *hipparchoi* with ten *phylarchoi* as subordinate officers.

Taking J.F.Lazenby's numbers for the Spartan army (*The Spartan Army* (1985)) e.g., six *morai* of 1,280 men each plus the king's bodyguard – the *Hippeis* – (300 men) we arrive at a total of nearly 8,000 hoplites. Each *mora* divided into two *lochoi* gives the twelve divisions and the numbers of men to make sense of the descriptions of actions within the scope of this book. Originally the recruitment would have been on a locality and year group basis but by the time of our review Spartiates would have been dispersed throughout the army due to diminishing numbers. All front rank men in the phalanx would have subordinate officer status as leaders of their file. There were commanders for each of the six *morai,* and for each of the subdivisions, twelve *lochoi*, forty eight *pentekostyes* and 192 *enomotiai*. All would come under the command of the king in time of conflict. In terms of operational efficiency no city state could match Sparta in terms of hoplite warfare in its heyday. This may be because it was the only near professional army on the mainland until the developments of specialist units and citizen training were instituted in the first half of the fourth century by other states.

Obviously no city state committed its entire forces at one time to the same endeavour and Sparta, like Athens, organised its 'call-up' on year groups. Mention should be made here of the *Skiritai*, a force of about 600 men who undertook the modern equivalent of SAS work for the Spartans and who lived on the northern border of Lakonia.

31

Some Points on Persia

Persia looms large within the activities of the Greeks throughout the period under scrutiny supporting first one and then the other antagonist as it had done for much of the fifty years before. It is extremely doubtful that the strategy was adopted to avoid Panhellenism which might lead to an invasion of Persia by a unified Greece. Greek city states were much too independent and perverse for that. Although much is made of Greek resistance and their final victories following the Persian invasion early in the fifth century, it is as well to remember that more Greek cities went over to the Persian side than made up the number which resisted. Persia's concern was to maintain control of the Asiatic littoral and limit interference from mainland Greece in support of the many Greek cities there.

Consistent support was given to Sparta by Kyros the Younger and this is what served to end the Peloponnesian War. This, however, is singular, as it was more the Persian custom to stop any of the mainland powers from becoming too dominant unless that state was, in part, of client status.

The Persian empire was vast, its communications superb and its culture enviable. However, not all areas within its boundaries were directly under its control. Mountain peoples were often independent, merely contained, left to their own devices and dissuaded from coming down into the lowlands. This proved to be a sensible policy and avoided the constant commitment of manpower for little return. It explains how Xenophon, with his companions of the *anabasis*, travelled through areas within the empire which were obviously not under direct Persian control.

Governing such a huge area was achieved by dividing the empire into regional *satrapies* and making the governor (*satrap*) of each area responsible for its security. These satraps were virtually autonomous and only finally answerable to the Great King himself. The system was feudal, with each satrap's main responsibilities being to provide men to serve the king in time of war and to collect tribute. This accounts for the occasional rivalry between satraps and differences in policy towards the states of mainland Greeks.

The Persian army was of variable composition depending on the opposition but its main components appeared in most major engagements. Its strongest arm was the cavalry. Two forms existed, heavy and light. The former was fully armoured with bronze scale chest and back protection and leggings to the ankle also of bronze scale. The helmet had cheek guards and the weaponry consisted of two javelins and a short sword. The chest of the mount was protected by a hanging apron of bronze discs sewn onto leather and its fore-head was covered by a sheet bronze protection. The light cavalryman usually wore a quilted cuirass over a tunic, felt or fabric headgear and his horse was unarmoured. He too had javelins, a short sword or battle-axe. Both varieties were missile throwers although the better protected heavy cavalry could come to close quarters with all except heavy infantry in close formation. Of the foot soldiers, the Immortals, a force which was maintained at 10,000 men, proved the most effective infantry. It was the Great King's guard in peacetime and the crack infantry section of the Persian army in battle. It was a wholly professional and formidable force in the right conditions. A body covering of bronze scales was worn under the knee length tunic, head protection was negligible, linen or soft fabric not unlike that worn by present day Arabs. This was so that it could be drawn across the face as a protection against the stifling dust raised during conflict. Armament consisted of a bow, a heavy spear and a short sword. Over the course of the fifth century the wicker shield was changed to a shield very similar in style to the *hoplon*, obviously as a result of regular contact with Greek forces. Brave though they were they proved vulnerable when faced with a Greek phalanx. Light infantry, slingers, archers, etc., were drawn from all parts of the empire in a profusion of fighting styles. Persia could raise a phalanx from its Greek subjects to counter that of any invading Greek force providing it maintained its relatively benign control over the cities of the Aegean littoral. The two difficulties with which a Persian commander-in-chief had often to contend were those of language and an unwillingness to fight from those lower orders who were forced to serve. Agreed signals would appear to be the only answer to an army made up of many nationalities. The Persian answer to those unwilling to engage is well attested – the lash. Herein lies a fundamental difference between Greek and Persian. The former, the committed citizen joined with comrade citizens fighting for the common good, their city and its gods, the latter, often the reluctant and coerced individual among many whose viewpoint was similar.

Battles

In the period under discussion set battles are few but significant. This was a period in which small scale actions often demonstrated high abilities among commanders. Experimentation abounds and developments in equipment led to a lightening of the panoply for the hoplite. Light armed forces too saw revisions in equipment which also led to greater mobility, e.g., peltasts. In consequence new tactical considerations were explored and the differing forces within armies became inter-dependent. The smaller engagements will be given discussion throughout the text.

The main set pieces on land were as follows:

Kounaxa, 401 BC

The attempt of Kyros the Younger to topple his brother Artaxerxes failed with his death in this battle. Persians were successful on one wing and much of the centre while the Greek phalanx within Kyros' army carried all before them. The difficulties of their return from the heart of Persia is dealt with in Part One of the main text.

Sardis, 395 BC

A large Persian cavalry force was destroyed by Agesilaos' astute use of inter-supporting units of his army.

Nemea, 394 BC

A battle in which both Spartans and Thebans were respectively successful on their right wings. Sparta won the battle largely through the failure of Thebes' allies not taking the opportunity to attack the Spartans in flank as the latter rolled up their line.

Koroneia, 394 BC

Another victory for Agesilaos using initially the Spartan lead to the right to outflank the enemy followed by the turn inwards to take the enemy in the flank. The succeeding progression across the battlefield led to the destruction of the opposition with the exception of the Thebans who had been successful on their wing. On the return of the Thebans from their pillaging of the Spartan camp Agesilaos chose to confront them head-on rather than adopt the much easier and less costly tactic of taking them in flank as they passed by. Both forces now faced each other in the opposite direction to that in which they had started the conflict. The significant outcome was, that despite being heavily defeated, the Thebans broke through the Spartan line by virtue of their density.

Leuktra, 371 BC

Epameinondas commanding on the left adopted a depth of fifty ranks in his phalanx and made effective use of his cavalry at the opening of the battle.

Pelopidas pinned down the Spartan attempt to lead to the right to outflank. The Spartan command position had to take the full brunt of Epameinondas' oblique approach and was destroyed while the remainder of the Spartan forces looked on, threatened as they were by the Theban trailing right.

Second Mantineia, 362 BC

A clever deception by Epameinondas led the Mantineians, Spartans, Athenians and other allies to believe that he was about to encamp. They too were about to stand down when Epameinondas launched his surprise attack, again with a massed left wing against the command point, this time spearheaded by a wedge shaped force of cavalry intermixed with peltasts and with the phalanx in close support. Had he not been killed, Epameinondas would have undoubtedly won yet another battle. In this engagement the trailing and threatening right dissuaded the opposition's left wing from taking part at the critical point of the onset.

The Main Text

The main text of the study is divided into three parts. The third, which can best be described as covering the theory of good command, serves as the standard against which the historical practices of the first and second parts can be measured. Indeed 'The Ideal Commander' categorises all that Xenophon wished for in his model general. It is indicative that, though splendidly informative, the *Kyropaideia* proved to be less interesting to the writer than the other main texts. Fact is indeed more fascinating than fiction. The main sources used in each part of the text are as follows:

Part One: Xenophon as Commander – *Anabasis* from Book III to the end with additional references from *Memorabilia* and *Oikonomicos*, 401–400 BC.

Part Two: Commanders in Practice – *Hellenika, Agesilaos* and Books I and II of *Anabasis*, 411–362 BC.

Part Three: The Ideal Commander – *Kyropaideia* and those relevant texts within the *Scripta Minora*, e.g., The Cavalry Commander, Horsemanship, Spartan Constitution.

In Part One, Xenophon gives a strikingly objective assessment of his own experiences. In Part Two, his personal view on the tactics and morals of his contemporaries highlights good and bad practice. In Part Three he makes clear what is to be expected of the ideal commander through the description of the practices adopted by the hero of his 'historical novel'.

The subheadings, which are common to all three parts, reflect those issues which Xenophon regarded as paramount to good command. The last two begin with a section on cavalry which he rightly recognised as being of growing importance during this period. As is indicated by the title of this monograph, the main text will deal only with what is found in the writings of Xenophon. References to other sources are given when they clarify or support an indisputable point. Those contentious or questionable references are given additional treatment in the end notes to each part of the main text. In so doing, the distinction of focus between 'Xenophon and the Art of Command' and what would otherwise be 'The Commander's Art 411–362 BC' can be maintained.

Sun Tzu

Frequent use is made of extracts from the writings of this Chinese general of the late sixth and early fifth century BC. His 'Art of War' is still used in officer training in the Chinese army. Russian military personnel too have long made use of it. The content proves remarkably similar to the opinions and tenets held by Xenophon in his judgements of what is required of a good commander. Its thirteen chapters define a doctrine which is simply stated at both the strategic and tactical level and is balanced by clear statements concerning the character and moral obligations necessary to be a good commander. Possibly written around 490 BC it is the first known work of its kind. Extracts from it are used in this book to highlight a commonality of approach to the essentials of warfare in both East and West.

References to cavalry action are absent from his writings. The first known cavalry to be used in Chinese warfare was around the 330s BC.

Some Problems with Sources

Xenophon, a friend of Agesilaos and his family, companion to many leading men of Sparta who had held commands in the successive actions taken by the Spartans, was well placed to write a history of his period (*Hellenika*). His own participation in a number of important events is deserving of attention from the point of view of an eye witness. Therefore it is no surprise to have graphic descriptions of some of the actions in Asia Minor, Thessaly and Koroneia and less than satisfactory coverage of events for which we might expect more detail. For other actions he is reliant on Spartan eyewitnesses, commanders or friends.

His sources seem not to go beyond those with whom he has direct contact. This accounts for some of the omissions. His critics ought to take his domestic and geographical situation into consideration when considering his methodology. He only discusses what he knows to be a sustainable truth. Obviously there is bias, but possibly less bias than some modern scholars' antipathy to the writings of Xenophon on whom they rely for their evidence, uncomfortable for them as it may be at times. This can explain, for example, the lack of information concerning Theban policy within northern Greece and Pelopidas' involvement in it. What is surprising, however, is the absence of comment on Tegyra. Mention should have been given even if lack of detail of the action made for a muddied description. More serious is that such important events as the founding of Megalopolis (see Map 3 on 'The Encirclement of Sparta'), the establishment of the Second Athenian League or the Battle of Knidos are totally ignored. Occasionally the chronology is a little suspect. Lack of specific detail because of the loss of direct participants did not stop him from attempting a description of Leuktra. Omissions and inaccuracies there may be within his writing of this continuation of Thucydides, but his judgement of men and their merits is splendid. Such are some of the problems within the *Hellenika* which is the basis of the second part of the main text.

The *Kyropaedeia* is a landmark in the history of literature. It proves to be the first work of historical fiction ever written and even includes a romantic element, though that will not concern us here. Based loosely on historical fact it gives an account of the life and strong principles shown by Kyros the Great throughout his life in the sixth century BC. Xenophon uses his hero to exemplify the virtues of the good ruler and excellent commander. It is in the examination of Kyros' actions as an ideal commander that we can discover Xenophon's theories on the subject. What the reader of the *Kyropaedeia* must decide is how Persian or Greek is the subject matter. Is Xenophon in his theorising trying to propose another form of warmaking? The answer must be in the negative. He must use the known artifacts, weaponry and formations of sixth century Persian warfare to strike an authentic note. He would never recommend the use of chariots for a Greek army after having seen them fail at the Battle of Kounaxa. The detail is there to give an Asiatic flavour against which the moral attributes of his hero and the universal principles of good command can be displayed.

Main Sources and Abbreviations

(All sources consulted: Loeb Classical Edition, Loeb Classical Library, Harvard University Press).

Xenophon: Kyropaideia = (*Kyr.*)
             Agesilaos = (Xen. *Ages.*)
             The Constitution of the Lacedaemonians = (*Lak.Pol.*)
             Ways and Means = (*Por.*)
             The Cavalry Commander = (*Hipp.*)
             The Art of Horsemanship = (*Peri Hipp.*)
             On Hunting = (*Kyn.*)
             Anabasis = (*Anab.*)
             Hellenika = (*Hell.*)
             Memorabilia = (*Mem.*)
             Oikonomikos = (*Oikon.*)

Plutarch: Agesilaos = (Plut. *Ages.*)
             Pelopidas = (*Pelop.*)
             Lysander = (*Lys.*)
             Alkibiades = (*Alk.*)
             Artaxerxes = (*Art.*)

Sun Tzu: 'The Art of War' (translated by Lionel Giles, (Shanghai and London, 1910)).

Lesser used sources
Frontinus = (*Front.*), Arrian = (*Arr.*), Polybios = (*Pol.*), Athenaios = (*Athen.*), Thucydides = (*Thuc.*), Herodotos = (*Herod.*), Oxyrhynchus = (*Oxy*), Aeneas Tacticus = (*Aen Tact.*), Diogenes Laertius = (*Diog.*), Pausanias = (*Paus.*), Diodoros Histories = (*Diod.*)

Glossary

agoge	the Spartan form of training their youth
aspis	a solid round shield
anabasis	'a going up'. (It came to mean 'an expedition from the coast especially into Asia'. In addition to Xenophon's *Anabasis* we have Arrian's *Anabasis* detailing the campaigns of Alexander the Great. Agesilaos' expedition into Asia Minor could well be described the same way.)
archon	an Athenian magistrate
Boeotarch	elective office of the Boeotian Federation of Cities led by Thebes. The Boeotarchs acted as generals in times of conflict.
emvolon	a wedge
enomotia	a unit of the Spartan army of around forty men
ephebe	an Athenian military cadet
ephors/ephoroi	appointed for one year only, the senior magistrates at Sparta
hamippoi	light infantry used in conjunction and interspersed within cavalry.
harmost	military governor
hegemon	leader (from which our use of hegemony or leadership emanates)
helots	slaves who provided the workforce on Spartan farms and estates.
hiera	signs based on the interpretation of various parts of a sacrificial victim, e.g., liver
hipparchia	cavalry unit
hipparch	supreme cavalry commander.
Hippeis	originally describing horsemen and suggestive of early aristocracy. (In Sparta it designated the 300 men making up the Royal Guard. They were, however, footsoldiers.)
hoplite	a heavy infantryman
hoplon	the round concave shield of the hoplite
kopis	short slashing sword
lochagos	the commander of a *lochos*
lochos	in the Spartan army this unit comprised 640 men. Other states had differing numbers in this unit.
medised	went over to the Persians
mora	comprised 1,280 men, the largest division of the Spartan army
neodamodeis	new citizens, probably freed helots available for service within the Spartan army. Limited voting rights.

peltasts	light armed infantryman, peltast
pentekoster	the commander of a *pentekostys*
pentekostys	a unit of 160 men in the Spartan army
perioikoi	free inhabitants of the towns and villages in Spartan held territories
pezoi	foot soldier
phalanx	a dense rectangular formation of heavy infantry
polemarch	the commander of a *mora*
polis	city state
sphagia	sacrificial rites based on the flow of blood from a sacrifice
strategos	general
syssition	Spartan military mess
taxis	an Athenian army unit
taxiarchos	commander of a taxis
trierarch	a wealthy citizen responsible for the outfitting and maintenance of a warship

PART ONE

XENOPHON AS COMMANDER

X enophon's vivid account of the long march of the Ten Thousand in which he was elevated to the position of commander-in-chief proves to be an invaluable insight into tactical thinking at the turn of the century (401–400 BC).

Chronologically, the events of the *Anabasis* predate the greater part of the *Hellenika*. The problems in relation to its writing are not of concern to the present study.[1] Rather, the content, in terms of tactical decisions and their execution as described by Xenophon, is the prime interest. Consideration of the first two books of the *Anabasis*, which dealt with the march inland up to the point of the Battle of Kounaxa, is given in Part Two of this text. The focus turns to the homeward march from the point of the election of the substitute Greek generals following the treacherous capture and killing of the former leaders. To have marched so far into the heart of the Persian empire within the army of the attempting usurper Kyros, and to have remained undefeated on the field of Kounaxa when all else was lost, was a predicament in itself. To have lost its leadership shortly thereafter could be described as the prelude to disaster for the Greek forces.

Given an overview, the tactics of both Greeks and Persians can be seen to emanate from two distinct strategies. That of the Greeks was defined by expediency, the necessity to return safely to Greece with as few losses to their number as possible. The Persians had more options. They had won the battle, compromised the Greek command and the Greek force could be regarded by them as ineffective as an offensive entity, so long as they, the Persians, maintained a large army in near contact. However, the Greeks were nonetheless potentially dangerous if left to their own devices.

There is no doubt that a large Persian army could have annihilated the Greeks but at considerable loss to themselves. Knowing that the Greeks' options were extremely limited and were likely to weigh heavily on the need to effect a withdrawal, there was no reason for the Persians to do anything precipitate. Therefore, while the Greeks had to be persuaded and encouraged in their intention to withdraw, no opportunity could be missed to make that withdrawal as difficult and as uncomfortable as possible, in the hope of dissuading others from similar adventures. The initial stages of the march can be likened to a dangerous beast being constantly prodded and kept on the move in a direction satisfactory to its pursuers. The Persians followed a perfectly sensible course of action. In the descriptions of their tactics against the Greeks, thereafter, they can be seen shepherding them out of the empire by the shortest route and over some hostile terrain, hoping possibly for a breakdown in morale among the Greeks which would give them the opportunity to destroy them piecemeal. There was no cowardice on the Persian side in pursuing such a strategy in this way, merely a different viewpoint. The avoidance of a major confrontation while achieving one or both objectives was a highly esteemed and long held eastern tenet of warfare and was here adopted by the Persians: 'Hence to fight and conquer in all your battles is not supreme excellence; supreme excellence consists in breaking the enemy's resistance without fighting' (Sun Tzu III.3. See[2] for further comments from this source.)

It is as well to review the position of the Greeks after the so-called truce following the battle and prior to their long withdrawal. Having lost five generals, twenty captains and 200 soldiers through the treachery of Tissaphernes, it is not surprising that morale was low. What was regarded as an act of treachery by the Greeks may not have been viewed in the same manner by the Persians. It was one thing to have a commonality of ethic and practice when Greek fought against Greek, but to those living further east such niceties in war may not have been held in such esteem. After all, in the view of the Persians, the Greeks had accompanied an attempted usurper and the fact that the Greeks only knew positively of the mission's purpose late in the march was of no concern. They were dangerous enemies and any advantage which could be garnered on any occasion must be seized upon. It may well be that cultural differences were not wholly appreciated at that time, much in the same way that the British misunderstood the attitude of the Japanese to prisoners of war, even though we had traded with them for a considerable length of time prior to the Second World War. The fact that death was preferable to surrender in Japanese eyes took a long time to be understood and accounts for the disregard in which the Japanese held their captives, who, in their belief, by the act of surrender had given up the right to be regarded as human.

The number of just over ten thousand hoplites is misleading. At *Anab.* I.ii.9 Xenophon gives approximate figures for the Greek force of 11,000 hoplites and 2,000 peltasts. Earlier in the same reference he had referred to 200 Cretan archers and at *Anab.* I.ii.3, light armed troops. These last would not be peltasts, but would have been similarly armed without the small shield (πέλτη – *pelte*). At *Anab.* I.vii.10, when Kyros' army was marshalled under arms there were 10,400 hoplites, 2,500 peltasts in the Greek contingent. These were the fighting men and excluded the personal servants, slaves, baggage carriers, women and possibly children who accompanied the expedition in addition to those fighting men. Following Kounaxa, Xenophon refers to 'a great multitude' (*Anab.* III.ii.36) and to a great number of women in the camp (*Anab.* IV.iii.19). It is not inconceivable that the total of this mass of humanity numbered thirty to thirty-five thousand. In Greek terms this was the size of a reasonably strong city state. There were not many Greek cities at that time which could put 10,000 hoplites and probably 2,500 peltasts into the field. This accounts for two later factors, namely that the Greek cities were not enamoured of the likelihood of the return of such a force, and the recurring idea on the march that the expeditionary force should found its own city.

At that point, leaderless, without supplies or cavalry, and encumbered by camp followers who threatened to be a further drain on available resources, the Greek hoplites must have appeared to the Persians an easy target to dismember should they pursue their chosen strategy. It is as well to bear these factors in mind when reviewing the analysis made by Xenophon and the decisions finally taken at his instigation. Such were the facts facing the Greeks, but there were further logistical imponderables to be considered. First and foremost was the question of provisioning such a moving community. Even on the inward march, with accompanying merchants and the peoples whose areas they traversed making markets for the troops and their dependants, there had been problems. The exorbitant price charged by the Lydian market forced the Greeks to subsist on meat (*Anab.* I.v.6). Again, after the Battle of Kounaxa, they slaughtered oxen and asses from the baggage train to subsist at a time when there could be no market for the normal necessities.[3] Decisions had to be made and it will be seen that some of those fly in the face of previous experience, denoting new thinking in the manner in which the progress of an army through enemy territory could be conducted.

Xenophon's position with the expeditionary force was unusual in that he was initially 'neither general, captain nor private' (*Anab.* III.i.4). He had accompanied the army as a friend of one of the generals, Proxenos. He was obviously well known to the men serving under Proxenos, and his abilities, even though he was a young man, led them to elect him as general in place of the dead Proxenos (*Anab.* III.i.26). Once elected, he lost little time in outlining his plan of action to the assembly. It reflected his analysis of the current circumstances and his view of what needed to be done and, as has already been noted, showed a willingness to consider options which had been rejected in earlier times.[4]

First, he addressed the question of morale and showed that it was best to lead by example to redress the present position (*Anab*. III.i.36–45). Xenophon obviously had a sense of occasion because he chose to be dressed in his finest armour for this meeting (*Anab*. III.ii.7). At that meeting he made it clear to all that reliance on arms was the only option when dealing with dissembling Persians (*Anab*. III.ii.8). Within the speech he recounted past successful encounters against the Persians with the intent of raising the morale of all concerned. He suggested, giving the impression that the Greeks themselves intended to settle in Persia as an act of concealment of their true purpose, to march home (*Anab*. III.ii.24). The Persians obviously feared such an option as had already been demonstrated when Klearchos had led the army to the fertile land between the Tigris and the canal (*Anab*. II.iv.21–22). A comment was made which found echoes elsewhere in Greek thinking following their return, that poor Greeks would find a much more comfortable living in the Persian lands which they had won from the Persians than remaining in their own impoverished communities (*Anab*. III.ii.26). Their example, together with that of Agesilaos a short time later, showed the long term inability of the Persians to deal effectively with a resolute Greek force within their territories. This fuelled the idea of a unified Greece waging war against Persia, a mission which was delayed by the hegemonic struggles through much of the fourth century and not to become a possibility until Phillip II, and an actuality in the time of Alexander.

Having steered the resolution of the army toward a homeward march, Xenophon dealt with the minutiae of the enterprise. First, the wagons had to be burned (*Anab*. III.iv.27). This decision looks at first sight to be precipitate, but there were good tactical reasons for its consideration. The army would be required to proceed at the slower pace of the baggage train and over terrain which could accommodate wheeled vehicles, thus limiting the choice of route. Roads *en route* would have to be repaired to allow their passage. Unlike the inward march, the baggage train would have to be with the army for protection at all times and they could not be sure that grazing and fodder would be encountered in sufficient quantities for both oxen and pack animals. In any case there were fewer beasts of burden remaining following the need to use some of them for food. Second, the tents were also to be destroyed, being too cumbersome to carry. Finally, any extraneous materials were to be abandoned and, apart from arms, only bare essentials were to be retained. On the proposal of Cheirisophos these measures were agreed by the assembly.

This was good tactical thinking under the circumstances, one might assume, but, on closer scrutiny, two issues emerge. Despite the agreement to destroy the wagons and superfluous baggage, Xenophon proposed that the march should be conducted in a hollow square with the *baggage train* and camp followers being protected within it (*Anab.* III.ii.36), a seeming contradiction of the vote. Indeed, their march started with just such an arrangement (*Anab.* III.iii.6) despite the report that wagons and tents had been destroyed (*Anab.* III.iii.1). To make sense of this it must be assumed that asses, mules and horses were used to carry what little baggage was retained together with the arms of those who were 'resting', unarmoured and relieved from duty on the march. Single pack animals would be able to go over rough terrain, through narrow defiles and move more quickly than ox drawn vehicles. No mention is made of *stromata* (bedding), an item of straw or similar material, bulky yet lightweight. It is likely that this was retained as an essential by all hoplites.[5] The matter of the tents, however, proves contentious. The direction of march had been agreed on Xenophon's suggestion that by travelling towards the source of rivers they would be easier to cross, and this could only be to the north. However, he notes Kyros' description of the Persian empire earlier and in this (*Anab.* I.vii.6) there is a clear indication of the rigours and cold to be expected. Whether this was taken to be hyperbole on Kyros' part, or whether Xenophon and the other new generals were only interested in the short term in losing contact with Persian forces, must be left to the individual reader to decide. What followed was an extraordinary feat by any standard, but before looking at the ways and means which secured the safe return of the Greeks, it is as well first to examine the beliefs and attitudes which coloured the deliberations in planning prior to action being taken.

Piety

Piety here denotes belief in, and of, ritual. One of the most significant allusions to shared piety is the case of the 'sneeze'. Xenophon's reaction is a fine example of an intelligent yet pious commander taking advantage of a situation which might otherwise have turned out badly for the Greeks. In its very description there is implied a particular response by all present to such an event at that time, namely obeisance to Zeus Soter (*Anab.* III.ii.9). It occurred during his morale

45

raising speech to the men. As he was urging them to put their trust in their weaponry and by so doing oppose the Persians and engineer their own deliverance with the help of the gods, a man sneezed. Xenophon was quick to channel the thoughts of all to the idea that, as they were talking in terms of their deliverance from their present condition, they must make sacrifice to this aspect of the god and to the other gods as well, once safe country was reached. To sneeze was believed to bring luck in the ancient world. Even today a 'bless you' might be the response emanating originally from a religious base. A unanimous vote to accept the proposed course of action was taken and the paean sung.

At this stressful time it would not be unusual for the psychology of the men to be easily targeted to fundamental religious beliefs. To the ancients pledges were sacrosanct, and we find them honouring those made at that time when the army reached Trapezus (*Anab.* IV.viii.25) with sacrifices and games. The degree to which vows and pledges assumed importance to the Greeks is best attested by Xenophon's early speech to the men (*Anab.* III.ii.10). Here Xenophon plays on the shared belief in honour among those listening.

Similarly, dreams and the reporting of dreams played a critical role. In many ways the dreams of someone in a position of command were of paramount importance to an army. By way of explaining his reason to propose himself as general to the men of Proxenos (*Anab.* III.i.25), Xenophon tells the reader that his analysis of the situation was made following a dream (*Anab.* III.i.11-12). Once in that position, he gave many examples of his piety and the responsibility he recognised to follow on from his assumption of office. Another significant dream came to him prior to the resolution of the problem of the river crossing (*Anab.* IV.iii.8) where the leg-irons he dreamed he was wearing fell away and he was able to 'make a stride' or 'stand with legs apart' (διαβαίνειν from διαβαίνω which has the shaded meaning 'to cross over' or 'step across'). He reported his dream to his general colleagues who took the matter seriously, signifying the weight given to such matters in divination. The depth of Xenophon's own belief can be judged when, on receiving the report of the two young men that they had discovered a river crossing, he poured a libation to those gods who had revealed the dream and subsequently the ford. He shared the ceremony with the agencies of the fulfilment of his dream, the young men (*Anab.* IV.iii.13).

Unlike other societies fewer sacrifices were made in propitiation. In terms of religious practice a Greek army was a microcosm of Greek society and sacrifices were made to seek guidance, endorsement of decisions made, or to make vows to be redeemed in the future. The supportive conjunction of the *hiera* and *sphagia* (*Anab*. I.viii.15) as broadcast by Cyrus may well have been more for morale than as a reflection of the truth, considering the outcome of Kounaxa, and perhaps give an idea of differing levels of belief in such matters between Persian and Greek. Commonality of viewpoint cannot be presumed to be shared by different cultures. This is not to say that Persians were less devout than Greeks, but their acceptance of signs and portents may not have been quite as wholesale. Much of our evidence of the religious practices of Persians and other peoples comes from Greek sources and is therefore written from a point of view which inevitably accepts the supreme will of the gods. It is not beyond possibility that expediency in both personal and national interest could take precedence over immediate signs and portents which in themselves were often ambivalent. To the rulers, or commanders in our present concern, superstition had to be held in check among those whom they led. Although in matters of generalship considerable agreement will be found between Xenophon and the Chinese general Sun Tzu, one, and one only, distinct difference emerges, and that is on the taking of omens. 'Prohibit the taking of omens, and do away with superstitious doubts. Then, until death itself comes, no calamity need be feared' (Sun Tzu XI.26). Here rather than risk a superstitious response to omens it is best not to have taken any omens at all. Both west and east followed a different practice for the sake of sustaining morale. The one from the point of view of sustaining the moral rectitude of the proposed action by having the endorsement of the gods, the other wholly from expediency in terms of keeping the minds of the soldiers focused and undisturbed. Persia, lying between the two, and borrowing from both, took omens and made sacrifice. However, it is unlikely that Persian commanders considered it necessary to share the results with the common serf serving in their armies. Until there is more evidence to hand, the shades of difference between the extreme polarities of the eastern and western way of thinking on such matters can only be conjectural. One has only to compare the differing attitude to warfare of Asoka in India, 150 years later, prior to, and after, his conversion to Bhuddism.

However there is evidence that some Greeks were not above thinking that even a Greek commander might manipulate the outcome of a sacrifice for his own ends. Admittedly this was at a time of shortage of provisions and no likelihood of ships coming to take them back to Greece from Kalpe. Morale was consequently low. Further, the Greeks had reasonable grounds for their suspicion, for Xenophon had wished earlier that he could found a city on the Euxine and had confided his desire to Silanos the soothsayer (*Anab*. V.vi.15).

The latter had reported the matter to the troops at that time and they would not countenance the idea. Following unsuccessful sacrifice for departure, some had accused Xenophon of persuading the soothsayer to say that the signs were unpropitious (*Anab.* VI.iv.14–16) and that his intention was to force the issue of founding a city. His response to this was to make public proclamation that anyone could attend the sacrifice on the following day. If any of those present happened to be a soothsayer he was invited to inspect the victims. Three sacrifices were made, all unsuccessful to the endorsement of departure, and the soldiers became angry. Xenophon was adamant that without favourable omens he was unwilling to lead the men in any enterprise. The following day another three sacrifices were made, all being unsuccessful. A further sacrifice was made the next day, again proving unfavourable but no further sacrifices could be made because of a lack of victims, until the soldiers brought a bullock from the baggage train in place of the sacrificial sheep. This too proved to be of no support to the enterprise.

From this we can discern that three sacrifices in one session of the day appeared to be the limit (three sacrifices (*Anab.* VI.iv.16) and 'up to three offerings' (*Anab.* VI.iv.19)). When compared to *Anab.* VI.v.2 where Arexion the soothsayer, on satisfactory completion of the first sacrifices by Xenophon, sees an eagle in an auspicious quarter of the heavens and encourages Xenophon to advance, we are aware that both hiera and sphagia have been propitious and that they have been further endorsed by a natural phenomenon. It is at this point that we have evidence that a commander may make the early morning sacrifices but that the seer can conduct those required later in the same day (*Anab.* VI.v.8).[6]

An example of the seriousness with which sacrifices were made in search of answers to propositions can be noted in the conduct of Kleander who is described as being desirous of becoming commander-in-chief. He sacrificed without success over the course of three days, and on that account relinquished any possibility of taking up command (*Anab.* VI.vi.36). Here again we have the figure 'three' being mentioned as a parameter. In like manner Xenophon himself, when wishing to travel home, sacrificed to Herakles and, against his own desires, followed the signs from the god and stayed with the army (*Anab.* VI.ii.15). Similarly, on being pressed to take up the overall command he was persuaded by the sacrifices he had made on this matter to decline (*Anab.* VI.i.22–24). He had remembered the omen of the eagle which had been noted at Ephesos by a soothsayer and this, together with the clearly unfavourable portents of the sacrifices, led him to his decision.

Rites of purification for an army were not a common occurrence, but the indiscipline which led to the unilateral actions of some of the men in relation to the Kerasuntians brought corporate guilt upon the entire force. Blood had been shed and the blood had been that of ambassadors to the Greeks. The common guilt had to be expunged. Further, this followed a series of rumours and counter-rumours running throughout the army as to the intentions of the generals and Xenophon in particular, fuelled in part by Silanos the soothsayer. Shortly after, Neon, deputising for Cheirisophos in the latter's absence, and not directly party to any planning decisions with the other generals, set it about that Xenophon had persuaded his colleagues to lead the army back to Phasis. The secret mission of Kleuretos and his volunteers, which had led to his own death and several of the men, was quickly followed by the fatal acts of gross impiety against the ambassadors. In a long speech (*Anab.* V.vii.5–33) which recounted the background to the problems besetting them, Xenophon points out the evil permeating the army (*Anab.* V.vii.11–12) and the dangers of following self appointed commanders to the exclusion of those who had been approved by the assembly. Suitably mortified, the assembly agreed to purification rites being undertaken, to the punishment of the instigators of the lawlessness, to make such future action a capital offence and to the setting up of trials for all who had committed an offence since Kounaxa (*Anab.* V.vii.34–35). The generals were not excluded from this mass expurgation, for their past conduct was also to be reviewed (*Anab.* V.viii.1).

In Greece, burial of the battle dead normally took place on the battlefield if on home or allied territory, or in the home city state after being transported there. Memorials naming those who had fallen were set up. Even an enemy, if Greek, would show due respect to the funeral rites of the fallen. This may have been a shared practice, but it was a comforting insurance that the same treatment would be meted out should similar misfortune occur to those taking upon themselves such a responsibility to honour the dead. Muster rolls would have been important and evidence shows it was a duty to honour those whose bodies were not recovered (*Thuc.* II.34.2–3). Further discussion on this matter is given early in the section on Piety in Part Two of this text.

Such practices were difficult to follow when involved in actions abroad. In the case of the action of the small group of the Arkadians where most lost their lives, Xenophon duly organised the retrieval and burial of the dead. They had lain for five days where they had fallen and those who were corrupting were buried where they lay while those who had fallen on a roadway, a less moist place, were able to be gathered and given the normal rites. It is those whose bodies were not found who are deserving of special mention. To those was given a large cenotaph decorated with wreaths (*Anab.* VI.iv.9).[7] The commanders arranged for the retrieval of the dead and gave them burial honours insofar as was possible (*Anab.* IV.ii.23). Likewise, in thankfulness on reaching a sight of the sea, the soldiers built a great cairn of stones on which they placed offerings to the gods (*Anab.* IV.vii.26).

Natural features and phenomena were subject to the consideration of the gods, particularly in adverse conditions. After marches through deep snow and a river crossing where the men were wet through to their waists, three further marches through deep snow saw the army struggling against a strong freezing north wind. One of the soothsayers suggested a sacrifice be made to the wind and this was duly done. Whether fortuitous or otherwise, or whether that particular soothsayer was also a student of climatology, the wind abated very soon after the rites (*Anab.* IV.v.4). At the point of the disputed river crossing (*Anab.* IV.iii.17) soothsayers deemed it important enough to perform sacrifices to the river while under missile fire. The opinion of the soothsayers held great weight as can be seen in the course of the attack on the stronghold of the Drilai, but only when their findings were in accordance with the principle sacrifices of the day. These had been made by Xenophon and, when the soothsayers stated that the expedition would continue to be fortunate so long as fighting continued, they echoed the outcome of Xenophon's sacrifice. He was prepared to press the attack rather than attempt a risky withdrawal (*Anab.* V.ii.9).

It could be supposed from the evidence thus far that the proposed action, which was the subject of the sacrifice, was to be undertaken immediately following the approval of the gods. In certain circumstances this proved to be far from the case. The sacrifice made after the generals had heard that, by passing through the land of the Karduchians they would come to Armenia, proved to be qualified (*Anab.* III.v.18). They sought approval for a march to be made at a time which they considered appropriate and, as it turned out, this was made at night for tactical reasons The gods would therefore appear to eschew tactical considerations and deal only with the mundane right or wrong of the issue. It can be argued that behind the organised delay, the generals were hoping for further intelligence concerning their safe passage through the intervening mountains.

One important issue is the tithe to Artemis of the Ephesians and Apollo. It was incumbent on Xenophon to ensure that the tithes reached their destinations. In the case of that of Apollo, he made this himself at Delphi, but that which was designated to Artemis he left behind with Megabyzos, a priest of

Artemis. This arrangement was to forestall any likelihood of his not completing his religious duties. Two facts emerge from this arrangement. The first is evidence from Xenophon himself that he was with Agesilaos in Asia and at Koroneia (*Anab.* V.iii.6) and that, such was the responsibility under which such matters were held, that Megabyzos travelled to Olympia, where Xenophon had his estate nearby, to give him the balance of his offering (*Anab.* V.iii.7). Megabyzos had obviously made the offering which Xenophon had left him to make as he considered fit, and had brought him the balance. The sum involved gives the measure of such donations, for with that balance Xenophon was able to buy a piece of land near his estate at Skillous, build a temple and create a festival.

The most important thing for a commander to do was to sacrifice on behalf of his men. If Xenophon is to be believed that he chose to remain behind in order to sacrifice to see whether the gods approved of taking the army to Seuthes, and was doing this solely for the sake of the men, he is to be applauded. It may well be that this proved to be the subject of the sacrifice, but it was no doubt also used as an excuse for not going into Perinthos, from where he had received intelligence that he would be arrested and handed over to Pharnabazos if he went into the city (*Anab.* VII.ii.14–15).

At *Anab.* VI.v.21 Xenophon gives a short list of what is consulted when taking measure of the will of the gods: sacrificial victims, of which the quality and conduct at the sacrifice should be of the best; bird omens when available; the reading of the hiera and sphagia of the victims themselves following sacrifice. To be mundane, the victims of the sacrifice also provided fresh meat at least for the use of the officers. Between one and three sheep could provide a portion for between thirty and one hundred men. A prime example of designing the choice of sacrificial victims to the needs of the table was the selection of captured cattle for sacrifice on the occasion when the Paphlagonian ambassadors were the guests at a feast in their honour (*Anab.* VI.i.4). The choice of larger animals for sacrifice was necessary to satisfy the needs of the greater number of men present.

Morale, Training and Discipline

Although there has already been some discussion concerning morale in the previous section, it is informative, before looking in some detail for examples in the *Anabasis*, to make a short review of Xenophon's views in some of his other writings, hitherto not yet covered in this study, relevant to this and other concerns in this section.

One of the strongest beliefs held by Xenophon was that a commander must inculcate loyalty in his men (*Oikon.* XXI.4–8) and this is a facet of command technique which he made a point of praising in others, as can be seen in Part Two of the text. A perusal of the *Memorabilia I–III* shows in what worth Xenophon also holds virtue (*Mem.* II.i.21–34 for the story of the training of Herakles). It is used as an example to the young aspirant to high office, including generalship. In like manner, his attitude to the treatment of men of all conditions, including slaves, is made plain. Willingness rather than coercion was the better way; work rather than indolence. But the most pointed list of requirements comes at the point in Book III where Sokrates engages in a dialogue with a young man aspiring to generalship who has been to a teacher of tactics. He admits, on Sokrates' questioning, that he has only learned tactics. Sokrates' reply listed all the important aspects of generalship, of which tactics is but a small part (*Mem.* III.i.6–7).

> For a general must also be capable of furnishing military equipment and pro-viding supplies for the men; he must be resourceful, active, careful, hardy and quick-witted; he must be both gentle and brutal, at once straightforward and designing, capable of both caution and surprise, lavish and rapacious, generous and mean, skilful in defence and attack; and there are many other qualifications, some natural, some acquired, that are necessary to one who would succeed as a general. It is well to understand tactics too; for there is a wide difference between right and wrong disposition of the troops... (*Mem.* III.i.6–7, Loeb edition translated by E.C. Marchant.)

There are parallels in the earlier writings of Xenophon's near contemporary Sun Tzu:

> In which army is there the greater constancy both in reward and punishment (I.7).
> The consummate leader cultivates the moral law, and strictly adheres to method and discipline; thus it is in his power to control success (IV.16).
> Bestow rewards without regard to rule, issue orders without regard to pre-vious arrangements; and you will be able to handle a whole army as though you had to do with but a single man (XI.56).
> Confront your soldiers with the deed itself, never let them know your design. When the outlook is bright, bring it before their eyes, but tell them nothing when the situation is gloomy (XI.57).
> Make forays in fertile country in order to supply your army with food.

Carefully study the well-being of your men, and do not overtax them. Concentrate your energy and hoard your strength (XI.21–22).

The principle on which to manage an army is to set up one standard of courage which all must reach (XI.32).

Unhappy is the fate of one who tries to win his battles and succeed in his attacks without cultivating the spirit of enterprise, for the result is waste of time and general stagnation (XII.15).

If soldiers are punished before they have grown attached to you, they will not prove submissive; and unless submissive, they will be practically useless. If, when the soldiers have become attached to you, punishments are not enforced, they will still be useless. Therefore soldiers must be treated in the first instance with humanity, but kept under control by means of iron discipline (IX.42–43).

If a general shows confidence in his men but always insists on his orders being obeyed, the gain will be mutual (IX.45).

When the common soldiers are too strong and their officers too weak, the result is insubordination. When the officers are too strong and the common soldiers too weak, the result is collapse (X.16).

Regard your soldiers as your children, and they will follow you into the deepest valleys; look on them as your own beloved sons, and they will stand by you even unto death. If, however, you are indulgent, but are unable to enforce your commands; and incapable, moreover, of quelling disorder, then your soldiers must be likened to spoilt children; they are useless for any practical purpose (X.25–26).

Do not repeat the tactics which have gained you one victory, but let your methods be regulated by the infinite variety of circumstances (VI. 28).

Personal knowledge of the men under the command of a general is seen to be an essential. In a short conversation which is a criticism of those who had set themselves up as teachers of tactics, Sokrates questions further. He leads the young man on from his statement that the best men in an army should be placed in the van and the rear with the worst in the centre, and asks him how he will know the good from the less able (*Mem.* III.i.9). The youth admits that he, the commander, will have to have knowledge of the men to be able to make judgement. Later, to another who has been chosen as general, Sokrates points out that it was the duty of a commander to look after the interests of those who had elected him general and who would be led by him *(Mem.* III.ii.3-4). In *Mem.* III. Sokrates persuades, by analogous argument, a newly appointed cavalry commander that it is not enough merely to take up his position, he has to train both men and horses and lead by example. In the dialogue with Nikomachidis, Sokrates sets out the similarities that both general and businessman had to face in the course of their duties: the need to make subordinates willing and obedient, to give the right man the right place (again the need to know his men), to punish the bad and reward the good and to win the goodwill of his subordinates (*Mem.* III.iv.8). To the younger Perikles, he suggests that what a general did not know he might glean from others (*Mem.* III.v.23).

With the foregoing we are aptly prepared to consider the actuality of Xenophon's suggestions and actions in what follows. Here was a tidy mind, only happy when matters were ordered and accustomed to deal with the minutiae. A stickler for order (*Oikon.* VIII.4–7), indeed one who saw a form of beauty in order (*Oikon.* III.3). An ideal person for a command position, who would look after the logistics, care for his soldiers and weigh every action that he required of his men. This indeed proved to be the case, but with such a preliminary character sketch comes the danger of having someone in a position of command who finds that his vision is impaired by the desire only for orderliness. In the case of Xenophon we find an imaginative leader willing to learn from initial mistakes, modify his planning and seek the best solution in the interests of the men under his command. In the speeches he made to the assembly of men, much of what he says finds an echo in what he wrote at a later date.

To take up the main concern of this section, morale was of the utmost importance throughout the withdrawal of the Ten Thousand. Much that has gone before has pointed to the need of commanders to lead by example. Nothing was made more clear by Xenophon to his commander colleagues at the time of his speech prior to the resolve to march home (*Anab.* III.i.36–37). This speech contains the kernel of his thinking with regard to those who serve under any commander and one may wonder whether he, as a very young man with limited experience of warfare, could have actually made such an analysis at that time. Whether the actuality was modified by later reflection and given more flesh by reason of experience at the time of writing can only be guessed at, but following on from the necessity to lead by example, he dealt with the question of discipline (*Anab.* III.i.38), the current low morale of the troops (*Anab.* III.1.39–46) and the basic essentials of a well ordered army. He was quick to preserve morale and to turn despondency to more positive ends when Tissaphernes' men adopted a scorched earth policy and seemed to be denying the Greeks any opportunities for forage. He showed that the Persians were burning the product of their own territories as if admitting that such lands were in the hands of the Greeks (*Anab.* III.v.3–5). The ploy of further diminishing the standing of an enemy prior to engagement in order to boost the morale of one's own men by implying that the Greeks were better men, is used (*Anab*. IV.viii.14). However, the soldiers themselves, under no orders to do so, disfigured dead Persians for the purpose of intimidating their enemy (*Anab*. III.iv.5) and to lower Persian morale.

The care of those under his command was paramount to Xenophon and went hand in hand with sustaining morale. This was not merely adopting successful tactics to ensure their safety, but meant looking after their day-to-day welfare. Book IV.v graphically recounts the problems encountered when the march had to be made through deep snow. Lack of food, snow blindness and frostbite proved to be major problems and Xenophon lists the means by which such sufferings could be avoided: looking at something black while on the march in order to avoid snow blindness; keeping moving to keep up the blood circulation; taking off footwear each night to avoid the leather thongs becoming embedded in the flesh (*Anab*. IV.v.12–14). Presumably a caring commander such as he would ensure that his men followed instructions. Thirty soldiers, slaves and baggage animals died at one point. Xenophon, who commanded the rearguard, came upon numbers of soldiers who had fallen out of line through hunger and exhaustion. His immediate action was to go to the baggage animals, disburse whatever was edible to the sufferers and to organise those who were sufficiently strong to continue the disbursement. His reward was to see those who had eaten rejoin the march (*Anab*. IV.v.7–8) when their strength was revived. The van, under Cheirisophos, had reached some villages and was followed there by as many of the army who were up to the effort. Those who could not complete the journey were forced to spend the night in the open without fire or food. Deaths were reported to have occurred in their number (*Anab*. IV.v.11). Meanwhile, Xenophon, with the rearguard, knowing that the enemy was in pursuit, came upon more men who, rather than go any further, appeared to prefer death. He came to the decision that to protect them he, with the fittest of the rearguard, should mount a pre-emptive attack on their pursuers. With the flight of the enemy, Xenophon told the sick and exhausted that men would be sent the following day to collect them and continued the march. Having gone no more than half a mile the route was impeded by troops lying in the snow without a watch posted for their protection. He discovered that the bulk of the army had settled for the night in like manner and he and his men were obliged to do the same, without fire or food, but not before guards had been set up (*Anab*. IV.v.21). At daybreak, Xenophon sent his youngest men to retrieve the sick, ordering them to force them to rise to continue the journey. With the arrival of men from Cheirisiphos, who had enjoyed the conditions of being fed and quartered in a village, the sick, now with Xenophon, were carried forward to the camp. Under the circumstances no commander could have done more, but Xenophon followed these actions by visiting and checking on the condition of the men now recovering and enjoying the plenitude found in the villages.

Obviously, lack of provisions was a constant concern to the commanders. A well-provisioned army was better able to cope with the unexpected hardship or engagement. This constant concern is readily understood on a march where no markets had been, or could be, easily arranged under the circumstances prevailing. While there had been a possibilty of the Greeks succumbing to the Persians' wish that they would surrender, provisions had been forthcoming, but, once their intention was clear, no further resource came from their enemy. So it was that the matter of provisioning this great host became a recurring problem. The matter was often solved by appropriating the stores of occupied villages, but harrassment from the Persians initially proved to be a problem and diminished morale (*Anab*. III.v.2–3).

In the mountains of the Karduchians the Greeks took what they could when the enemy had taken to flight but, when in Armenia, concluded a truce with Tiribazos to do no harm to property in return for provisions. This smacks of Tiribazos looking after his own interests rather than those of the Great King (*Anab*. IV.iv.5–6), however, see under 'Secrecy' and 'Tactics' for further discussion. Other examples of the manner in which provisions were acquired follow. In the foregoing, which dealt with the passage through snow, the villages reached by Cheirisophos were exceedingly well provisioned, but the Greeks had ensured good conduct from the inhabitants by virtually placing the headman, his daughter and other members of his family under arrest during their stay. Later (*Anab*. IV.viii.20–21) with provisions taken from villages the soldiers succumbed to a sickness after eating honey. At that time the army was probably at its most vulnerable, the greater part being unable to stand or conduct themselves in a manner in which they could have defended themselves. Thereafter, they plundered Kolchis while living for thirty days in villages nearby, presumably being provisioned from these. Trapezus provided them with a market and gave gifts (*Anab*. IV.viii.23) and after a successful attack on strongholds the Greeks discovered stores of food which they presumably took for their own use (*Anab*. V.iv.27–29). It is indicative that in the same action Xenophon reported that the force which made the attack was followed by some of the army, not under orders from a commander to do so, but merely going for the possibility of acquiring plunder (*Anab.* V.iv.16). This prompts the question to what degree discipline held sway in a Greek mercenary army. Was this common practice, or unusual because Xenophon makes allusion to it? Or does it imply a limit on the commander's control of his forces?

The fundamental choice of how discipline was sustained was between coercion and loyalty built up through humanitarian practices. Xenophon's manner and reported practice favoured the latter, but it remained unreported under whose direct command these mavericks campaigned for their plunder. The commanders were therefore securing the requisites by any means possible. Klearchos had declared that without provisions both general and private were good for nothing (*Anab.* I.iii.11) and Xenophon's anger at Herakleides on his shortfall in provisioning was understandable because discipline depended upon it (*Anab.* VII.v.5). The link between general and soldier was an unspoken contract of care.

A curious passage is encountered at *Anab.* VI.i.1. While staying at Kotyora the soldiery seemed to be divided between some who bought their supplies from the local market provided, presumably organised by the commanders, and others who acquired theirs from pillaging expeditions against the Paphlagonians. It is highly unlikely that there was a shortage of supplies at this market for it would necessarily be held on a regular basis. The prices must have been reasonable otherwise there would have been few customers. There can be only three related answers to this: the group who pillaged had run out of money or goods to exchange for provisions; they preferred to keep their nest-eggs and run the risks involved in such a practice; or the matter had been ordered in such a fashion. Several were captured while conducting their raids. This provoked Korylas, the ruler of Paphlagonia, to send ambassadors to the Greeks who laid on the feast alluded to earlier, the outcome of which was a non-aggression pact between the Greeks and the Paphlagonians. The pillaging could be regarded as a tactic to achieve a desired end ordered by the commanders. The middle option again prompts the question of discipline. What commander could allow men to put themselves, and eventually the whole army, at risk by such actions, unless there was a breakdown in discipline. In support of the first premise is the comment at *Anab.* VI.i.17, where the Greeks wondered how they might reach their homes with something to show for their labours. This was why they decided to offer Xenophon sole command at that point to ensure secrecy and to quicken decisions rather than wait for those from a committee of generals. It is likely that limited personal resource was the true reason for the pillaging, and it may well be that it was so ordered by the commanders to be done by contingents so that those resources could be supplemented in turn.

The closer they came to Greece the more easily provisions seemed to be acquired, mainly because they were dealing with Greek colonists. Whether the hospitality and gifts were given out of true 'guest friendship' or from fear of what an army of such size might do if not treated in a kindly fashion, is debatable, but we find Herakleia sending a huge quantity of grain and wine together with twenty cattle to the army on its arrival in Heraklea's environs. However, once they were within the Spartan controlled Bosphoros area, provisions proved difficult to come by. Indeed Anaxibios, then commanding for the Spartans there, suggested that they take provisions from Thracian villages (*Anab.* VII.i.13) but made no offer to help otherwise. This provoked a near sack of Byzantion and discipline was difficult to restore. A Theban, Koeratidas, desirous to become a general, appeared on the scene with an offer to provide for the men if they followed him. He was voted into office which lasted until it was discovered that his supplies were insufficient for the army. It was only by coming to an agreement with Seuthes, to aid him in the enterprise to recover his father's kingdom, that the army was assured of food and promised pay.

Such were the tribulations which faced the army and particularly their commanders at a time and place where it could be expected that life would be easier. It is as well to rehearse here the uniqueness of the long march. In terms of Greek warfare there had been nothing to match it up to that time. The normal Greek campaign would see an army set off, well provisioned for the proposed and limited action, usually within a relatively short time-scale. It was a rare occurrence for anyone to go hungry or not to have the promise of adequate provisions forthcoming. A Greek army operating on the mainland would not be encumbered by such a quantity of camp followers. We have in the *Anabasis* a veritable moving city state. The fighting element had servants and slaves to help with the baggage which was deemed normal to a Greek army. However, much of the baggage had been abandoned and, as has already been noted, there was a large number of women, whether concubines or wives, acquired on the inward march, and, by that time undoubtedly, infants. All looked to the soldiery to support them and provide them with sustenance. Such was the ever-present problem facing men and particularly the command structure. When reviewing the actions taken at times by sections of the army which might sometimes smack of indiscipline it is as well to remember that the immediate problem of survival for self and dependants could well have taken precedence over orders.

The order made by the generals at *Anab*. IV.i.12–13 to free recently taken captives was a measure to address the issue early in the homeward march but, as can be seen at *Anab*. IV.i.14, the response to the order was not entirely effective. Even when a check was made as to what was being given up, men smuggled women and boys for whom they had developed an affection. Men who acted in self interest were not an unusual problem for commanders to face as the case of Klearatos (*Anab*. V.vii.13–17) demonstrates. An independent adventure against a peaceable people such as the Kerasountians was not to be approved of, but was difficult to legislate against. The matter was further exacerbated by the surviving Greeks on this escapade who killed three of the ambassadors from Kerasous as they were on their way to the main body of Greeks to inform them of the action, and to request them to come to reclaim their dead. The problem which arose from this unilateral act of gross indiscipline was dealt with by Xenophon in a speech to the men which demonstrated the need to follow orders of appointed commanders or run the risk of chaos (*Anab*. V.vii.27–30). Xenophon proved himself fair in his judgement of the indiscipline shown by the men at *Anab*. VI.iv.7, for, ostensibly, he had been the cause of it. He and other generals, having been associated with the idea of founding a city, were faced with the refusal of the men to encamp on the spot where such a possibility was obvious. This level of mistrust for their commanders was neither good for discipline nor morale.

A moral issue arose, although it is not dealt with as such, and one may question the thinking of the commanders at the time of its happening. Had the problems of obtaining provisions also muted accepted practices within the group of Greek commanders? At *Anab*. V.v.2–3 when in the territory of the Tibarenians, the latter sent messages to the Greeks offering gifts of hospitality. Initially, these were refused until the Greeks made sacrifice. It had been the intention of the Greek commanders to plunder the coastal strongholds of the Tibarenians and the arrival of this offer of guest friendship had obviously taken them aback. The fact that they left it to a sacrifice to decide whether or not to accept the gifts is a measure of the degree to which their honour had slipped. Luckily, or in this case by the design of the seers whose morality may have been less corrupted, the sacrifice was declared to be firmly against war and the Greeks accordingly accepted the gifts. It is as well to compare this episode with the conduct of the army in relation to the Kotyorites and Sinopeans (*Anab*. V.v.7–12) where relations were strained, even Greek against Greek. Xenophon states the case of the army very succinctly. Whether the land was barbarian or Greek, where there was no market, they took provisions, not out of cussedness but out of necessity (*Anab.* V.v.16). Xenophon countered the threat of war by the Sinopean ambassadors by threatening war on them in turn (*Anab.* V.v.22–23). Although much annoyed by his words, the ambassadors resolved to show hospitality to the army. In the final analysis, the needs of the men must be paramount for any commander.

In action, the sustaining of morale was an imperative. So it is that Xenophon recommended engaging the Persian force under Spithridates and Rhathines sent by the satrap Pharnabazos, rather than effecting a retreat, and this was purely on the grounds of morale (*Anab.* VI.v.17). So in action as well as speech, it was important to lead by example. At the same reference Xenophon personalised the matter by declaring that he would rather advance with half as many soldiers as retreat with twice as many.

In the *Anabasis* Xenophon understandably is the focus of any action. There are three prominent occasions when he led by example. The first was the occasion when, covered in snow and warm against the cold conditions, the men were unwilling to rise from their sleeping places and face the cold. Xenophon made the point of getting up, although he admitted the need to summon up courage to do so, and started splitting wood for a fire. His example was followed and soon many were doing likewise and annointing themselves with the only available substitute for olive oil, pork fat mixed with almonds, sesame and turpentine (*Anab.* IV.iv.11–13). The second was the successful race to capture the summit of a hill to secure an advance. Xenophon, encouraging his men forward while on horseback, was criticised by a certain Soteridas for being mounted while he, on foot, was tired because of carrying his own shield. Xenophon's reaction to this was to dismount immediately, take Soteridas' shield from him, push him out of line, take his place and march with the men. Wearing his cavalry breastplate he was more encumbered than the rest of the men and exhorted them to pass him by, if necessary, because it was difficult for him to keep up with the pace of the leaders.[8] The reaction of the men to this was to hurl abuse at Soteridas and to pelt him, presumably with small stones and clods, until he reclaimed his shield and allowed Xenophon to remount (*Anab.* III.iv.47–49). This was a similar situation to that encountered at *Anab.* II.iii.11, where Klearchos had involved himself directly with a mundane activity which the men had been ordered to complete. There was obviously a school of thought which recommended that commanders should be as well, if not better, skilled than their men, that they should never ask their men to do anything that they themselves were not willing to do and that, as a consequence, they expected complete compliance from the men when orders were issued. The third, and possibly most obvious example, was when Seuthes, prior to the attack on the villages, questioned Xenophon's reason for dismounting from his horse when there was a need for haste (*Anab*. VII.iii.44–45). Xenophon declared that the hoplites would move quicker and with better spirit if he was seen to be leading on foot. The commander had to establish himself in the good opinion of his men and to do this he had to be a model for them by setting an example in the endurance of hardship (*Anab*. IV.iv.11–12), by showing confidence (*Anab*. III.ii.18–19), by leading by example (*Anab*. III.iv.37–49; VII.iii.45–46) and by being accessible to his men (*Anab*. IV.iii.10).

Training does not arise as an issue in the *Anabasis*. The need for training in an army of battle hardened veterans became a personal matter for the individual hoplite, that of honing personal skills. The day to day activities of keeping alive proved sufficient incentive. Fitness would be no problem in view of the marching and fighting they had to do. Hunger, sickness, adverse weather conditions and the receipt of a wound were the major problems for the soldiery. If Xenophon's colleagues were as assiduous as he, and there is little reason to doubt this, dealing with such adversities loomed large in the responsibilities undertaken by the generals. However, the conduct of a general could be reviewed, indeed censured by the army in times of hardship. Lykon, an Achaean, pointed out that there was an insufficiency of supplies or money with which to proceed onward from Herakleia and laid the blame for this at the door of the generals. He proposed to the Assembly that the army demand money from the city for the journey (*Anab*. VI.ii.4). This, after Herakleia had already supplied them with three days' supply of provisions and laid on a market. Cheirisophos and Xenophon refused to be their ambassadors, and when others were sent in their place, the citizens withdrew within the city walls taking their property and market with them, making it clear that they intended to defend themselves by force of arms. This development was, in turn, again blamed on the generals and in the resulting discussions, the Achaeans and Arkadians decided to elect new generals from their own fellow citizenry.[9] The result of this disaffection was the breakup of the army into three groups: the first made up of Achaeans and Arkadians numbered over 4,000 men, the second under Cheirisophos of 1,400 hoplites and 700 hundred peltasts, and the third under Xenophon with 1,700 hoplites, 300 peltasts and a force of forty cavalry, the only one of the three groups to have horsemen. This total number of just over 8,000 men when set beside the figures given earlier in the account for Greeks within Kyros' army indicates the casualties or desertions from an original force of possibly just under 12,000 hoplites and 2,300 peltasts and archers.[10]

Xenophon himself faced accusations in the inquiry into his conduct following the purification of the army. He easily rebutted the prime accusation and what followed in his speech demonstrated clearly the occasions and reasons behind his use of corporal punishment. It was applied solely at times of indiscipline, for the good and safety of the individual in the case of those who through exhaustion or hunger were unwilling to go on, for forcing warmth and circulation of the blood in those who took no precautions against frostbite and for those whose indolence slowed the march, thus endangering the army (*Anab.* V.viii.13–22). All actions were committed in times of hardship or peril and for the common good. Xenophon drew the attention of the men to the fact that in less stressful times such as they then enjoyed he had never struck anyone.[11]

Some argue that the army of the *Anabasis* was like a city state.[12] Admittedly, there are grounds for this in the make-up of the personnel in terms of accompanying slaves, servants, womenfolk and children, but there was no opportunity for purely public issues to emerge. The conditions of the march prohibited such niceties unless Xenophon has ignored making mention of them in his account. They might have done so had Xenophon's idea of founding a city been adopted. Shared functions of state were observed, such as the constant need to consult the gods, but the votes at assemblies have been given too much weight in the argument for democracy. The men were mercenaries and had to be consulted on issues which affected their well being both in health and pocket and these had nothing to do with a commonality of political belief. It was not democracy which led to the break-up of the army but the self assertion of personal wishes and needs. At home the Achaeans and Arkadians, to name but two of the major contributors to the army, had not yet tasted true democracy. The establishment and maintenance of morale and discipline can only be treated in military terms from the evidence of the *Anabasis* and no wishful thinking in civil terms can be realistically countenanced.

A picture emerges of the character of Xenophon from his writings. A fair minded, ascetic, practical personality who holds a firm view of the attributes necessary in an ideal commander and one who, in his own actions, tried to emulate his own vision. It is in the many analytical speeches which Xenophon reported he made that we discover the problems faced by the army and the planning which led to their resolution, often reiterating the need for discipline and morale.

On the March and in Camp

Technically the whole of the *Anabasis* was what its title suggests, a march. However it was a march interspersed with actions, tactical manoeuvres and periods of rest. It became a campaign by virtue of the line of the march but not a campaign against a specific enemy. The enemy was only he who proved confrontational to the aim, that of strategic withdrawal, or rather in modern terms, *operational objectives and the end-state*.[13] There is no reference to contingency planning by Kyros in case his plans went awry and no references in sources up to that time of any commander previously having given them consideration. The likelihood is that all good commanders must have given some thought to such contingencies, but for the sake of morale kept those ideas to himself. It is therefore obvious that much which happened on the march will be addressed under the section on tactics and that the current section will address itself to factors which will complement that area of discussion.

The initial analysis made by Xenophon, as was seen earlier, was made to boost morale but contained a balanced view of the pros and cons of particular courses of action. The most discerning suggestion was that of burning the wagons and inessential baggage so that routes would not be restricted and the pace of the march not determined by that of the oxen. Provisions were to be garnered *en route* rather than carried, so that as many men might be kept under arms as possible.[14] The initial formation for the march followed a suggestion that the hoplites form a hollow square within which the remaining baggage train and camp followers would be protected.[15]

This formation did not last long. The experience of the difficulties encountered when the road narrowed or when a bridge or narrow crossing had to be made, led to the wings drawing together thus creating congestion to such an extent that confusion resulted. Similarly, when sufficient space was achieved so that the wings could move apart, gaps emerged which an enemy could also exploit. The response to this problem was to create six units of a hundred men, each under a *lochagos* together with subordinate commanders. Their duties were to drop back behind the wings when they came closer, and to fill the gap between the wings when they drew apart. The gap on each occasion would be variable so that flexibilty of formation by these forces was an imperative and would be conducted, depending on the size of the gap, by the subcommanders deciding on the appropriate number to provide the infill.[16] Although further discussion of this arrangement really lies under tactics it is as well to complete it here. It would appear that these counter measures were the product of discussion among the generals (*Anab.* III.iv.21). Xenophon detailed the arrangement and, because he made special mention of it, this might imply that it was a new development. However, as it emanated from the joint discussion of the generals and no individual was given the credit for creative thinking, it could well be that this was one of several known and tried options for such a problem. What is most significant is that this special force whose duties were designed as a corrective to any foreseeable problems, can only be described as a *reserve*. An unusual and early reference to such special forces which is indicative of the new thinking which was pervading the military man. While a teacher of tactics in the safety of his city states could codify as much as he wished, the practitioner in the field itself was the creative element in the development of warfare.

Ideally, a Greek army was happiest when it could march in battle order or in column, at the ready to deploy in line of battle as it did through Armenia (*Anab.* IV.iv.1). But this required the conditions of a broad plain which was also conducive to cavalry action, the most effective arm in the Persian forces. Indeed it is indicative that early in the journey, because of cavalry and light armed harrassment, the Greeks avoided having to march and fight at the same time and chose the easier option of defending their encampment from any attack during the day. When the Persians decided to retire late in the day, orders were given to the Greeks within easy earshot of the Persians, to make ready for a march thus delaying the Persian withdrawal. With the eventual and much later Persian retiral, the Greeks made a tactical night march with the intention of putting as much distance as possible between themselves and the enemy (*Anab.* III.iv.37). This they succeeded in doing and benefitted from three days of unhampered marching thereafter. However, night movements were not confined to the Greeks alone. For the Persians, with cavalry, it was possible to overtake and pass the Greeks by making their move also by night in order to take up a forward position threatening the Greek route.

Although initially casualties were sustained, the decision to make a march through the Karduchian mountains, rather than try to bridge the Tigris at one of its deepest points at the ingenious suggestion of a Rhodian (*Anab.* III.v.8– 11), was sound in that it was not terrain suitable for cavalry deployment. The order of march for entering the mountain chain saw the rearguard, under Xenophon, made up solely of hoplites. All the peltasts were with Cheirisophos in the van. Xenophon remarked that it was arranged in this manner because of the unlikelihood of any pursuit but, more importantly it might have been

Cheirisophos' assessment that the peltasts would be of greater use in dislodging the Karduchians from high positions.

A repeat of the order to discard all superfluous baggage, animals and personnel was made to quicken the march (*Anab.* IV.i.13–14). Even so, this was not entirely successful. Many of the captives were released but, as the march progressed in bad weather, the very issue which had made for the order still remained, a shortage of provisions. The march was slowed almost to a stop-go pace so that enemy attacks might be repelled. The dash for a pass made by Cheirisophos was a calculated risk but endangered the rearguard which was subject to severe harrassment as they tried to keep up with the column (*Anab.* IV.i.17). This was counter to the arranged usual practice that the van would wait until the rearguard was comfortably in touch. Cheirisophos' valid reason was that he had hoped to occupy the pass before the opposition took possession of it.

Wherever possible, encampment was made in villages (*Anab.* IV.iii.1; IV.v.23). No doubt this was mainly because of the availability of provisions but was also useful for defensive purposes. At a time when security was paramount, the Greeks made even more stringent provision for safety by going to an easily defensible site, digging a trench across the line of approach, in this case an isthmus, and building a palisade with three gates, presumably for sorties (*Anab.* VI.v.1). The issue of encamping in a strong place was forced upon the serving soldiers by circumstance. They had come to the region of Kalpe suspecting that the generals intended to found a city. Finding an ideal site suitable for either a city foundation or a camp on the isthmus, with rich soil, copious quantities of timber, sheltered anchorage and adequate spring water, the men had been suspicious and had encamped on the beach rather than at the more obvious location for their safety. Only when a foraging force had suffered serious casualties on being surprised by the cavalry of Pharnabazos, and later, when outposts to the Greek camp itself had been attacked by Bithynians, was there an acceptance of the original choice of site. The series of mishaps was the result of the breakdown of the essential trust of men for their commanders. It can be argued that the seed of that mistrust was the responsibility of the commanders who permitted it to grow to a point where discipline was greatly at risk.

When Xenophon chose to visit Seuthes' camp at night, he noted that there were unmanned watch fires and presumed that Seuthes had moved his encampment, only to discover that these fires had been lit in advance of the pickets to conceal their numbers and locations (*Anab.* VII.ii.18). The pickets, however, could see any advance which was made toward their positions.

Xenophon obviously states this as being unusual for the time but later incorporates a more developed version of the principle in the *Kyropaideia* where fires are lit to front and rear of the encampment (*Kyr.* III.iii.33; III.iii.25). No fires are lit within the camp, but this seems to be normal practice for the time for at *Anab.* VI.iii.21, fires are extinguished after dining and the encampment at that time is in total darkness. In camp Seuthes is found ensconced in a tower with his horses ready bridled in case of night attack (*Anab.* VII.ii.21–22). This was because he was encamped in the territory of the Thynians, a people accustomed to making attacks by night. Such care, which ran to the extent of feeding the horses by day in order to have them at the ready by night, impressed Xenophon sufficiently for him to note it (*Anab.* VII.ii.21). As a measure of security Seuthes was requested not to allow any of his Thracians to enter the Greek camp by night (*Anab.* VII.iii.34), an obvious precaution to be taken when friend and foe alike were Thracians. Seuthes adopted the Greek practice for a night march whereby the slowest led the way so that no part of the whole might be separated from the other (*Anab.* VII.iii.38). It is at this point that the alternative forms of Greek marching formation are prescribed. The daytime march was made with the leaders of the march being chosen from those best suited to the terrain, either peltasts or cavalry. Seuthes also suggested that he and his cavalry take their place at the rear of the march, being able to come to the van quickly if needed. He also provided guides from the oldest of his men who knew the country well (*Anab.* VII.iii.39).

A model example for marching and encamping for the period is provided at *Anab.* VI.iii.4–21 at a time when Xenophon sought to rescue those Arkadians who were cut off and beseiged by Thracians. The organisation of the advance is undertaken with extreme care. The cavalry under Timasion went ahead of the main force to reconnoitre the terrain over which they must pass, always keeping in touch with the command point. On the flanks Xenophon sent out peltasts to the higher ground to do the same. All groups, cavalry, peltasts and the main body of hoplites burned everything combustible which they encountered, giving the impression of the advance of a very large force. When the enemy camp was in sight some three miles distant, they encamped on a hill lighting as many fires as was possible. Having given the impression of being a large relief force they extinguished all fires after they had eaten their evening meal and set up guards. With such care it wasn't discovered until the following day that the enemy had withdrawn from their position.

Much that is pertinent to the march is best discussed under tactics where the balance of interest favours the latter.

Secrecy, Spies, non-combative Deception and Intelligence

First and foremost a commander must build on a body of knowledge concerning his adversaries, the nature of the terrain which must be traversed, the places where provisions can be replenished, the likely response of the peoples through whose lands the army must make passage and, in the case of Xenophon and his colleague generals, a constant use of guides and local informants, willing or coerced. Given the meagre information to hand at the commencement of the march, normally nobody in his right mind would have undertaken command responsibility had not the situation been so desperate. It attests to the leadership qualities present within this corporate body of Greeks and to the basic organisation of the command structure within a Greek army, that there was an ever present willingness to demonstrate initiative and acceptance of responsibility.[17] Indeed it is that quality of initiative which caused problems from time to time on the journey, when individuals took it upon themselves to arrange unilateral plundering expeditions, or were willing to take up command positions when the army divided temporarily. A constant secondary level of intelligence had to be maintained, that of internal security, in order to contain and direct this spirit of individualism.

This individualism was present among the common soldiery and had to be taken into account by commanders. It has been seen that a hoplite could grumble about his commander quite openly as was the case with Soteridas, and herein lies the difference between the Greek and Persian armies of the time. A Greek army was made up of like minded individuals, notionally free men, whose position in an army could be variable. For his city state he could be in a position of command on one campaign and serve as a journeyman soldier the next. It was a question of the common good. Not so with the Persians, whose nobility retained the command positions and whose subjects made up the army and were under compulsion to serve without question.

Under the changing conditions of the march any intelligence gathering structure would necessarily have to be simple. Language problems would be a constant issue when dealing with ever changing local populations. A heavy reliance on scouts and information from prisoners was essential to derive information concerning the habits, attitudes and resources of the areas they sought to traverse. Information gathering of all kinds had to be made and the commanders' responsibility was to sift it and plan the next course of action. In Xenophon's case, he made it quite clear that anyone with information which could be of use could come to him at any time, be it day or night (*Anab.*

IV.iii.10). His style of command, like that of Kyros in the *Kyropaideia*, was one of open access to all comers. However, it can be noted that the bulk of received information is of immediate or short term use only. Constant observation proved to be the key to success.

At the outset, few hard facts were known other than the obvious, that to cross rivers it was best to do so nearer their sources which meant marching north (*Anab*. III.ii.22) and that there were peoples dwelling within the territory of the Persian empire who were not subject to the Great King (*Anab*. III.ii.23–24) though not neccessarily on that northerly route. The only useful piece of information other than the conviction that the Persians were out to do them harm was that there were villages where provisions could be had lying about two and a half miles away from their position (*Anab*. III.ii.34); not an auspicious start to an intelligence structure. However, early in the march it was observed that the Persians made camp no less than seven miles away from the Greeks. This was in case of a night attack by the Greeks when the Persian horses were tethered and hobbled (*Anab*. III.iv.34–35).

The first tangible piece of intelligence was derived from prisoners who gave them information concerning the surrounding area for all points of the compass (*Anab*. III.v.14–16). From this the line of march was decided, even though it would take them through the territory of the warlike Karduchians who had, it was reputed, destroyed an army of the Great King numbering 120,000. The prisoners had indicated that as soon as they were through Karduchian lands they would be in Armenia with the option of going in any direction they chose. Further, they would there be able to cross, or go round the waters of both the Tigris or Euphrates rivers. This line of action suited them better than attempting the difficult river crossing faced with cavalry on the further bank. It may also have been very acceptable to the Persians that the Greeks decided to do so, for theirs was a damage limitation exercise with the hope that the eventual destruction of the Greeks might be achieved. Proof of this strategy may rest with the non-aggression pact made by the Greeks with Tiribazos, the lieutenant-governor of Western Armenia. The terms were that the Greeks could acquire all the provisions they needed provided that they left properties unharmed as they passed through the region. Further, Tiribazos elected to leave the Greeks unharmed in their passage. Despite some adverse weather conditions the army enjoyed a short period when foraging or plundering was unneccessary, with requirements being plenty and readily available. This was a time when the Greeks must have felt infinitely more secure than at any time since Kounaxa. However, the first worrying report came when men, who had wandered from the camp, reported seeing many fires at night (*Anab.* IV.iv.9). The direction of the fires was ahead of the Greeks in the direction of their march towards the mountains (*Anab.* IV.iv.15). The result of this accidental piece of intelligence brought greater measures of security within the Greek forces. It was decided to have all divisions of the army together rather than in separate encampments within villages.

A brief digression is required to cover the questions raised by this seemingly innocuous description of events. Had those men who had seen the fires gone beyond the line of pickets which would normally have been placed in advance of an encampment? Why had the pickets themselves not reported the matter, for it was their duty to be on watch? Had the Greeks relaxed so much that they had dispensed with the need for anything other than daytime scouts? An explanation is that those men who had seen the fires had indeed, for whatever reason, gone forward in advance of the pickets; the pickets themselves would have been beside fires and, because of the effect of adjacent light on the retina, were unable to see any distant lights; there were no night time scouts. The proof that Greek watch fires were manned at that time lies with the surprise expressed by Xenophon much later when he came upon those unmanned watch fires of Seuthes placed well in advance of the unseen pickets (*Anab.* VII.ii.17–18). (See earlier under 'On the March and in Camp'.)

Returning to the further developments from this kernel of intelligence, severe weather conditions forced the commanders to reverse their decision to encamp together and they sent the men back to their former billets in the several villages. The army was not moving on from their present position until further clarification was received. It is at *Anab.* IV.iv.14 that Xenophon lets slip the comment that, whereas many of the men were exceedingly happy to return to a good billet with plenty of provisions, there were some who had burned the houses they had left and were now forced to put up with inferior accommodation. It may well be that those men had made a practice of destroying each and every house they had stayed in at each stage of the march through Western Armenia. If so, this was in direct breach of the agreement with Tiribazos and may well have accounted for his reaction. Again it prompts the question of discipline, for there is no reference made to any punishment for the misdemeanour. Mere acceptance of the fact and a hint that, on this occasion, the men got their deserts for being so precipitate in thinking that they would be moving on.

It is at this point that a personality is revealed who is deemed a specialist intelligence officer. There must have been several employed, for Demokrates is described as having a reputation for accuracy and sound interpretation, implying that he was the best of a number (*Anab.* IV.iv.15). This too adds to the evidence of a basic intelligence architecture. He is given the responsibility for a reconnaissance to investigate the fires in the mountains. On the return of the reconnaissance force during the night, he admits not to have seen any fires but had with him a captive Persian. When questioned, the Persian said he was from Tiribazos' camp travelling to arrange for provisions. He added that Tiribazos had an army made up of his own men and Chalibian and Taochian mercenaries, and that the plan was to attack the Greeks on the only road which led through the mountains (*Anab.* IV.iv.18). The action taken on receipt of this intelligence is dealt with under 'Tactics' below. The only unresolved issue lies with the reason behind Tiribazos' intended attack on the Greeks. Was it in response to the shameless breach of the treaty by some of the Greeks, or was it a continuance of Persian strategy? If the latter, it was in Tiribazos' interest to safeguard his fiefdom from damage and also to play for time so that mercenaries could be mustered. Had it been his intention at the outset to attack the Greeks? He was also described as being very close to the Great King. Therefore, while there is perfidy on the side of the Greeks in this affair which provided adequate excuse for Tiribazos' reaction, the balance of evidence suggest that it was always his intention eventually to do harm to the Greek army.

That the Greeks sought information from every source available is obvious, but the methods of acquiring it differed with circumstance. A covert conversational method proved useful for Cheirisophos with women and girls at a well outside a village wall. Using an interpreter speaking in Persian and pretending that the Greeks were travelling to the satrap from the Great King, he elicited that the satrap was about a *parasang*, some three and a half miles, distant. In the prevailing weather conditions, a safe distance (*Anab.* IV.v.9–10). Information derived under mild coercion followed the possession of a village. Although treated well, both headman and villagers would know they were at the mercy of the Greeks. Useful information as well as direct intelligence on the locality was forthcoming, such as the tip to place bags on the feet of horses and baggage animals when travelling through deep snow (*Anab.* IV.v.36). The 'mild coercion' extended to taking the headman as guide to the army with his son in the keeping of Pleisthenes of Amphipolis for good conduct (*Anab.* IV.vi.1) and suggests a common practice where possible. The fact that the headman did not, or could not because they were unavailable, lead the army to villages, led to Cheirisophos striking him, and having left him unbound thereafter, allowing him to escape leaving his son behind (*Anab.* IV.vi.3). At the other end of the spectrum, ruthless and brutal methods were applied to the two Karduchians captured by Xenophon. They were questioned separately (*Anab.* IV.i.23). When no information could be gained from the first as to a prospective route, he was killed in front of the second who thereafter willingly divulged the required information and offered to act as guide. Other captives proved more fortunate. Those taken prisoner by Xenophon (*Anab.* IV.vi.17) had obviously readily divulged information on how to pass over a seemingly impassable mountain. An insight into how such prisoners were caught is at the same reference. The rearguard set an ambush of peltasts to capture some from the following enemy.

Information from friendly sources was always welcomed. The planned march through the territory of the Mossynoekians was resisted by the inhabitants when application to do so peacefully was made through Timesitheos, a Trapezountian, who was the city's ambassador to these people. From Timesitheos the Greeks learned that fellow Mossynoekians further on were enemies of those in the immediate vicinity and the ambassador was sent to them with a proposal for an alliance against a common adversary (*Anab.* V.iv.3–10). This was accepted, and an attack from both sides of the territory, with allied reinforcements being sent directly by sea to the Greeks, was arranged.

Reported deception is minimal in Xenophon's account once the army was clear of the Persian army. This should not be regarded as unusual. This was not a campaign, but a march through successive territories whose inhabitants were, in turn, hospitable, compliant through fear, or vehemently hostile. On a campaign it was the duty of a commander to know as much as possible about the character, methodology in warfare and likely reactions of his opponent. This was garnered both by intelligence and direct experience. Time was something the Greek commanders did not have for this purpose. They did what they could on what little information they had. What small deception or ruse is reported is of the simplest kind, such as that of disguising numbers. The occasion of the relief march undertaken by Xenophon in aid of the Arkadians *Anab.* VI.iii.14–21 has been dealt with under the section 'On the March' but it is as well to suggest here that Xenophon was undertaking a ruse to disguise the strength of his forces. The Thracians at that time would have little idea of the strength of any likely relieving force and would assume, at first sight of the fires, that it was greater than its actuality. One could argue that Xenophon's reluctance to go to Perinthos (*Anab.* VII.ii.15) was a self-preserving deception perpetrated on his colleagues, but this would be to split hairs. What was a splendid ruse was the inversion of the signalling system at the time of the river crossing to enable the men to have additional time to complete their crossing. This followed the discovery by the two young men of a ford across the river referred to earlier. The safe crossing was effected by a simulated short charge against the Karduchians on the normal signal from the *salpinx* and then a quick crossing of the forces thereafter. The prearrangement had been that the signal to charge upon the enemy was limited to a show of aggression by which additional time could be gained for the crossing of the remainder of the army. The signal had in effect been one of retreat rather than one of attack as would be expected from the call (*Anab.* IV.iii.29).[18] The fact that it worked may well have rested on the aggressive false advance of the troops rather than on the signal itself. Xenophon presumed, and how are we to know whether he was correct or not, that the signals of the Greeks were known to the Karduchians, and was staking the success of his tactic on this factor (*Anab.* IV.iii.29).

Again, it could be argued that the dissimulation of the Greeks concerning their initial intentions on the march could be considered as a ruse but this would be to stretch credulity a little too far. The opposition was well aware of the limited options available. What was more pertinent was a specific tactic to mislead the enemy adopted by some Cretans under the command of a man from Mysia called, appropriately, Mysus. The ten men involved pretended to keep out of sight from the enemy but their flashing bronze shields gave the impression that there was a far bigger force lying in ambush. This allowed the main body to withdraw without problem (*Anab.* V.ii.29).[19]

A more subtle and underhand ploy was attempted by Herakleides. In suggesting that the other generals could lead the Greeks as well as Xenophon, Herakleides was trying to exclude Xenophon from influence (*Anab.* VII.v.9) for fear that Xenophon had caught him out in the matter of wages to the troops. The support of the other commanders brought Seuthes to believe that Xenophon was being maligned. Similarly, the antagonistic Thracians themselves made a truce with Xenophon on the grounds that they would be obedient to Seuthes, only to use the time bought by this arrangement to spy on the forces ranged against them (*Anab.* VII.iv.13).

Xenophon himself led a reconnaissance with chosen captains from the army to assess whether it was possible to press an attack (*Anab.* V.ii.8). The deciding factor was that to withdraw would lead to a greater loss of life than if an attack were made. A description of the whole episode against the stronghold of the Drilai is given later under 'Tactics'.

In the event that the content of this section might appear somewhat lightweight, it is worth considering the value of the accumulated knowledge for future operations. There can be no doubt that the information passed on to Thibron by Xenophon and others was important, and that Xenophon must have been an invaluable source of information to Agesilaos on both Pharnabazos and Tissaphernes, in particular, and on tactics in general. Having set down his account, the Greeks had at hand more detailed information on conditions within the Persian empire, a factor which gave credibility to the growing pan-hellenic desire for a campaign of revenge against the Persians. Such a campaign, when prepared for by Phillip, and undertaken by Alexander, owed a great deal to the summation of Xenophon's intelligence report, the *Anabasis*.

Tactics

Unlike Parts Two and Three of the main text, which each have a separate section on cavalry, it has been deemed better to subsume its activities in the *Anabasis* under tactics. This is not to denigrate its role, for its achievement far outweighed the number of men involved. In the latter two parts the treatment for cavalry should be seen as developmental, the third (The Ideal Commander – *Kyropaideia*) in terms of theory, the second (Commanders in Practice – *Hellenika*) in actual practice over a period of time, changing from an arm with the limited but essential needs of screening, skirmishing and pursuit, to a strike force in its own right. Indeed, Xenophon ordered his few horse thus to charge the enemy along with footsoldiers when Mithridates confronted the Greeks (*Anab*. III.iv.4–5). But the circumstances on which that order was based were unusual. To the Persians the appearance of any cavalry from the Greek force would be a total surprise. This contingent had only been formed two evenings before and this was its first appearance in the field. Further, the charge was made against cavalry, archers and slingers, the last two being wholly ineffectual at close contact. We can rest assured that Xenophon would not have employed similar tactics against a line of heavy infantry. Thus surprise and a knowledge of an enemy's strengths and weaknesses were the keys to success here, but no more than the astute order to make the charge at the time when the enemy's missiles first found their range.

From the assumption of his command Xenophon made repeated analyses from which answers to practical problems emerged. These analyses were more often that not shared with his co-generals and he was not unwilling to admit an error in his judgement as in the case of the 'hollow square' formation alluded to in the section 'On the March'. Often within these analyses, and in the reported actions following, the tactical considerations of the antagonist can also be discerned. It was unfortunate for Tissaphernes that he allowed Mithridates to spoil his own tactical plan to destroy the Greeks at long range by allowing him to put the Greeks on their guard and clearly show to them in what areas they were glaringly deficient. The attack made by Mithridates under the guise of friendship with a force of only 200 horse and 400 archers and slingers so mauled the Greek troops that it led him to believe that he could bring about their surrender if given a larger force. Having come out of that engagement unscathed because no pursuit made by the Greeks was successful, and no Cretan archer could achieve an adequate range of shot in reply, Mithridates presumed that the next force he brought, of 1,000 cavalry and 4,000 archers and slingers, would be more than adequate (*Anab*. III.iv.2). However, the first attack, though effective, showed the Greeks the Persian's hand, and they were quick to seek a remedy to their needs by creating the small force of fifty cavalry and, by inducement, some two hundred slingers, mainly Rhodian (*Anab*. III.iii.20). A slinger at that time was still regarded as of inferior status within an army so that the undisclosed inducement would have had to be significant, and in no way could the previous standing of the volunteers be diminished. Rhodian slingers also used lead missiles which had a greater range than those of stone used by the Persians.

To have background knowledge of such facts speaks volumes for the young Xenophon who must have showed early to the troops in general his capacity for adaptation and firm leadership in times of low morale. He rightly pointed out (*Anab*. III.iii.14) that they had been extremely fortunate not to have been attacked on the first occasion by a large force.[20] So it was that, too late to be successful in his tactical aim, Tissaphernes took to the field with a large army. His deployment is interesting. An open 'half tile' arrangement wherein the rear and flanks of the moving Greek force were covered by Persians with only the van being unimpeded, e.g., ⌐■⌐. This is an inversion of the battle line adopted by Croesus at the fictional battle of Thymbrara of an open half tile surrounding the flanks and opposing line of the dense 'tile' formation chosen by Kyros, and may have given Xenophon the seed for his invention. The tactic was obviously to create disruption by pouring in missiles over a considerable time until a rout ensued, during which his cavalry would create mayhem among the survivors. The direction of the rout, had it occurred, was preordained. There was only one free escape route and that was forward, a direction in which cavalry could easily overtake and attack fleeing hoplites at their most vulnerable, out of formation and in their rear. A good tactical plan, had not his subordinate already given the game away. In the event, the density of the Persian ranks led to substantial casualties on their side as the Rhodian slingers, whose range was greater than that of the Persians, inevitably found their marks. Similarly the re-use of Persian arrows by the Cretans allowed them to keep up a long distance fusilade of such intensity that Tissaphernes was obliged to retire beyond range (*Anab*. III.iv.15). Xenophon mentioned that the Cretans practised firing into the air for the purpose of increasing their range (*Anab*. III.iv.17) but it is likely that, given that Cretan and Persian bows were of a similar size, the arrows of the Persians were probably a little longer and thus more effective for longer range work, hence their re-use by the Cretans. At *Anab*. III.iv.14, Xenophon makes the point that Tissaphernes did not wish to risk a decisive battle and did not have the courage to do so. This sums up the differing viewpoints of the two command structures. It shows that even Xenophon had yet to appreciate, if he ever did, that face to face contact, man to man, was not within the thinking of the Persian commander if there were other options, and then only as a last resort. Why risk all on a single engagement, when the secondary objective to force the Greeks to leave the empire was still in process?

As always, peltasts proved invaluable in mountainous terrain but obviously only when faced by enemy light infantry inferior to themselves. It proves illuminating to view the actions which took place on the journey home in terms of the effective use of both light and heavy infantry, as well as the tactics of the opposing forces on such ground. At *Anab*. III.iv.24, the Greeks were heartened to see hills at last. This was country which would give them respite from cavalry attack. However, the light troops ranged against them on the first hill pursued them, admittedly under the duress of being coerced by whips, and dislocated the Greek peltasts to such an extent that they had to take cover within the main body. Pursuits made by hoplites were ineffective because of their slowness and they suffered attack when they made a return to the ranks. Thus the rear of the Greek force was always under attack as they made their descent on the first two hills. On the ascent of the third hill, however, no attack was made on the enemy until a large body of peltasts had taken up a position higher than that of the enemy which threatened the rearguard of the main body. So it was that the march continued along the road over the hills, the rearguard being covered by the peltasts travelling in parallel higher up the mountainside, threatening any enemy which might appear between the two Greek forces (*Anab*. III.iv.30). It is as well to note the effectiveness of the Persian light armed troops in such terrain.

A forward position to the line of the Greek march was taken by the Persians on a spur of a mountain overlooking the road. A dilemma for the Greeks was that the peltasts with the rearguard could not leave their position to come forward because of the threat of the enemy coming up on their rear, another good tactical ploy by Tissaphernes. So that a significant force could be deployed to capture the summit of the mountain above the position of the Persians thereby making their location untenable, Xenophon led the peltasts from the van supplemented by the 'special forces' stationed there (*Anab.* III.iv.43). These 'special forces' were those referred to earlier in relation to solving security problems when marching in a hollow square. It would appear that the six units of a hundred each had been divided into two. Three sets of a hundred were under the command of the general of the van, Cheirisophos, and the remainder were presumably with the rearguard, under Xenophon. It became a race for the summit which the Greeks won, leading to the withdrawal of Tissaphernes with his following forces (*Anab.* III.v.1). It is worth noting that Ariaios, one of the former commanders of Kyros the Younger's forces, was with Tissaphernes at this time.

So, to secure a safe advance it was deemed essential to be in possession of any heights in close proximity to the line of the march. This led to the obvious conclusion that such heights should be taken in advance. However, the Greeks were reliant on information concerning the terrain from whomsoever they captured or who willingly offered such facts. They themselves knew nothing of the topography to be encountered and the obvious and normal procedures often proved difficult. They often only knew of high ground problems when they came upon them or from informants within the locality. Such information (coming their way only after the ruthless killing of one prisoner in front of another) was a description of a high route which passed by a position that they must occupy in order to safeguard their march (*Anab.* IV.i.25). So it was that the Greeks had initially to develop tactics often by trial and error, often in response to a given situation in which they found themselves rather than by pre-emptive action.

The Karduchians had proved impressively effective against the rearguard in the gloom of the early evening (*Anab.* IV.i.10). The Greeks had tried the tactic of trying to be friends with this people and of doing no harm within their villages, but to no avail.

In order to cover the advance on the proposed position to be occupied, Xenophon made an advance with the rearguard along the expected route of the army to be met by huge boulders being sent against his force by the Karduchians from above. His feint worked in that the Karduchians were unaware of the presence of the other Greeks as they made their way to dislodge them from what was, at that time, a lower position on the mountain. On the following morning, under cover of mist, the Greeks moved up against the Karduchian position held by their main body which fled before contact (*Anab*. IV.ii.7). All but the rearguard had by now penetrated and successfully passed the Karduchian positions. However, Xenophon and his men in charge of the baggage animals, could not follow the same higher route as their comrades without abandoning the baggage train. He was faced with a succession of hills from which the enemy first had to be dislodged and which then had to be manned by Greeks to safeguard the passage of the baggage train on the lower route. The ease with which the third hill was captured was soon turned to alarm when the reason for the Karduchians quitting this position became clear. The remainder of the rearguard had come into view and the occupying force had abandoned its position with the intention of mounting an attack on it as it moved through the pass. Xenophon also received the grave news that the first of the hills on which he had left a small force had been retaken. At this point Xenophon entered into a dialogue with the Karduchians in respect of reclaiming the Greek dead. To this the Karduchians agreed but only if the Greeks vowed in turn not to burn their houses. Following the agreement, the Greeks under Xenophon continued on their way only to be attacked in force by the Karduchians rolling yet more stones against them. In due course, however, the whole of the army was reunited.

The tactic which was pursued by the commanders of van and rearguard is worth noting (*Anab*. IV.ii.24–27) in terms of mutual aid. Whenever the van was impeded Xenophon would come forward to take ground higher than the enemy, thus facilitating the forward movement of the march. Similarly, when the rearguard was attacked or impeded, Cheirisophos would come from the van to take up a higher position than the Karduchians and thereby break any blockade. Thus it was that by protecting the flanks of the march from high positions the security of any advance was assured.

Returning to the Tiribazos episode which was introduced under 'Intelligence', its completion here illustrates the virtue of pre-emptive strikes at an enemy.[21] Security measures demanded that the Greeks come together in one camp rather than being dispersed among villages. Leaving Sophainetos in command of a garrison-sized force within the camp, presumably the bulk of the army set out under the guidance of the captured Persian for the enemy's position. The fact that the enemy was seen to be encamped implies that the forward move of the Greeks was made before the enemy had established its positions. The brief description of the action in which the peltasts charged forward without waiting for the hoplites, suggests a certain laxity in command whereby contingents such as peltasts could take it upon themselves to initiate an attack without a direct command or close support of hoplites. There is no reference to a command to do so in the source. The fact that the enemy fled leaving a great deal of plunder to be taken is irrelevant. The question remains as to whether subalterns often acted on their own initiative. This could be extremely useful at times of duress, but could also be taken as a weakness in the command structure at times when coordinated action was deemed a necessity (*Anab.* IV.iv.20). The proof of this is that the generals learned of the success of the action without being part of it (*Anab.* IV.iv.22). The recall to return to the Greek camp led to the decision that the whole army should proceed before the enemy had time to regroup. The march forward was undertaken the next day over the pass with a large group of guides, presumably captured from the camp the day before. The basic planning of the operation was sound. It was an essential, and still is, in any attempt at a pre-emptive strike, that the force involved has a secure base to which it can return in case of failure, or a less than wholly successful outcome to the operation. Therefore the initial establishment of a secure camp was an essential basis for such an operation and shows excellent contingency planning. To some it might appear that the entire army should have advanced and gained time by passing over the pass a day earlier but this is to presume success in the venture, and any competent commander would never make that assumption. His plans must cover all aspects, positive and negative. Another pre-emptive attack was made on those attacking the rearguard (*Anab.* IV.v.18), but in this case, the Greeks were seeking to protect the invalids within their forces who, under force of circumstances, were having to be left behind temporarily. They were buying time so that a retrieval of the sick could be made.

Tissaphernes lost no opportunity in the early stages of the march to discomfort the Greeks. His cavalry successfully attacked foragers in search of plunder by making a sudden appearance at a time when pitching camp would be uppermost in the minds of the Greeks and when they had acquired herds of cattle from the area (*Anab.* III.v.2).

Having worsted the Greeks, Tissaphernes set about burning the villages from where the Greeks expected to be provisioned (Sun Tzu VII.11: 'We may take it then that an army without its baggage train is lost; without provisions it is lost; without bases of supply it is lost'). At that point Xenophon had a clear difference of opinion with Cheirisophos as to what tactic to adopt in these circumstances, this after the latter had returned from relieving the foragers. Xenophon proposed leading an action against the fire raisers whereas Cheirisophos suggested that by burning the villages themselves also, they might make the Persians desist from the practice. No report is made of any action being taken and it is likely that, given the despondent meeting of the commanders later that evening, none had been undertaken. The Drilai adopted a similar scorched earth policy (*Anab.* V.ii.3) but their motive was defensive rather than offensive. They were attempting to make conditions as difficult as possible for the Greeks in the hope that they would eventually retire. As it was, by burning their weaker strongholds, they denied the Greeks ready provisions or plunder apart from the occasional animal which had made its escape from the conflagration.

Terrain obviously played a great part in the final decision on any deployment of forces be it on a plain, advancing uphill, or at a contested river crossing. At a time when provisions were running out, an attack on a Taochian stronghold proved problematical because of its location. Cheirisophos was unable to establish a continuous line around the stronghold because of the precipitous nature of the terrain (*Anab.* IV.vii.2). The problem lay in the route of access to the fortification which was overhung by a large outcrop from which the Taochians sent down boulders on any attackers. Several men had received broken legs and ribs in the attempts before Xenophon arrived with the rearguard. Xenophon's analysis and suggestions therefrom proved profitable. His assumption that the supply of boulders had a limit led him to a plan to persuade the Taochians to use it up as quickly as possible. Having seen trees scattered across the line of advance he proposed that men could shelter safely behind these when stones were let loose and run on to the next in the intervals between showers. This tactic worked and seventy men started the advance in safety. Rivalry between the captains emerged and, at each dash between trees, Xenophon reports that more than ten cart-loads of stones were wasted (*Anab.* IV.vii.10). On eventual entry to the stronghold, the women threw their children to their deaths over the precipice and then followed immediately, along with their menfolk. One Greek officer, a Stymphalian called Aeneas, attempted to stop a man from doing the same but was carried over the precipice along with him. It is likely that Aeneas was motivated more by the fine robe worn by the individual than from any humanitarian spirit. To put the matter into perspective, although presenting a tactical problem, at the end of the day, there were probably fewer than a hundred defenders trying to deny access to an army of thousands.

When it came to an enemy in strength the Greeks were less successful. The Chalybians, through whose lands the march proceeded, also lived in strongholds. However, the Greeks had no success in capturing provisions there, and had to rely on the cattle they had taken from the Taochians for provender. There is no direct report of any engagement, but there is more than a hint that the Greeks suffered severe casualties at the hands of the Chalybians in what was recorded about these people. Xenophon states that their soldiers were armed with a very long spear and a short slashing sword, being protected by greaves, helmet and a linen corslet fringed with plaited cords at the groin and that they were the only enemy they encountered which was ready to come to close combat. There is no mention of a shield. The fact, however, that Xenophon states that they decapitated their enemies indicates first hand experience (*Anab.* IV.vii.16). Although their attacks are described as having occurred after the passage of the Greek army past a town or stronghold, and in pursuit of that force, the inference is that this was the only occasion when the Greeks were faced by an enemy who approached the category of heavy infantry. Had Xenophon given further details of the use of this long spear and the formations adopted by the Chalybians we would have been indebted. A force which came to close quarters suggests that the spear was not thrown. A long spear would in any case have been unsuitable for such purposes. That they were effective fighters suggests some form of disciplined organisation. That they were effective against Greek hoplites, even if it was in pursuit, suggests that Xenophon, as commander of the rearguard, sustained losses and grudgingly acknowledges the fact without going into detail.

The other stronghold which required capture was the capital of the Drilai, the preliminaries to which have already been described. It should be made clear that the Greeks had insufficient time to make a full investiture of any fortified place on their march. Their role was transient and at this point in time they were acting on behalf of the Trapezountians who directed them against a people who had proved troublesome and from whom the Greeks could secure provisions by force of arms. Even so, only half of the army was committed to the enterprise because it was necessary to maintain half the force in camp to defend it against an army of Kolchians who had taken up a threatening position on the heights above the camp (*Anab.* V.ii.1). The terrain was difficult highland country and, when eventually the Drilai had fallen back on their strongest fortified position, their capital, it can be seen from the description of its defences that the precipitate advance of some of the Greeks had led them into danger. The stronghold itself was of palisades interspersed at regular intervals by towers constructed of wood set upon a rampart, presumably of earth and stone, and surrounded by a broad trench. This in turn was fronted by a very deep ravine which made access and, as it turned out, withdrawal, extremely difficult, for, according to the messenger who took news of the Greeks' plight to Xenophon, retreat back down into the ravine had to be made in single file, an impossible task given the frequent sorties made by the enemy. The initial advance on the stronghold had been made by a force of peltasts, presumably in pursuit of the retreating Drilai. They in turn had been closely followed by a force of spearmen. Xenophon uses the word δορυφόροι (doruphoroi) at this point and one ponders such use. He had already stated that the hoplites were three quarters of a mile behind and indeed reports at *Anab.* V.ii.6, that the messenger sent back from the attacking force came to him at the head of the hoplites. One can come to the conclusion that Xenophon uses this word as another way of describing hoplites, but this would imply another force of hoplites acting independently of the main body and who were in support of the peltasts, yet the hoplites are clearly stated as being led by Xenophon some distance behind. Or perhaps, because this group of spearmen was in close support of the peltasts, it was another body of light armed infantry with spears. Further, since the use of the word is not casual, and was not made in a place in the text where it was necessary to avoid tautology as a matter of style, one can conjecture that this was a force with special duties, such as its meaning suggests: a bodyguard, perhaps, in this case of the commanders. Still further, at *Anab.* V.ii.10, when marshalling the erstwhile attackers while waiting for the hoplites to come over the ravine to join them, there is no mention of hoplites being present in the force. Nonetheless, the question remains.

That an enemy in retreat should be hotly pursued is a good tactic, but that pursuit had to be conducted with the safety of the pursuant force firmly in focus. A general pursuit may have been ordered by Xenophon but one must question how a thousand or so Greeks found themselves in a position from which withdrawal was perilous. The subcommanders must take responsibility for the predicament they found themselves in, where to retreat in single file invited death from sorties made by the defending force. Had a general order not been given, this would be yet another example of minor insubordination on the part of subcommanders. On the other hand it can be presumed that when the aim of the mission was made known at the outset, the subcommanders were expected to exercise discretion in its achievement.

So, with the attacking force of Greeks being unable either to take the stronghold or to make a safe withdrawal from its vicinity, Xenophon and his accompanying captains crossed over to assess the problem. At this point Xenophon did not commit further troops to the attack. Only after discussion and agreement between himself and his captains was the decision made to bring the hoplites across the ravine. That decision rested on the conclusion that it would have been well nigh impossible to make a withdrawal without great loss of life, whereas a concerted attack could lead to the capture of the fortification. At this point it can be observed that the whole conduct of the operation is tightened up and given focus. Xenophon first ordered the peltasts to draw back and cease firing at long range. With the arrival of the hoplites he allowed the captains to draw up their own companies in the manner they thought most effective, relying on the competitiveness which abounded between the officers to produce the best outcome. He then issued an order for a coordinated fusilade from bowmen and slingers to be made at a given signal, providing at the same time that men were given the responsibility for ensuring a ready supply of ammunition. Only then was the deployment for attack made. This appeared to have been in a crescent formation which would have made all sectors of the line equidistant from the perimeter of the stronghold (*Anab.* V.ii.13). At the call of the *salpinx* and after the paean to Enyalios, the attack was made under the massive concerted fusilade of missiles. The outer defences were taken and the light armed troops rushed into the stronghold to plunder what they could. Again we see the virtue of having an alert commander in charge of an operation. Xenophon did not allow the hoplites to enter, but took charge of the gates. His reason for caution was that he had seen the enemy appearing on surrounding heights. However, when those within, who had been in search of plunder, came pouring out, followed by a number of wounded who reported that the enemy had counter attacked from a citadel, Xenophon ordered that any of the hoplites who wished to take plunder from within could now do so. In this way a complete reversal of the flow occurred and, having caused the enemy to retreat to their citadel, the Greeks found themselves in possession of all that was portable within the fortification. After manning the ramparts and the approach roads to the citadel, which was deemed impregnable, preparations were made for a withdrawal. The outer defences were dismantled and the wounded and those carrying loads were sent off first along with the greater part of the hoplites. Those picked troops who remained, when it came to their turn to retire, were subjected to yet another sortie from the citadel with the enemy manning rooftops and casting down logs on the Greeks.

Pinned down as they were, with night coming on, a stroke of luck occurred when a house went up in flames, causing the enemy occupying adjacent houses to take to their heels. Xenophon ordered the firing of other houses in the vicinity thereby cutting off those of the enemy from additional support from the citadel. Being faced with a force which could endanger their withdrawal but who could not easily be reinforced, he ordered that all men out of missile range should bring up logs and combustible material to be placed between them and the enemy (*Anab.* V.ii.26). Having established a wall of fire, and also set fire to those houses which stood near to the original ramparts, the Greeks completed a safe withdrawal.[22]

The foregoing shows clearly a series of decisions which Xenophon had to take, most on the spur of the moment, demonstrating his clarity of evaluation, his ongoing concern for the safety of his men and his methodology, i.e., nothing was done until total discipline was present.

Again, in action against a stronghold on the approach to the chief city of the Mossynoecians, Xenophon turned an earlier mishap to advantage. The ill-disciplined and precipitate attack made on this fortification by some Greeks intent on plunder, in the company of the newly arrived local allies, sheds light once more on problems within a mercenary army. The chief motivation had been personal gain and discipline could often be sacrificed to the satisfaction of that end. Xenophon states as much at *Anab.* V.iv.16, but more importantly alludes to the large number of Greeks involved in the adventure, without orders to do so from any general. They had been put to flight, a thing unheard of up to that point in the march, had suffered fatalities and had brought indignity upon the whole Greek army by having the heads of their fallen comrades displayed in triumph along with those of their barbarian allies. Worst of all, they had engaged the enemy in no standard form of battle order. Obviously the use of the word ἀτάκτοις suggests that the men were acting as individuals and not in concert. Xenophon addressed the army on these issues as an object lesson in the need for discipline and order, and called on the troops to restore their reputation (*Anab.* V.iv.19–21).

Some unresolved issues emerge, however, from the description of this first action. Who followed the barbarian allies in the attack? It would only make sense if this group, referred to only as Greeks, had been peltasts because of their greater mobility. On the other hand, a hoplite out of formation and in flight was an easy target for any pursuer. Furthermore, as the barbarian allies had marched straight through the Greek encampment directly to the attack (*Anab.* V.iv.14), it may well have been that the Greeks who followed were a mixture of peltasts and hoplites who had snatched up arms to join them in this unexpected attack. This was the only way they could have kept up with the attackers and been in a position whereby flight was the sole option. Being opportunist may have led the hoplites not to don their full panoply, thereby reducing further their effectiveness when counter-attacked.

Because the approach was uphill, the following day saw the Greeks and their barbarian allies deploy in column. The barbarians were placed on the left, also in column, with archers positioned between all columns. The duty of the archers was to hold the enemy at bay while the advance of the heavy infantry took place. Xenophon couples the peltasts with the bowmen in this duty, but is not explicit about the position in which the former were placed. It is likely from the evidence of a slightly later reference that the peltasts were ranged in front of the main body of hoplites, having the opportunty to retire, if necessary, in the spaces between the columns of hoplites. The interesting point is that the van of the hoplites is described as being a little further back (*Anab.* V.iv.22). The position of the peltasts is further confirmed by the fact that the enemy engaged them in battle prior to the arrival of the hoplites (*Anab.* V.iv.24) and that, on the flight of the barbarians with the arrival of the heavy infantry, the peltasts pursued them to the city followed relentlessly by the *lochoi* in column. At the point of their arrival at the city the enemy had obviously regrouped and, with reinforcements, engaged the Greeks. Xenophon makes it clear that although the barbarians came to hand to hand battle they were ill equipped to do so. Having thrown their javelins they tried to defend themselves with their spears. The description of these as being so thick and long that a man had difficulty in carrying one suggests that such weapons were better suited to a form of fighting similar to that of the phalanx. Perhaps the Greeks pre-empted their enemy's opportunity to get into whatever formation was best suited to their use? The outcome of this description gives evidence that artillery was used to blunt any enemy advance and that the peltasts, advancing under covering fire, were used in battle for more than mere skirmishing. They were the cutting edge of the attack matching the mobility of their antagonists. Indeed they can be credited with the victory. An astute use of light infantry and recognition that away from the conditions of mainland Greece, evaluation of enemy forces was a constant practice on the march home.

It is hardly surprising that constant adaptation to the demands of the moment was a prevalent feature. The Greeks had met so many adversaries, all with differing approaches to warfare against which they had to contend, that their penchant for experimentation must be applauded. The imaginative solutions to specific problems undertaken by commanders leading troops best used to that ritualistic form of battle familiar to the Greek soldier at home, can only be admired. In Xenophon's description of this last engagement no mention is made of slingers or cavalry. One can presume both arms were there. It would have been strange if the artillery were deficient of that strong Rhodian arm which had given such good service in the past. Similarly, cavalry, highly effective uphill in terms of pursuit, would be advantageous. But the most telling statement concerns that of the following heavy infantry. The trailing hoplites, positioned in such a way, suggests more sophisticated tactical thinking than the period in question has attested elsewhere. This could only be possible if a commander could dispense with the skirmishing activities of peltasts and use them as a disrupting agency in the van against the opposition, a tactic guaranteed to lead to disaster in any formal engagement in Greece, but which led to success here. The accrued knowledge of the weaponry and likely tactical response of the enemy is seen to be of great advantage to the commander.

The interest in adaptability to terrain continues but now moves on to the deployment of other battle lines in response to a variety of different locales. Having been conducted through friendly Makronian territory, the Greeks found themselves faced with an army of Kolchians in battle order on a mountain in defence of their border (*Anab.* IV.viii.9). Initially, the Greeks formed up in line to make the advance, but obviously the commanders had doubts concerning their adopted formation because they chose to have a meeting to discuss tactics (*Anab.* IV.viii.9). The other option would have been to march in column, the troops within a company, one behind the other. They would then have had their best or younger, and more agile, soldiers to the front. However, with the initial suggestion of deployment in battle line, the men of a column moved into line abreast of one another. At the meeting, someone, and it may well have been Xenophon who mouthed the words as he reported he did, pointed out the options, that advancing in depth of line would give the enemy the chance to outflank the Greek forces, that by advancing with a thinner extended line would give the enemy the opportunity to break through, and that, in any case, an advance on such terrain would lead inevitably to a dislocation of the line which the enemy could exploit. His suggestion was that the army should form up in columns, leaving sufficient space between each company so that the front would overlap the enemy's wings. This meant that the best soldiers were, as has been noted, at the front and that, should the occasion arise, companies to the left and right could come to the aid of beleaguered colleagues. The suggestion was adopted and, in the approach to the action, with Cheirisophos on the right wing as behoved the commander of the vanguard, and Xenophon on the left, as commander of the rearguard, both arranged their peltasts in positions beyond the wings of the enemy. The opposition tried to remedy the overlap by directing men to both wings, but left their centre denuded (*Anab.* IV.viii.17). The Arkadians, under Aischines, who presumably were at the Greek centre, thought that with this movement the enemy was in retreat and made their successful charge, peltasts being closely followed by hoplites. Thus, the necessity of creating an overlap was seen to be an essential, and the pre-battle discussion had centred on the means by which an outflanking action could be achieved. What should also be appreciated is that advancing uphill was better done in column than in battle line, a tactic which Archidamos adopted at Kromnos but without success (365 BC).[23]

The deployment chosen for the passage over the pass blocked by the Chalybians, Taochians and Phasians was in line of battle (*Anab.* IV.vi.6). This was presumably because there was sufficient room to do so with the terrain ahead of a nature not to compromise the integrity of the line even though the advance would be uphill. Here we have the 'old chestnut', the need to secure the flanks before an advance could safely be made. The displacement of an enemy force from heights would, by this time, have been a regular occurrence on the march, and the Greeks would be well practised in the art. When it was necessary to do so in a situation where those commanding the heights were in contact with substantial allied forces on the ground, however, more circumspection was needed. What was true for the Greeks was also true for the allied forces barring their way in this example. They too could not afford to be outflanked. So possession of heights was both offensive and defensive, and was the key to success. Both sides needed to achieve security on the flanks and not permit an outflanking movement to develop. In the present case, the enemy position at the pass was a strong one, with control of the immediate heights on the approach to their main body. No other force was seen to have been ensconced elsewhere on this large mountain stretching as it did some six and a half miles within the view of the Greeks. Xenophon's analysis is clear sighted (*Anab.* IV.vi.10–14). His priority was to secure the advance with as few casualties as possible and, with this in mind, he proposed an alternative to that of immediate battle. He points out the problems of an advance in daylight against a strong position with the dangers of missiles thrown from above. Better by far to attempt to take possession of heights during the night, unobserved, but in a locale which would threaten the enemy position. This was preferable to fighting directly against a strong position manned by a well prepared enemy ('It is a military axiom not to advance uphill against an enemy, nor to oppose him when he comes downhill.' Sun Tzu VII.33. 'So in war, the way is to avoid what is strong and to strike at what is weak.' VI.30). The occupation of high ground was successfully completed before the enemy could take counter measures. For them it was a serious threat and caused them to keep many fires burning throughout the night. It would have been illuminating in quite another way to have known the disposition of these fires and the arrangements of the pickets, but Xenophon does not, or perhaps could not, give this information. The importance attached by both sides to the possession of heights was seen in the strongly contested fight by the enemy detachment sent against the Greeks which ensued the following day. The enemy force sent to thwart the Greek advance along the heights must have been significant because Xenophon suggests that the division of enemy forces left the majority at the pass, suggesting the commitment of a strong minority. Thus the forces facing the Greeks were divided in response to the Greek initiative. The defeat of the enemy on the heights, prior to the closing of the Greek army with those of the enemy at the pass, led to a recognition by the enemy that their position had now been turned and their withdrawal was immediate with little loss of life (*Anab.* IV.vi.25–26).

River crossings were a dangerous area for a force of the size of the Greek army. Such a crossing took a considerable period and was vulnerable to attack at any time. Orontas, the satrap of Armenia, opposed one Greek crossing (*Anab.* IV.iii.4). At their rear it was observed that the Karduchians were poised ready to attack once they commenced their crossing. As has been seen, a mixture of piety in relation to the dream and intelligence in connection with the two young men led Xenophon to propose the manner in which the crossing should be made. The plan was for the vanguard to cross first followed by the camp followers and baggage, then Xenophon with the rearguard. The van crossed under Cheirisophos and proceeded to advance against the enemy infantry. Xenophon, with his quickest troops, presumably peltasts and the youngest years of the hoplites, ran along the river bank and made as if to cross at the point at which the original road had indicated there would be a ford. The enemy cavalry, fearing that they might be cut off by this feint, retired towards the mountains thus removing any danger to Cheirisophos' flank. Greek peltasts and cavalry from the van pursued them. With the camp followers and baggage train crossing, Xenophon, having returned to his rearguard command, ordered them to wheel, facing the Karduchians, with the file closers next to the river. Assuming that this meant the last man in file, it suggests that when moving into the line of battle the Greek rearguard had their backs to the river (*Anab.* IV.iii.26).

At this point Cheirisophos sent back his slingers, archers and peltasts in support of Xenophon. Xenophon sent instructions to them to wait on the other side of the river in readiness to discharge missiles and ordered his own men to await the point at which enemy missiles found their range, at which time they themselves were to charge. The *salpinx* call to charge which followed was the prearranged signal for the Greek force to about face and, led by the previously last in file, to cross the ford as quickly as possible in formation. This was duly completed without problem and the reunited Greek army advanced in battle line until such time as it arrived at a large village which provided provender.

At this point it is as well to review an action involving unsupported hoplites, at the division of the army into three by virtue of the bloody-mindedness of the Arkadians and Achaeans. Following their disembarkation at Kalpe (*Anab.* VI.iii.2), this force proceeded to march inland a mile and a half or so against the nearer Thracian villages with intent to plunder. At dawn, having agreed a high point at which they would rejoin each other at the end of their actions, each general led his force against a village. In the case of those villages which seemed stronger, forces combined so that two *lochoi* made the attack. With the escaped defenders of each village gathering together, the divided Greek force found itself facing a formidable array of light infantry which pursued and destroyed two *lochoi*, in possibly two separate engagements. This interestingly enough at a gorge where the hoplite formation, retiring with its plunder, presumably in a hollow square, would have been dislocated because of the terrain. It is likely that both actions took place in sequence at, or around, the same locale, considering the significant loss of life. The remaining *lochoi* rejoined on the appointed hill and sat out the night while the Thracians invested the hill as more and more reinforcements arrived. The following dawn saw attacks on the Greeks by peltasts and cavalry in considerable numbers at various points of their encampment. The Greeks, unable to extricate themselves from this predicament, and continuing to lose men while being unable to cause casualties among their assailants (*Anab.*VI.iii.8) sued for peace. The negotiations broke down and, had it not been for the relieving force under Xenophon (see also under 'Postlude'), it could well have meant the total demise of the Arkadians, cut off from any water supply as they were. This shows that hoplites were an endangered species when not accompanied by one or more of the ancillary arms, a form of military dinosaur when out of its homeland and without support from peltasts or cavalry.

One of the most important actions reported by Xenophon requires a brief description of the preceding events. This too suggests that a balanced force was not in use. Being without provisions and Xenophon unable to agree an expedition for procurement owing to the lack of supportive sacrifices, the army followed Neon, the deputy in place of Cheirisophos in his absence, on a foray. They were accompanied by 2,000 volunteers. Being attacked by Pharnabazos' cavalry and losing a quarter of their force, the remainder took to the hills from where they were relieved by Xenophon. The base camp was attacked at night by Bithynians and the Greeks moved to a stronger position which they fortified. Leaving behind those over forty-five years of age to defend the camp, the remainder set out and marched to the area where the initial action had taken place. Whether the original intention was to reclaim their dead to give them burial as well as acquiring provions, is not stated. Having buried the dead as they came upon them, they saw enemy forces of horse and foot under Spithridates and Rathines in battle formation (*Anab.* VI.v.7) just over a mile and a half away. These last had been designated by Pharnabazos to collaborate with the Bithynians in an attempt to destroy the Greeks. Obviously avoidance of contact was impossible. At this point (*Anab.* VI.v.9) Xenophon suggested to his colleagues, after immediate and successful sacrifice, that they should station companies of men behind the phalanx so that any part which was hard pressed would be given immediate support and could exploit any disorder in the enemy. The main body led on while Xenophon took the last three battalions from the rear, each consisting of 200 men, and ordered them to follow the phalanx, supporting its right, centre and left, at a distance of some hundred feet to its rear (*plethron*). These were genuine reserves, planned to be such, given a specific reserve role and organised to be withheld from the opening action of the battle and to react to whatever contingency or opportunity arose thereafter. What is surprising is that there seemed to be no query of Xenophon's suggestion. The principle seemed to have been known and taken as matter of fact as if it were an everyday occurrence. It may well have been a regular arrangement in actions on the march but there are no other references which suggest this to be the case. Nor is there anything recorded in other sources prior to this time in such detail which suggests a common practice. It must be left to the individual to decide whether a modest Xenophon is understating what may have been a brilliant piece of innovative tactical thinking. The numbers involved may also suggest the use of those same 'special forces' employed for security on the march, i.e., 600, but this would be to stretch credulity too far. The numbers coincide neatly with those of the formations present within the army at that time.

The advance having got under way highlights another recurrent problem for the Greeks on their homeward route, namely reconnaissance. It should come as no surprise to discover, yet again, a problem with a ravine, unknown until the point of arrival at its side. The advance was halted while a decision was made as to what to do next. Xenophon points to the advantages to morale of advancing rather than retreating. With the ravine to the Greek rear Xenophon's analysis of such a situation echoes much that is in Sun Tzu: 'Throw your soldiers into positions whence there is no escape, and they will prefer death to flight. If they will face death there is nothing that they may not achieve, officers and men alike will put forth their uttermost strength'. IX.23. 'Soldiers when in desperate straits lose the sense of fear. If there is no place of refuge they will stand firm. If they are in the heart of hostile country, they will show a stubborn front. If there is no help for it, they will fight hard.' IX.24.

The order Xenophon gave for crossing the ravine showed him alert to the possible dangers at such a time. Eschewing the normal procedure of crossing in file over a bridge, he ordered every man to cross the ravine at the point at which he now found himself stationed. In such a way the crossing was quicker and greater numbers were earlier intersupportive on the other side. As the advance slowly proceeded the peltasts were ordered to each flank. The attack was conducted at a march and not at a run, spears at the right shoulder until the signal from the *salpinx* gave the order for lowering into attack mode. There was a unilateral charge by the peltasts, again without orders to do so, and they were put to rout. The phalanx marched on, raised the battle cry and the enemy took flight. At this point the forty or so Greek cavalry did sterling work in dispersing the enemy left. This is the first reference to their presence (*Anab.* VI.v.28) and it indicates that they were stationed on the Greek right wing. One has to assume the Cretan bowmen and Rhodian slingers were present. The enemy right however, which had not been subject to such a pursuit, had gathered on a knoll and did not retreat until the phalanx turned its attention to them. The Greek peltasts had not been wholly effectual in the pursuit, achieving only dispersal of the forces, but fearing to press home the attack in fear of the enemy cavalry. Meantime what was presumably the centre of the enemy force, containing Pharnabazos' cavalry together with Bithynian horse, had remained uncommitted on a hill as spectators to the action up to that point. The Greeks reformed their line and marched upon them. Without waiting to engage, the enemy fled, presumably down the slope of the hill in the opposite direction to the Greek advance at the foot of which was another ravine. Had the Greeks known of this declivity they might have summoned up the energy for a pursuit, but again, foreknowledge of the terrain was lacking, and the enemy cavalry escaped in terrain wholly unsuited for a retreat of horsemen and ideal for pursuit of cavalry by footsoldiers, particularly peltasts.[24]

On the evidence of what a few cavalry could do against forces in large numbers, it must have been its absence from Xenophon's initially private plundering raid on Asidates, a wealthy Persian landowner, which created such problems for the Greeks on their retreat with slaves and booty. To give him his due, Xenophon does not in any way seek to excuse himself for the debacle. Having tried to do friends a good turn by including them in a night raid to raise personal wealth, the small group was greatly enlarged by interlopers from the army who wanted to share in any wealth that was likely to be forthcoming (*Anab.* VII.viii.11). The force of 600 which did make the abortive attack on Asidates' fortress was only partly successful. The defenders, shouting and lighting beacons, attracted help and support from the surrounding district, and the Greeks found themselves hard pressed to defend themselves from attacks from all quarters. Xenophon lists the participants in this relief and, at a considered guess, the Greeks were facing a force of infantry and peltasts of possibly 3,000 men including archers and slingers, together with about 200 cavalry, many of whom would have been mounted bowmen. To extricate themselves from this shambles Xenophon decided it best to form a hollow square within which the slaves, booty and animals could be driven along. His reasons were valid. To have left the product of their pillaging would have given the enemy heart and caused a loss of morale among his own men, possibly leading to a rout. His troops were the more likely to fight for the retention of their possessions if they took them with them. Although initially in a hollow square, the formation on the march was later conducted with the line curved to give greater protection from arrows and other projectiles. What does this mean? The sequence of the description gives the clue. The hollow square was retained until the support from Gongylos and Prokles for Xenophon's force arrived, and it was the time spent within that formation which accounts for the fact that half the force suffered from wounds. The greatest number to have been wounded would have been those on the right unshielded flank and those to the rear who had little or no protection against arrows and sling shots. With the arrival of support, presumably including cavalry, the Greeks were now able to change formation to adopt a curved advancing line providing greater protection from missiles with their wall of shields, knowing that their rear would be covered by their allies. Once again, the lack of a few additional words which would have given specific detail concerning the composition of the original force or those of their relieving allies, leaves us with the problem of deciding on the most probable scenario. Further information concerning the crossing of the river would have been illuminating to the problem of how a retreating force under great duress managed to achieve it. Indeed, without the opportune arrival of Gongylos and Prokles, could it have been achieved it at all? The fact that the retreat is dealt with in the space of *Anab.* VII.viii.16–19 bears significant comparison to the long detailed tracts used to describe attacks on a few Thracian villages in the company of Seuthes. Xenophon included it for completeness to his narrative and must be applauded for his honesty. This was a debacle he would have wished to omit if it were not for the fact that it served as a prelude to his personal enrichment the following day when, with the whole army, he captured Asidates, his family and possessions, encamped in villages near Parthenion.

These last actions by Xenophon as commander prior to handing over the army to Thibron could best be described as banditry. The relative safety of his circumstances at that time led him to abandon the careful planning and astute selection of appropriate forces for a task which had brought signal success on the long march home. In this escapade, wholly motivated by the desire for personal gain, he put at risk not only an enviable reputation but also his very life. He too could have joined those illustrious generals such as Lysander and Marcellus who died ignominiously in unnecessary actions.

Postlude

An opportunity is taken here to clarify certain issues which have arisen from the whole of the foregoing. In defence of the fact that, overall, in Parts Two and Three, the present study gives cavalry a separate section denied to the like of peltasts, or other arms, it should be pointed out that the latter has been given adequate coverage under sections such as 'Tactics'. To defend the approach more positively would be to highlight the ineffectualness, in this part of the text alone, of peltasts at such points as the attack of Mithridates (*Anab.* III.iii.7) where the lack of cavalry was of the greatest import and again at VII.viii.16, where an absence of cavalry led to half the force of foraging Greeks being wounded. Similarly at VI.iii.7–8, the Arkadians without any ancillary forces, peltasts, slingers, archers or cavalry, were beleaguered by Thracians and were extricated from their plight by Xenophon who had with him a balanced force. Had the Arkadians had with them even a small force of cavalry their position would have been very different. A force could be without peltasts but could be still be effective with cavalry. A force with hoplites and peltasts but with no cavalry was vulnerable. The ideal scenario for any commander was to have at his disposal a force containing hoplites, light infantry, archers, slingers and cavalry, so that his options were variable. A force of hoplites supported by cavalry alone was to be preferred to one supported only by peltasts by virtue of the former's greater mobility. For those who would cite the Lechaion (see Part Two) as a rebuttal, this in turn can be equally rebutted by the evidence of the inadequacy of command, particularly on the part of the cavalry commander, on that occasion. The importance of cavalry cannot be overstressed in light of the important part it was to play in Hellenistic times where the major tactical developments in terms of armed forces were in heavy infantry and cavalry and where the key component was the cavalry itself. In the melange of fourth century military development, the most striking feature is the ever greater effectiveness of the cavalry arm when used to its potential. Even small cities like Phleious could rightfully boast of success (Part Two). The prowess of the small force of Syracusan cavalry (*Hell.* VII.i.21) which made a Theban army 'dance to its tune' attests the increasing values and skills of this arm (Part Two). To counter the argument that it was only under Macedonian command, wherein the status of that arm was elevated by the leadership of the commander-in-chief, is to deny the experimentation which had been going on in Greece itself. The ἔμβολον (*emvolon*) was no accident at Second Mantineia, and shows the interest in experimentation which was current during the mid fourth century in particular relationship to this arm. (See Part Two.) Xenophon, although guilty of neglect in detail in what may have been essentials in the descriptions of battles, does not miss the implication for the future suggested by what was to become a strike force. Add to this the fact that Xenophon himself, as a cavalryman and lover of horses, gives to us more technical information on the subject of horsemanship and cavalry tactics than can be found in virtually the remainder of ancient sources. He is more likely to pick up on such developments and rightly gives numerous references and citations of its use. Although he could not know the direction of its development at the time, he was quick to recognise its potential. This arm was soon to become the battle winner in Alexander's battles and those of earlier Hellenisitic times, until reliance on elephants as the shock corps led to a falling off in the use and quality of a cavalry arm. The development of the cataphract and medieval horse in imitation of Samartian practice shows a later predilection for this arm up to the time of the emergence of the tank and air power which took over its role. The greatest commander of all time, Hannibal, was defeated by Scipio Africanus only because the latter had managed to detach Hannibal's Numidian cavalry from their former allegiance.

An intriguing point to consider is the failure of the Greeks to capitalise later in the fourth century on the direct experience gained in terms of artillery. In two places Xenophon makes special mention of the effectiveness of the Karduchian archers (*Anab.* IV.i.18; IV.ii.28). There, the high torsion of their large bows required them to place the left foot on the bottom of the bow to stabilise it and give additional purchase to the left arm for the backward pull of the bowstring by the right. The added velocity, together with the use of longer and, consequently, heavier arrows, proved capable of passing through both the shield and breastplate of a hoplite. Indeed, the Greeks used these long arrows as javelins when they came to hand. In the second passage Xenophon notes the good service performed by the Cretan archers in this region albeit against agile light troops, but one wonders why the lesson of this armament was not acted upon. An advancing hoplite phalanx could have been broken at a distance by an organised corps of such archers acting in concert had the technology been transplanted to the plains of Greece. It was lucky that the Karduchians were not subject to, or immediately available to, Tissaphernes. Such advances in technology were ignored on the Greek mainland and indeed by the Persians themselves.

The frequent references to wicker shields used by those who opposed the Greeks on their march may be initially intriguing but with knowledge of the capabilities of such armament, their preferred use becomes clear and has little to do with a lack of metal technology. First and foremost, the shield would be light to carry and ideal for light infantry operating in mountainous areas. Depending on the weave of such shields, and taking into consideration the use of archery butts up to present, it can be seen that the degree of penetration of such defensive protection could be of a limited nature. More likely the arrows or missiles lodged in such a shield could be re-used. It could well be that the arrows of the Karduchians would be less effective against these wicker shields than against the *aspis* (a solid round shield).

Without the evidence of Xenophon we would probably not be aware of the high incidence of insubordination in Greek armies alluded to in the *Anabasis*. To a greater or lesser extent Greek armies were subject to such limitations to the command structure which went far beyond the occasional heroic bravado of members of the first rank of hoplites making an individual sortie against the enemy. We have been witness to Xenophon almost wringing his hands in despair at some unilateral action taken by sections of those forces under his command. In the available reported actions which took place in the fifth and fourth centuries, can we be absolutely certain that the outcome of any engagement was not the result of some unilateral action by subordinates?

Finally, the problem of identity of the spearmen in the attack on the stronghold of the Drilai remains. Perhaps the answer is simpler and more mundane than that suggested earlier. Xenophon describes these men as having 'rushed out after essentials' ἐπὶ τα ἐπιτήδεια ἐζωρμηένοι (*Anab.* V.ii.4). In their haste they may well have been only partly armed and could not be described as hoplites without the full panoply. Carrying their hoplite spears the use of δορυφόροι describes them as they were, spearmen. Clearly they should not have been there and should not have found themselves in such a predicament.

End Notes

1. Whether Xenophon was writing an Apologia or not, is of little importance to the substance of his description of the events of the *Anabasis*. Modified truth or biased opinion has little effect on the subject matter which is sought. It matters little to the study whether the responsibility for the decisions taken have their origin with Xenophon or another, or that his descriptions of certain actions may have been coloured by subsequent events prior to writing. The fragments of Ctesias, the lost accounts of Sophaenetus and Ephorus, or their influence on such writers as Diodoros, and to a lesser extent, Plutarch, are neglible to the present purpose, which is to give an account of good and bad practice in command to be found in Xenophon's writings.

Anderson's *Xenophon*, pp. 105–112, deals with the dilemmas caused by Xenophon's description of Kounaxa and with other contradictory sources, he makes a telling comment in attempting to fathom some of the causes for these contradictions. 'One cannot help wondering, once more, whether Phalinus, the Greek professional in the service of Tissaphernes, was not the ultimate source for Diodorus and claimed that his master was the man who really won the battle.'

Under 'Tactics', Part Two of the present study deals with the kernel of what

Xenophon described from *Anab*. I.vii.20 to the end of Book VIII, and also the content of Book X. See also Plut. *Art* 7.

2. 'To secure ourselves against defeat lies in our own hands, but the opportunity of defeating the enemy is provided by the enemy himself.' Sun Tzu IV.2.

'If he is taking his ease, give him no rest. If his forces are united, separate them.' Sun Tzu I.23.

'Attack him (the enemy) when he is unprepared, appear where you are not expected'. Sun Tzu I.24.

3. *Anabasis*, Loeb Edition, note 4, p. 49 states misleadingly that 'The Greeks in Xenophon's time ate comparatively little meat under any circumstances, and that in the Arabian desert a diet of meat constituted a real hardship.' This is a somewhat extreme view. The Greeks enjoyed eating meat of all kinds otherwise they would not have taken the opportunity to do so when occasion arose (see *Anab*. IV.v.31) when all kinds of provision was available including a remarkable amount of meat, e.g., lamb, kid, pork, veal and poultry. The Greeks, like most people, enjoyed a mixed diet and to be deprived of vegetables, fruit and bread would have been an annoyance but no real hardship. In the absence of potatoes (not available in Europe for some centuries to come) that annoyance would probably stem from having no bread to soak up the gravy accompanying the meat.

4. See Nussbaum, 'The Ten Thousand', p. 40:

> Most striking is the case of Xenophon himself – still under thirty, presumably with next to no military experience, and until then not even a fighting member of the army, he is chosen officially to be one of the seven or so generals and unofficially to be, with Cheirisophos, chief leader of the whole army; and he is chosen on the strength of his leadership in a crisis, without any reference to military technicalities whatsoever.

A statement which, though accurate in much of what it describes, seems to suggest that Xenophon had played an entirely passive role up to the point of his elevation. He obviously had more than one set of armour with him (*Anab*. III.ii.7) and was close to the main action of the battle of Kounaxa when it was joined. It is hardly likely that he would merely sit on his horse and watch from the sidelines. Being directly involved in the fighting could well account for much of the contradictions in sources. It is not easy to see the full picture if you are a participant.

5. See Lazenby, in *War in History* 1(1), p. 9. An excellent introduction to contemporary logistics.

Also Pritchett, *The Greek State at War*, Part V, p. 159 indicates the obvious, that markets were provided by friendly peoples but very usefully gives a list of references of the nature and distribution of the booty taken on the *Anabasis* and from whom it was seized.

6. This matter is dealt with fully in Pritchett, *The Greek State at War*, Parts I and II. The competent commander knew enough about conducting sacrifices and reading signs but often had a seer to interpret. The decision for action or inaction remained the responsibility of the commander.

7. For a comprehensive view of Greek attitudes to the battle dead see Pritchett, *War* Part IV pp.139–45 and Vaughn, *The Identification and retrieval of the hoplite dead*, pp.38–62.

8. See Anderson, *Xenophon*, p. 75.

9. More than half the army was made up of Achaeans and Arkadians. (*Anab.*VI.ii.10.)

10. At *Anab*, IV.viii.15–16 Xenophon indicates that the forces available were 8,000 hoplites, 1,800 peltasts and archers and at V.iii.3, states that the total number of men was 8,600, noting that the remainder had fallen at the hands of the enemy or in the snow, but with only a few dying from disease.

Discrepancies arise within the various totals which Xenophon offers in the course of his narrative. See also Anderson, *Military Theory*, p. 86 for his note on *Anab*. I.ii.9.

11. See Anderson, *Xenophon*, p. 123. This suggests that corporal punishment was used as a last resort to maintain discipline. Xenophon approvingly cites the case of Klearchos' fairness in picking the right man to belabour for indolence when speed of movement for the army was of the essence (*Anab*. II.iii.11). Anderson is correct in pointing to the demoralising effect of indiscriminate beatings (*Hell*. VI.ii.18–19).

12. Anderson, *Xenophon,* pp.120–121, stresses the democracy in the army of Cyrus (*Kyr*. III.2.37–38), and in the accompanying footnote suggests that, whereas in the *Anabasis* the army was organised like a city state, in the Kyropaideia the state was organised like an army. See also Nussbaum, 'The Ten Thousand', pp. 41–61. However, studies of Greek Commanders in the

fifth and fourth Centuries BC, (see Lengauer, *Studia Antiqua*; cf. Nussbaum, p.87) suggest that the choice of command positions was from a purely military point of view. On p. 83 Lengauer further declares in his rather repetitive study that a *strategos* is first and foremost a military man divorced from a political role, and on p. 93 states that 'the military leaders in the *Anabasis* are to him (Xenophon) already military commanders and there no longer exists identity of the military man and citizen. In the conditions of the fifth and fourth centuries the appearance of professional military leaders coincided with breaking away of such military commanders from the former structure of the polis.'

On p. 151 Lengauer rightly points to the evidence of Xenophon acting as a typical mercenary commander by going with his army into the service of Seuthes.

13. 0325, Army Doctrine, Vol.1: *Operations*. 'Operational objectives are the military goals that need to be achieved in the campaign to achieve the desired end-state.' An interesting omission is that the same document gives no consideration to withdrawals, strategic retreats, etc.

14. 'Bring war material from home, but forage on the enemy. Thus the army will have food enough for its needs.' Sun Tzu II. 9. ' Hence a wise general makes a point of foraging on the enemy. One cartload of the enemy's provisions is equivalent to twenty of one's own, and likewise a single picful of his provender is equivalent to twenty from one's own store.' Sun Tzu II. 15.

15. Xenophon undoubtedly had knowledge of Brasidas' formation for his retreat from Thrace (*Thuc.* IV.125). However, in Brasidas' case, the hoplites protected the peltasts and other light armed troops.

16. *Anabasis*, Loeb Edition, pp.234–5, makes suggestions as to how this was done but limits the options to three.

17. The command structure for the various Greek armies on mainland Greece differed little. It is likely that, when Klearchos was commander-in-chief, the structure mirrored that of the Spartan army. This is made even more likely by the number of Arkadians and Achaeans present, who made up at least half of the expeditionary force of Greek hoplites and who, at that time, were still subservient to Sparta. Further, another Spartan, Cheirisophos, took Klearchos' place and would be unlikely to disturb arrangements which were familiar. Xenophon, who became an inveterate admirer of all things Spartan would have had no reason to make changes when he assumed that position. For a thorough

and detailed description of the command structure, its functions and activities in the field see J.F. Lazenby, *The Spartan Army*.

18. Also Anderson, *Military Theory*, p. 80.

19. ibid., p. 113.

20. ibid., p. 116.

21. 0214, Army Doctrine, Vol.1: *Operations*. 'To preempt the enemy is to seize the opportunity, often fleeting, before he does, in order to deny him an advantageous course of action.' It is also described at 732a in the same source as 'attacking the enemy's will'.

22. Anderson, *Military Theory*, p.138. Here his point is that of the cooperation between mixed forces. The real issue, however, is that those forces could not successfully operate unless under clear direction from a commander well versed and talented in the exercise of assessing a developing engagement. Quick thinking, a knowledge of the capabilities of those arms and of the individuals within each, timing and the commitment of appropriate force to particular points to achieve the *end point* are the prerogatives of a successful commander.

23. Anderson, *Military Theory*, p.109. Although at that location Anderson is dealing with *Anab*. IV.viii.9–13, his remarks are pertinent to the general tactic.

24. On the deployment of the Greek forces at this battle see also Anderson, *Military Theory*, p.180.

PART TWO

COMMANDERS IN PRACTICE
411–362 BC

The historical writings of Xenophon show a selective approach to what he regards as good and bad practice, largely on personal grounds. It is no surprise that many of his examples of good practice are taken from those he holds in the highest regard, e.g., Agesilaos, Archidamos, Teleutias and Iphikrates, although he does eventually give unreserved praise to Epameinondas prior the second battle of Mantineia (*Hell.* VII.v.8; VII.v.20). To be fair, he also levels criticism at his favourites when the occasion arises, e.g., against Iphikrates (*Hell.* VI.v.51). When not at first hand, for he was a likely participant in the campaign leading up to, and including, Koroneia, he obviously took detailed information from his immediate circle of Spartan friends. This may in part explain the charges of bias laid against him by some modern commentators.[1] His treatment of naval engagements is usually perfunctory and descriptions of minor land engagements often omit the name of the commander even when he has praise for the action, e.g., the several references to the Phleiasians. Nonetheless, unsatisfactory as it may be in some ways for good historical reporting, his commentary provides the thread of good practice even when the commander is anonymous.

What is significant in the reportage of this period is that the Spartans were not alone in the training of militia. Gone were the days when the citizen turned up with his armour to serve the city state in times of crisis, only to return to his previous occupation until the next danger threatened. There is clear evidence that other states were forming specialist forces for use when danger presented itself.[2] The example of the Sacred Band is well known and had been in existence for some time before the period in question as is that of the thousand Argives at Mantineia (*Thuc.* V.67.2). However, following Leuktra, military training had obviously been instituted for all Boeotians (*Hell.* VI.v.23). States such as Elis, with their three hundred and four hundred soldiers, were now dealing with specialist troops, obviously under regular training (*Hell.* VII.iv.13;

VII.iv.31), Arkadia with its *Eparitoi* (*Hell.* VII.iv.22; VII.iv.32), Phleious with its *epilektoi* (*Hell.* VII.ii.10&12) and the mercenaries of Jason of Pherae (*Hell.* VI.i.5–6) (see Appendix 1), suggest that the practice was becoming commonplace, and makes the appearance of the national army of Macedon, under Phillip, less of a surprise and more the natural outcome of the growth of professionalism of this century.[3]

The example of Iphikrates becoming a specialist in the handling of light infantry indicates new thinking (see below), as does Agesilaos' attack on the Theban cavalry with his own cavalry intermixed with the younger hoplites (378 BC) (*Hell.* V.iv.40). The latter disposition may have been made because of the casualties suffered by Agesilaos' peltasts in the initial attack made by the Theban cavalry, but is no less significant for being the quick answer to an emergency required of a commander. However, see below for earlier purposeful use of hoplites and cavalry by Agesilaos during his Persian campaign.

The command position is clarified during this post Peloponnesian War period, and it is only those commanders with heroic views, such as Kyros the Younger, who unduly exposed themselves. Fighting at the very forefront at the outset of a battle was highly unusual.[4]

Much of what follows below under one subheading often has different weight, but equal relevance, under another. The issues are dealt with thematically and not in chronological order. Often, it is the minor events which show good and bad practice. While it is easier to segregate issues from a novella like the *Kyropaideia*, the reflections of actuality are not so accommodating. Although reference is made to other sources, either in support, or in dispute, of an historical point throughout the text, it is as well to remember that it is the opinion of Xenophon himself, within the Hellenika and the first three books of the *Anabasis*, which is being sought on the issue of what constitutes the art of command.

Cavalry

The numerous references to cavalry in the *Hellenika*, and the increasing number of reported tactical roles it had to fulfil, justify the conclusion that talented commanders, in the fourth century, were giving this arm serious consideration and were elevating its importance. Those who did not, and retained the fifth century attitude of limiting cavalry to brief skirmishing, pursuit and screening activities, were doomed to failure, e.g., Kleombrotos (371 BC). Obviously, accident, trial and error played their parts in this period

101

of experimentation, and the good commander is clearly the one who learns from experience.

In dealing with the cavalry of the period, it is as well to rehearse the physical limitations which circumscribed its use at the time, all the more to admire the superb horsemanship which sometimes prevailed. Relying for control on bridle and bit, the rider's major problem was retaining his seat. Without a saddle and stirrups, this required not only balance but strength in the legs. The riding position would have been more forward on the animal than is usual to a saddled mount today (*Peri Hipp.* I.11–12; VII.5). Two reasons for this are obvious. The first, to place the weight as near to the forelegs as possible and to minimise stress on the back of the animal. The second, for a more secure position when needing to use the javelin arm. The mount itself was smaller than might be expected, no more than fourteen hands, or a good pony size. Under such circumstances, the charge which a cavalry formation could achieve at a gallop with security for the rider, and some semblance of formation, was the product of rigorous training. It is a matter of rhythm between the body of the rider and the horse. Speed apart, it is easier to keep one's seat at a gallop than at a fast trot. With this in mind, the use to which cavalry was put becomes an issue.[5] Although unsupported by any direct evidence from sources, there are implications in the accounts of the use of cavalry to suggest that in the period under discussion, two forms of cavalry were present. Today, we would use the terms light and heavy cavalry, but these would be misnomers. The difference would have been in the standard of corporate horsemanship within a contingent, permitting a commander a greater choice in its tactical commitment in any action, and would not have seen any differences in armour or weaponry. Some cavalry regiments would have been useful only in screening and skirmishing, activities requiring less cohesive formations. Increasingly, however, we note in sources references which indicate cavalry mixed with other forces, differentials in the speed at which cavalry is used and, at its most disciplined, in terms of animal and man, descriptions showing its use as a strike force in attack. These will become apparent in the examples which follow in this section. With mixed forces, a charge would proceed at a pace at which light armed infantry could match at a run, over a limited distance, sometimes holding on to the tail of a horse.

It should be noted that only an aggressive mount which is highly trained and well controlled will come to close quarters with a massed wall of humanity. It is in the nature of the beast to pull up well short of such an apparent obstacle. This, in spite of all efforts of its rider to make it continue on its path.

Only if it has been extremely well schooled will success be achieved in making the animal clash against an obstacle. It is clear that, in the changing tactical use of the cavalry arm within this period, there must have been some training undertaken with horses to address this particular issue. The wedge formation and its use as a shock force, adopted by Epameinondas to open his attack at Mantineia (362 BC), was a natural outcome of tactical thinking.

The exhortation of Xenophon that a cavalry commander should make use of infantry with cavalry, and to show that this mixed force is superior to one of cavalry alone (*Hipp.* V.13), may well have been made for additional reasons other than the obvious tactical one. It is well known that a horse, which is unwilling initially to take a jump or move forward, can be persuaded to do so by a sharp whack on its rump (*Peri Hipp.* VIII.4). This may have been one of the duties of the accompanying peltast; or his very presence, being dragged along by the horse's tail, produced sufficient discomfort for the animal to continue on its path.

The developing roles which the cavalry arm came to fulfil are various and are based on its superior mobility. The occasional reference from the *Anabasis*, which should correctly be within Part One, is given to illustrate singular instances. On the march, it gave a protective screen to the flanks and rear, and undertook scouting and reconnaissance duties in the van (for the vanguard (*Anab.* VII.iii.43; VI.iii.10 and 22); rearguard (*Anab.* IV.vii.22–24); for both van and rear (*Hell.* IV.iii.4)). The last reference is to the order by which Agesilaos attempted to protect the hollow square he had formed on the march against cavalry harassment. An experienced commander would wish to have forward scouting for a variety of reasons: reconnaissance (*Hipp.* IV.4), locating the enemy (*Hell.* VI.v.52) (although there is criticism of Iphikrates, the intention was good, but could have been better had he had the benefit of the suggestions for the correct size of force (*Hipp.* II.9; VIII.12–14)) and raiding (*Hipp.* VII.7–10 & 14-15).

Its use in attack is dealt with below, but it is as well to note its use as a deterrent, when supported by hoplites. Epameinondas' stationing such a force on his right to threaten any move made by Athenians coming to the help of their beleaguered neighbours, at Mantineia (*Hell.* VII.v.24), was a classic deployment.

A greater involvement in the planning for the use of a cavalry arm can be seen from the above tactical deployment. No longer was it merely an appendage to the main force of infantry, but a viable, battle winning, unit on its own. From a position of screening, flank attack, and defensive activities on the march, it became the agent by which gaps in an enemy line could be exploited, to one by which those gaps or weaknesses in an enemy line could be created by frontal assault.

Like Kyros, Agesilaos found himself without a sufficiency of well trained horse in the initial phase of his Persian campaign. Following the Greeks being worsted in a cavalry clash by a force no larger than theirs (*Hell.* III.iv.14), Agesilaos returned to the coastal cities of the Asian littoral, and required the richest citizens to provide armour, men and horses, in exchange for their being excused active service (*Hell.* III.iv.15; see also Plut. *Ages.* 9). He saw to it that regular training was instituted, with rewards for horsemanship (*Hell.* III.iv.16). Much the same is stated in Xenophon's monograph on Agesilaos (Xen. *Ages.* I.23–24) with the confirmation that the new force was of high quality. Here is a clear example of a commander who recognised that his earlier assessment of what was to be needed on campaign did not meet the conditions under which he sought to operate, and who lost no time in making the necessary adjustment.

The following year, having outwitted and outmanoeuvred Tissaphernes, Agesilaos' army was at last overtaken by the Persians near Sardis and its foragers attacked. With the support of the whole army following, Agesilaos ordered his new cavalry to attack, closely followed by peltasts and the youngest hoplites. The Persians were obliged to desist from their pursuit of the foragers and come into formation to rebut the attack, which they were initially successful in doing. However, they had no supporting infantry, a fact which had been duly noted by Agesilaos, and were cut to ribbons when the footsoldiers arrived.[6]

Timing is of the essence in any attack and decisions for deployment need to be quicker for cavalry than for infantry. Opportunism is essential to any successful commander, but even more so in the handling of a mounted corps. A brilliant example of this is to be seen in Agesilaos' action against the Thessalians. Xenophon, as a cavalry commander himself, shows clearly Agesilaos' skill at reading the available possibilities in a developing situation (Xen. *Ages.* II.2–5; *Hell.* IV.iii.3–9). Moving in the formation of a hollow square, with his cavalry force divided to protect both the van and the rear, Agesilaos found his progress annoyingly slowed by Thessalian attacks on his rearguard. With the exception of his own personal escort, Agesilaos sent the vanguard cavalry to join those at the rear. It is obvious that the whole army came to a halt, about faced and presented a line of battle. In such circumstances, the Thessalian cavalry wisely chose to retire, rather than to indulge in a cavalry engagement against an enemy whose cavalry was either closely supported by hoplites, or had hoplites intermingled with them. The retiral was slow, and the pursuit equally so. At that point, Agesilaos, recognising the vulnerability of his enemy and the over cautious reaction of his officers, sent his personal mounted escort to join the cavalry with orders for all to charge the enemy at full speed. The very slowness of the Thessalian retiral allowed the ground between the two forces to be covered by the speedy shock attack of Agesilaos' cavalry, and they were engaged before the majority had an opportunity to turn to face their attackers. With the fall of their commander, the Thessalians were routed.

Xenophon makes direct comparison of the quality of the cavalry used by the respective armies prior to Leuktra. He makes the point that the Theban horse was in good battle training as a result of the wars with Orchomenos. He is clear in his condemnation of the ability of the cavalry used by the Spartans, and blames this on the method by which it was raised (*Hell.* VI.iv.11) – the least strong on horses owned by the richest men. This is a damning statement from a friend of Agesilaos on the continued practice of raising a poor quality force for minimal use. The lessons learned by the Spartans from the successful actions of allied cavalry from the Asian Aegean littoral on Agesilaos' march south through Thessaly, prior to Koroneia, had been ignored by the Spartan command. Their continued reliance on the hoplite phalanx at a time of diminishing citizen manpower and their blindness to the development of cavalry and light infantry tactics led to the demise of Spartan invincibility. It is as well to remember that Sparta in comparison to other states was very late in raising a cavalry arm and was only provoked into doing so by the loss of Pylos and Kythera, c.424 BC (*Thuc.* IV.55.1–2). At that time, the need for greater mobility to protect the seaboard led to the raising of a force of 400 cavalry. The point has been well made[7] that economics played a part in the relative size of the cavalry arm available to each state. Horses were expensive to maintain and, south of Thessaly, fodder was better applied to other livestock, including that which could be eaten. Similarly, attitudes and political views can be seen to dictate differences between the varying strengths available to a state, from one time to another, e,g., democratic Athens could find the raising of cavalry from the oligarchic class a little distasteful, and Sparta's whole social structure was to support the hoplite. Such conditions produced forces, the size of which either permitted or prohibited the use of certain tactics, and it is to be expected that the examples of good practice come from the well endowed, e.g., Thessaly, Boeotia, Olynthos, or the hard pressed, e.g., Phleious.

Leuktra is sometimes regarded as being Epameinondas' most brilliant achievement (however see below). While not wishing to detract from the success of his innovative manoeuvres, it is as well to look at the unimaginative approach of his opposing commander. Xenophon makes it clear that Kleombrotos had placed the Spartan cavalry in front of the phalanx (*Hell.* VI.iv.10). The facts are stated baldly, with no suggestion or explanation being given for this deployment, possibly because he did not know of one. The Theban cavalry was also placed in front of its phalanx, but this was possibly in order to cover the manoeuvre which led to the adjustment of their phalanx to a depth of fifty men, a formidable and unstoppable weight (*Hell.* VI.iv.12). Certainly, it is unlikely that the Theban cavalry was deployed in this manner in response to the appearance of Spartan cavalry, but more probably to provide a screen of dust and moving figures behind which the infantry manoeuvre could be made.[8] Having condemned the quality of the Spartan cavalry, Xenophon leaves his reader with the problem of understanding why Kleombrotos placed an ineffectual force in front of, and in a position eventually to impede, his phalanx. Was it an inept command, or was it because he too wished to screen a manoeuvre? The latter seems the more probable. It would appear that in what followed, either the timing of the manoeuvre in the case of Kleombrotos was at fault, or, more probably, Epameinondas second guessed what was happening, and ordered an immediate advance, while Kleombrotos was in mid-manoeuvre. The Spartan horse were not unexpectedly routed by the Theban cavalry, which presumably retired to the wing as the Theban phalanx advanced. The disruption caused to the Spartan hoplites, as their fleeing cavalry appeared among them, further weakened their line (*Hell.* VI.iv.13).

Poor handling of cavalry contributed to the Spartan disaster at Lechaion (390 BC). An initial error, made by the polemarch, was to detach the entire cavalry mora from that of his hoplites, so that they could escort the Amyklaians further, when they passed Corinth. Left without peltasts or a cavalry screen, he openly invited attack on his return march. Iphikrates and Kallias were quick to take the opportunity. The Spartans were aware of strong forces being present in Corinth (*Hell.* IV.v.12) and it would appear that arrogance had replaced tactical sense. The Spartan hoplite *mora* was progressively mauled by the brilliantly led peltasts of Iphikrates, any pursuit of whom was threatened by Kallias' Athenian hoplites. The eventual return of the Spartan cavalry saw further tactical mishandling. When pursuit of the peltasts was made by both Spartan hoplite and horse, the cavalry merely kept pace with the footsoldiers and proved, unsurprisingly, ineffectual (*Hell.* IV.v.16). The significant order as recorded by Xenophon was that the peltasts were to retire, before the Spartan hoplites had an opportunity to make contact (*Hell.* IV.v.15).

Xenophon censures Iphikrates for the misapplication of forces for specific tasks (*Hell.* VI.v.51–52). He rightly makes the point that instead of sending all the cavalry for the purpose of scouting, a few would have done the job satisfactorily and not have led to the loss of twenty men (370 BC). It is pointless sending a large force for a task if it is still less in number than the enemy, particularly when its task can be achieved by a much smaller and more mobile contingent. The problems of selecting an adequate route for a large force, and effecting a safe withdrawal, are exacerbated. On the other hand, praise is given to the Syracusan cavalry, numbering only fifty horse, which harried the lines of the Theban and allied forces (369 BC) (*Hell.* VII.i.21). After charging along the Theban lines and discharging javelins, they would retire and dismount to rest. Those of the Theban army who pursued them would find the Syracusans remounting and retreating further. If the pursuit was pressed further, the cavalry would turn and counterattack. In such a manner were these tactics employed that the whole Theban army was made to move to and fro, much at the will of those few cavalrymen. Initially, the Athenian and Corinthian cavalry did not take part, because of the size of the Theban army. Even though Xenophon excludes them from the action in his description, it seems likely that they would have followed the example given. No mention is made of the commander here, but the tactic is clearly noted.

Xenophon further shows the effective use of cavalry in relatively small numbers against larger forces, when he describes the action of the sixty Phleiasians against the retiring Argives (369 BC) (*Hell.* VII.ii.4). After successfully disrupting the defensive screen of Argive cavalry, the Phleiasians put the whole rearguard to flight. In the following year, 368 BC, Phleiasian and Athenian cavalry were prominent in defeating invading Argive and Arkadian forces at a river crossing. They forced the invaders to retreat along the foothills, avoiding the cultivated areas (368 BC) (*Hell.* VII.ii.10). The place of the engagement was well chosen and the continued threat of attack led to the safeguarding of crops. It is when manoeuvre succeeds in its objective, in this case the saving of the harvest, that command is to be seen at its best.

The ultimate decision for the deployment and duties of cavalry was in the hands of the general. Once orders had been given, the *hipparch* exercised authority within his terms of reference but these did not mute his ability to show enterprise when the occasion demanded. The key factor lay with the initial orders and herein rests the measure of good generalship. Had Thibron

(391 BC) made intelligent use of cavalry for scouting and reconnaissance and given his cavalry commander orders to carry out these duties, he would not have suffered the surprise and disaster at the hands of Struthas, whose intelligence gathering was well in place (*Hell.* IV.viii.18–19). By comparison Agesilaos had his *hipparch* suitably briefed in a flexible role and whoever was in command of the Olynthian cavalry on Agesilaos' march to Thespiai, following the king's highly successful wasting of Theban territory, was alert to opportunity. Mercenary peltasts, harrying the rearguard on the march, were put to flight by the cavalry, in a location which the *hipparch* had recognised as good ground for horses. The pursuit uphill maximised enemy casualties (377 BC) (*Hell.* V.iv.54).

While at this time the quality of Thessalian and Theban cavalry was generally regarded as being superior to that of other city states, they must have been dumbfounded to have been the object of a surprise attack by Athenian cavalry, in a force smaller than their own (362 BC) (*Hell.* VII.v.16). Again the commander is not named by Xenophon, but it is likely to have been Kephisodoros who was the *hipparch* at Second Mantineia (*Paus.* VIII.ix.10; *Diog.* II.55). The Athenian cavalry came quickly to the aid of the Mantineians collecting their harvest outside their walls, and inflicted a defeat on Epameinondas' cavalry arm in an action in which Xenophon's son, Gryllos, was killed. This setback, so soon after his unsuccessful assault on Sparta, must have proved a problem of morale for the Theban commander. In the second battle of Mantineia which followed soon after, however, the imaginative disposition of cavalry made by Epameinondas, which should have brought him total victory had he not been killed early in the engagement, shows genius. His enemy had deployed its cavalry six deep in the customary Greek rectangular phalanx formation. The Theban formation was organised so that its column appeared as a wedge, (ἔμβολον – emvolon) (*Hell.* VII.v.24) and unlike that of his opposition, interspersed with peltasts, or, more accurately, *hamippoi pezoi* καὶ ἀμίππους πεζοὺς συνέταξεν αὐτοῖς (*Hell.* VII.v.24). The surprise attack of this striking force, followed by the very deep formation of hoplites, was the cause of the initial disaster to the enemy's right, whose left could not come to its relief, threatened as it was by the uncommitted Theban right. There is no doubt that Xenophon supports the practice used by Epameinondas (*Hipp.* V.13). As at Leuktra, an opportunist attack on the enemy's command position proved successful. An object lesson which Alexander was to make habitual.

In this battle, it is to be assumed that the 'wedge' formation was similar to that of the Scythian practice, which was adopted by the Thracians and Macedonians, and not the full rhomboid of the Thessalians, which would present a wedge both at the front and the rear.[9] This formation would still be comfortable to the Thessalians within the cavalry present, but they may have been on the right wing, with only Theban cavalry on the left. Although backed by the element of surprise, which Epameinondas achieved by making his attack at a time when his enemy thought he was about to encamp, the result of the successful cavalry attack on the phalanx was predictable. The small gap in the line, achieved by the point of the formation, would be gradually widened as the wedge forced its way forward. The horsemen thrusting or throwing javelins, following up with the *kopis*, turning to the left and, particularly, to the unshielded side on their right to disrupt the line further, together with the action of the accompanying peltasts, prepared for the closely following onslaught of the Sacred Band and the Theban infantry. After the initial charge, the process would be gradual, unlike the charges of later cataphracts and medieval cavalry.[10] Xenophon makes no mention of the action of the Eleian cavalry which averted disaster for the Athenian hoplites in this battle (*Diod.* XIII.109.5). So the gradual development of cavalry deployment by a commander is seen to move from merely exploiting gaps in the line, to creating such gaps for exploitation. Mantineia, possibly, was the first planned use of cavalry as shock troops.

An interesting observation is made by Xenophon with regard to supportive deployment of cavalry and infantry as a rearguard. It is obvious, from his brief mention, that the withdrawal of the Argives from Phleious in 369 BC, referred to earlier, was covered by a rearguard composed of a cavalry screen, with infantry dedicated to their support (*Hell.* VII.ii.4). The fact that it was put to flight by only sixty Phleiasian horse attests to the quality of cavalry produced by this small state. It is regretted that a detailed description of the action is not given, so that the tactics used would be known. Again, the Phleiasian cavalry proved decisive in forcing the Mantineians to abandon their pursuit of fleeing mercenaries (370 BC), by riding around the force and threatening the rear (*Hell.* VI.v.14). This was a clear sighted analysis by the commander of what was needed to redress the problem, without undue danger to his own men.

Teleutias, commanding the allies sent against Olynthos in 382 BC, like his brother Agesilaos, ensured that he had with him an effective cavalry force. It is significant that he stationed Derdas and his 400 cavalry beside him in the battle line on the advance on Olynthos. In case it is presumed that the command point was always on the right in Greek warfare until Epameinondas, here is an example of the commander-in-chief taking up his position on the left wing (*Hell.* V.ii.40). There was a tactical reason for this positioning. The left of the line covered the gateway to the city which the opposition forces would have to use. The remainder of the line stretched to the right on which wing were stationed the Spartan, Theban and Macedonian cavalry. The cavalry of both armies figured significantly in the action that followed. The Olynthian cavalry, after a spirited engagement, put to flight the cavalry on the allied right wing, killing the Spartan hipparch and threatening to roll up the line. Xenophon uses the word συσπειραθέντες (*Hell.* V.ii.41) in describing the Olynthian formation, 'being in close order' or 'having closely come together', as he does in his description of the Theban phalanx at Koroneia (*Hell.* IV.iii.18). To note this as he does suggests that it was uncommon. It would also suggest that the weight of a massed charge, presumably in wedge formation, certainly among those living to the north of Greece, was becoming a tactical option. However the action of Derdas in making straight for the gateway, with Teleutias advancing in the same direction in battle order, led the Olynthian horse to see that the safety of any retiral that they might wish to make was threatened. The tight formation they may have maintained hitherto would obviously have been lost in the scramble to reach safety and, in consequence, many were killed as they made their way past Derdas' front.

The following year, Derdas had another success against the same opposition. Having arrived at Apollonia early, he later observed some 600 Olynthian cavalry pillaging the area around the city. Being emboldened by the lack of any opposition they appeared ever closer to the gates. Throughout the raid, Derdas had kept his force at the ready (*Hell.* V.iii.1) and eventually sallied forth putting the Olynthians to flight. What is most significant, is that he sustained a pursuit for just over ten miles, killing about eighty of the enemy. Such success indicates strong leadership, discipline and the farsightedness to take the opportunity in pursuit of greatly weakening what had been the enemy's strength. Xenophon notes that this action had the effect of keeping the Olynthians very much within the proximity of their city, even to the extent of leading them to cultivate only a small portion of their land (*Hell.* V.iii.2).

Although the following is equally relevant under the section dealing with tactics, it is better discussed here, considering the significant cavalry contribution made to the action. In seeking to destroy the Olynthian crops,[11] Teleutias had led his army towards the city and was confronted by the Olynthian cavalry which had crossed the river and approached his forces. He ordered the peltasts to charge and the Olynthians retired and recrossed the river. When only a portion of the peltast force had crossed in pursuit, the Olynthians turned and charged, killing the commander Tlemonidas and more than a hundred men (*Hell.* V.iii.4). Tlemonidas, himself, must have been naïf in being lured into what was known, at the time, to be an elementary error. Compare the successful crossing of a river by the Ten Thousand when threatened to front and rear at *Anab.* IV.iii.8–34, (also Sun Tzu IX. 4: 'It will be best to let half the army get across and then deliver your attack'; also *Hipp.* 7.11). For the remainder of the engagement see 'Tactics' below.

It has rightly been noted that cavalry in this period was most effective when employed in actions which allowed it to benefit from 'missile fire, and from hand to hand combat in the melee or the pursuit'.[12] Several instances have already been cited to show the effectiveness of cavalry against infantry, whereas frontal attack on a phalanx was unusual.

Piety

A commander's responsibility for his men did not end with the death of those who served under him. His pious duty was to retrieve their bodies under truce and ensure their burial. It is significant and correct, under the unusual circumstances, that Xenophon should devote such coverage to the failure of the Athenian commanders to recover as many bodies as they could following the battle off the Arginousai islands (406 BC) (*Hell.* I.vi.35 to I.vii.35; II.iii.32-35; *Diod.* XIII.100.1–2; *Paus.* VI.vii.7; *Athen.* V.218A).[13] The public outrage and distress is evidenced by the precipitate action of executing six of the eight commanders who were present in Athens, in a hurried abuse of the existing laws. The remorse felt by the citizens, when they assumed that they had been deluded, led to Kallixeinos starving to death in his own city on his return (*Hell.* I.vii.35). The Greek attitude to the recovery of the dead following a battle is better understood by such an example. The reaction of the Athenians, possibly fuelled by the animosities of previous commanders of the fleet who had served in this action as subordinates, was to what they believed to be an act of gross impiety.

In tandem with the foregoing is the popular belief which gained currency in succeeding years that the Athenian commanders, Adeimantos and Tydeos, had been bribed by the Spartan commander-in-chief, Lysander. Later sources such as Pausanias say as much following the latter's description of Lysander's monument at Delphi; while Plutarch (*Lys.* XI.1) makes it clear that the great Athenian Alkibiades suspected treachery in the Athenian forces.

111

Another contentious issue is that of Lysander's attitude to the Athenian prisoners in the final phase of the Peloponnesian War. Because of allegations against the Athenians, based on the threats they had made against the Spartans and their allies, all prisoners of war were put to death. One of the Athenian commanders had thrown overboard the crews of a Corinthian and an Andrian trireme and he was executed by having his throat cut (*Hell.* II.i.31–32). Such was the attitude taken by the victors at the outrageous threats against, and treatment of, fellow Greeks. In their reaction to such threats, the Spartans could be deemed no less guilty of impiety in denying funeral rites to the victims (see also *Paus.* IX.32.9; *Lys.*13).[14]

As a conservative and devoutly pious individual, Xenophon deplored the actions of the allies, in particular Argives and some Corinthians, against their fellow citizens (*Hell.* IV.iv.2–6), in their attempt to keep the city from suing separately for peace with Sparta (392 BC).[15] He is vehement in his condemnation of the massacre made at the time of the festival of Artemis Euklea, citing the custom that not even a convicted felon was put to death by the State at a time of religious observance. The sacrilege went further, for those who had fled to holy places were pursued and killed as they sought sanctuary. Breaches of public morality on such a scale suggest a seed change in collective belief, where local political need overwhelmed those beliefs which had, hitherto, united all Greeks. Xenophon labels this as sacrilege in the extreme (*Hell.* IV.iv.2).

Such actions indicate the progressive breakdown of the ritualistic formulae and mores which had characterised Greek society and pervaded the encounters between Greek forces hitherto. With this new thinking, and the formulaic practices being gradually set aside, the first half of the fourth century saw commanders experimenting with tactics outside those of the accepted hoplite engagement. They came to use, often with significant success, those sections of an army which had hitherto been regarded as very much of secondary importance, such as peltasts and cavalry, as prime components in successful encounters. Although there is no direct evidence, it seems unlikely that new thinking and attitudes were limited to tactics alone, but pervaded many aspects of Greek society including belief in gods and ritual. Democracy encouraged this and changes in attitude came more quickly when it was present, than under a strictly conservative regime.

Ritual in other aspects of activity can become habit and an excuse for not thinking. The fact that, apart from Agesilaos and, to a lesser extent Teleutias, Spartan commanders continued to rely very heavily on the traditional heavy

Remains of the Theatre at Megalopolis, reputed to be the largest in Greece.

The restored Theban Victory Monument at Leuktra. Note the shields at the top. It was probably surmounted by a bronze statue.

One of the original sculpted shields from the Monument.

Above: The battlefield of Leuktra. The Spartan camp was on the hills in the background.

Below: The area of the Battle of Koroneia. A typical flat terrain suited to the deployment of the phalanx.

Remains of the outer defensive walls of Messene.

The remains of the City of Messene.

The view towards Lechaion from Ancient Corinth.

infantry practices, the norm for more than a century, to the neglect of the useful employment of auxiliary forces, contributed to Sparta's inevitable decline during this period. This, together with a diluted rather than diminishing reservoir of manpower, and perhaps a deeper reverence for, and stricter observance of, ritual than other states at this time, contributed much to its nemesis.

In a short digression on the so called shortage of manpower, the unresolved question of the *neodamodeis* must surface ('νεοδαμώδων') (*Hell.* III.i.4). From the outset of its imperial period this new class within Lakedaimonian society played a significant role in overseas and mainland wars. To date, no wholly conclusive identification of these men has been made. If, as has generally come to be accepted, they were freed helots, the reasons and opportunities for them to be granted freedom still remains an issue. Did they come into being, originally, by means other than those associated with war, such as reward from a grateful state, or as the result of Spartiatai who could no longer afford to pay their mess bills, or maintain estates? Whatever the reasons, this class, once created, was eligible for army service. Reliance on such a reservoir proved, eventually, to be shortsighted. What was needed was a total overhaul of the constitution. It also meant that the Spartiatai became an increasingly protected class, barely having a presence in overseas operations. Out of the 8,000 men in the forces required for the Asian expedition of 396 BC, as suggested by Lysander, 2,000 were of this new class, and only thirty Spartiatai were included (*Hell.* III.iv.2; Xen. *Ages.* I.7; Plut. *Ages.* 6). After the disastrous losses to the ruling class at Leuktra, Sparta's reliance on mercenaries and freed helots became almost total.

At the time of Epameinondas' 370 BC invasion Xenophon makes the forcible point:

> ... but the Spartiatai, their city being without walls, were posted at intervals, one here, another there, and so kept guard, though they were, and were seen to be, very few in number. It was also determined by the authorities to make proclamation to the Helots that if they wished to take up arms and be assigned to a place in the ranks, they should be given a promise that all should be free who took part in the war. (*Hell.* VI.v.28).

The 6,000, who did so at this time, can be contrasted with the large desertion of the peroikoi to the Theban side at the later incursion.[16]

There can be no doubt that the *neodamodeis* were effective soldiers. However, their training would not lead them to be the equals of the Spartiates. Nor would emancipated helots, with even more limited experience in the arts of war, have given many Spartan commanders reason for tactical experiment. With the exception of mercenaries, the problem for the Spartans was an ever increasing dilution of quality in the forces it fielded.

In the symbolism of the priest king, the bodies of Spartan kings were always protected and carried back to their homeland. That of Kleombrotos, at Leuktra, was extracted from the battle with tremendous loss of life (*Hell.* VI.iv.13–14; see also *Diod.* 15.56.1) showing that the person of the king was of prime importance in more than royal terms. The body of Agesipolis, who died of a fever, possibly malaria, whilst on campaign, was placed in honey for the homeward journey, no doubt to suppress the smell of decay in summer (*Hell.* V.iii.19; see also *Diod.* 15.93 and also Plut. *Ages.* 40, where he describes Agesilaos' body being covered in wax in the absence of honey for the journey back to Sparta). Pausanias points to the possibility of disgrace should the body fall into enemy hands (*Paus.* 9.13.10). However, his is a view which reflects the beliefs of his own time and neglects the substance of the still strong religious beliefs of fourth century Lakedaimon.

The importance in Sparta of the priest king is best shown in time of relative peace, when Agesilaos made sacrifice as a normal procedure in state matters. Because of the adverse signs (*Hell.* III.iii.4) the conspiracy of Kinadon to overthrow the ruling Spartiates was uncovered. Agesilaos' duties as priest king were completed, but he was ready, as the commander of Spartan forces, to deal with any of the insurrectionists (see also *Lak.Pol.* XV.2–3). Sacrifices, libations, rituals, the taking of omens, etc., were part and parcel of everyday life. In no way were they the subject of superstition, rather they were part of the fabric of a practical society and, as such, had their place in association with any endeavour, whether it be for household or State.[17] In such circumstances, the constant reportage in sources of ritual in association with military matters carried out by the commander in chief reflects a perfectly normal occurrence. When on active military duty, the duties of the kings of Sparta were reduced to the two essentials, as seen at that time, of general and priest (*Lak.Pol.* XIII.11). After the ban had been called by the ephors, and all preparations for an expedition completed, the king made sacrifice to Zeus and the Dioscuri. Given that the signs were favourable, fire was taken from the altar by a fire-bearer who led the army to the border, where the king made further sacrifice to Zeus and Athena. Only when the signs were propitious, was the border crossed (*Lak.Pol.* XIII.2–4). The fire-bearer was to maintain an unquenched flame possibly for the duration of the campaign. When morning sacrifice was made, two ephors were present to ensure that those officers attending maintained due respect for the occasion.

In Athens responsibility devolved on the three senior Archons for the major part of religious practices. The *basileus*, as the name suggests, carried out those civic duties which had formerly been the prerogative of the king. These were traditional in nature, and involved all sacrifices within ancestral cults, such as the Eleusinian and the Lenaia, maintenance of the religious calendar and presiding over cases involving impiety. The Eponymous Archon determined the procedures for civic festivals of more recent origin such as the City Dionysia; that of Zeus Soter, set up in thanksgiving for the outcome of the Persian War; the processions for Asklepios established in 420 BC and the festival of Pythian Apollo; the Thargelia.

Important, for our present concern, was the Polemarch, whose responsibilities were those cults which had military connotations; those of battlefield sacrifice to Artemis Agrotera, Enyalios; the festival celebrating the victory at Marathon; the sacrifices in honour of Aristogeiton and Harmodios, the liberators of the city from the tyranny of the Peisistratids; and the public funerals to honour the war dead.

One of the most curious observations of piety occurred at the retaking of Peiraeus in 404 BC, where the paean was delayed by Thrasyboulos, on the exhortations of a seer, until their forces sustained a casualty (*Hell.* II.iv.18). Is this an echo of a ritual from former times? In the same action it should be noted that the depth, in which he formed up his men, was one of fifty shields (*Hell.* II.iv.11). The reason is unlikely to have been tactical, given the confined area of their advance.

The movements of armies, or indeed fleets, were subject to the favourable outcome of sacrifices and it is evident that, although commanders had seers in attendance, the responsibility for the sacrifice and the action thereafter was, more often than not, wholly that of the commander. In the case of the Spartans, it was usually the priest-king who commanded. Therefore, he merely took his all-embracing priestly responsibility to the battlefield. Again at Sparta, when the king was not commanding, that responsibility remained and was taken up by the commander-in-chief, e.g., Brasidas, Teleutias and Lysander, who was sometimes a member of the royal household. In other Greek states, where democracies or oligarchies had long since replaced kingship, the commander was elected or appointed, but his responsibilities reflected those of a surrogate priest-king in terms of expected religious practices.

It should, therefore, come as no surprise that the circumstances for a commander to undertake rites were almost limitless, from crossing borders (*Hell.* III.iv.3); Agesilaos crossing the border of Lakedaimon (*Hell.* III.v.7); Pausanias doing the same (*Hell.* IV.vi.2–3); Agesipolis sacrificing at the border and going to consult the oracles at Olympia and Delphi for sanction to invade Argos, (see below)) to sacrifice immediately before battle. The duty to sacrifice at borders prior to hostilities, however, did not inhibit Agesilaos from making arrangements to secure a line of advance into Boeotia, prior to the successful outcome of sacrifices (*Hell.* V.iv.47). For the sequence of events involved in the extended ritual for crossing borders see *Lak.Pol.* XIII.2–4.

The failure of a commander may be explained by his ignoring the auspices of the day, as is described in the case of Anaxibios, whose return march was ambushed by Iphikrates, an action, in which Anaxibios lost his life, on the day of his adverse omens (*Hell.* IV.viii.36) (dealt with more fully later). This would be termed foolhardy rather than impious, for sacrifice in such matters was not seen as a propitiation, but as a search for guidance and endorsement in an enterprise. The choice for action rested with the commander who, in this case, chose a course of action contrary to that which was indicated. By contrast, the well known delay of Pausanias, in ordering the advance at Plataea while awaiting favourable *sphagia* (*Herod.* IX.61) was made to look insignificant, some eighty years later, when Derkylidas held up his attack on Kebren for four days, while awaiting favourable *hiera* (*Hell.* III.i.17).

Delay in another manner is present in the actions of the Spartan ephors who, on hearing of the calamity of Leuktra, insisted that the Festival of the Gymnopaidiai should not be interrupted, but should be allowed to come to its natural conclusion (*Hell.* VI.iv.16). As all artistic expression was in honour of the gods, be it musical, dramatic, or movement in terms of dancing, when organised on behalf of a *polis* at the time of a festival, one glimpses the priorities working within the Greek mind. Perhaps this example is the most powerful in showing that, in the midst of what was Sparta's greatest disaster up to that time, honour to the gods took precedence over human needs. The 'iron' in the Spartan makeup would not allow news of a disaster to interrupt a formal ceremonial but it was not only a 'stiff upper lip' attitude.

It is not wholly clear how many daily sacrifices were the duty of command, however it does seem likely that, when on campaign, and in close proximity to an enemy, sacrifice would be an extremely regular occurrence. Topography, water crossings or the appearance of disturbing natural phenomena, would provoke some sacrificial response. Whether the sacrifice at daybreak by Agesilaos, prior to his breaking through the defences of the Thebans and laying waste to their land (*Hell.* V.iv.41) was particularly noted for its being even earlier than the normal time, or was reported as a normal procedure, is conjectural. The daybreak sacrifice was normal (*Lak.Pol.* XIII.3) but the timing was probably earlier, on this occasion, for tactical reasons. The examples of a daybreak sacrifice by Agesilaos, recorded also at *Hell.* V.iv.49 and VI.v.17, implies accepted practice divorced from tactical consideration.

Such was the piety of the Spartan kings that, following the Battle of Koroneia, Agesilaos went to Delphi to offer Apollo a hundred talents in thanks for his successful operations in Asia Minor, his return journey and the successful outcome of Koroneia (*Hell.* IV.iii.21). However, there is a discrepancy in the reported amount within the writings of Xenophon. Agesilaos is reported to have subscribed to Delphi no less than 200 talents (Xen. *Ages.* I.34) and it is not clear whether the latter is the cumulative total of offerings, or a reference to the same occasion.

It is clear that, even when a tactical decision had been made, the need for reassurance by sacrifice was paramount, even in the course of an engagement. The Akarnanians, in possession of the heights commanding Agesilaos' withdrawal from their territory, caused such mayhem with their missiles that the Spartan army was forced to a halt. At this point Agesilaos sought confirmation, through sacrifice, that his decision to pursue the Arkarnanians in an uphill attack was feasible. It is implied that the order for the younger men of the phalanx to attack was given only when a successful outcome to that sacrifice had been elicited (*Hell.* IV.vi.9–10).

Much of the reportage seems to stem from the actions of Spartan commanders, and this may well be because the sources of information used by Xenophon were from the Spartan viewpoint and, therefore, neglect the ancillary activities of their opponents. There is no doubt that commanders from other city states were no less meticulous in their duties, for, when Xenophon himself had command, he was equally rigorous in his observance of ritual (see Part One). Nor in his reporting does Xenophon imply that this was anything but commonplace.

Thus, when the Persian emissaries came to the Greeks, after the inconclusive battle in which Kyros the Younger met his death, Klearchos left to finish the *hiera*, examining the organs of a sacrificial victim (*Anab.* II.i.9). This had been his concern prior to their arrival, and he returned to the conference only after the completion of those duties, to give an inconclusive reply to the Persian King's representatives (*Anab.* II.i.22). The sacrifice took precedence over the meeting and its conclusions had to have an effect on the final outcome of that meeting. And so it transpired that, when Klearchos gave his report to his fellow officers, it became clear that the omens had been unfavourable concerning an action against the king, but were supportive of joining with the remainder of Kyros' army, encamped some distance away (*Anab*. II.i.3). On balance it should be noted that Klearchos' piety went hand in hand with an extremely tough and professional attitude to soldiering (see *Anab*. II.vi.1–15 for his character sketch by Xenophon).

The fact that Klearchos was a Spartan of the 'old school' is significant. His piety, and belief in the paramount importance of any matter involving the gods, was demonstrated by his simple trust and belief in the binding qualities of the oaths of Ariaios and his officers (*Anab*. II.ii.8) in which a bull, boar and ram were sacrificed over a shield to catch the blood. Into this mixture the swords and spears of the participants were dipped in mutual pledge. Likewise, Tissaphernes, and the brother of the King's wife, swore oaths on behalf of the Persians (*Anab*. II.iii.28) to lead the Greeks safely back to their homeland. Being later reminded by Klearchos, at a time of mutual distrust, of the consequences of breaking such an oath (*Anab*. II.v.7), Tissaphernes concurred with the view that it would be an act of gross impiety so to do (*Anab*. II.v.20–21). For a man who was exceedingly careful with tactics in the field, Klearchos proved ill fitted to match the treacherous deception (see introductory paragraphs in Part One) which later cost his life and that of four other *strategoi* and twenty *lochagoi*. His piety, and assumption that others fully shared his principles, led to the temporary loss of the Greek command structure, and could well have sealed the fate of the Greek army.

Such sacrilege proved beneficial in the longer term, however, because Agesilaos never believed anything coming from Tissaphernes, and was not surprised when the latter broke the initial truce following his arrival in Asia Minor (*Hell*. III.iv.6; Plut. *Ages*. 9). In fact, he turned the situation to moral advantage by claiming that, by breaking his oath, Tissaphernes had caused the gods to take the side of the Greeks (*Hell*. III.iv.11; Plut. *Ages*. 9). Shortly after, Agesilaos was persuaded to retire to the coast, rather than to advance, because the sacrificial victims produced incomplete livers. The *hiera* or signs led him to deduce that his army was lacking in cavalry (*Hell*. III.iv.15; Plut. *Ages*. 9). A seemingly formidable decision to make for the movement of an army, after perusing the guts of an animal, but the terms in which it is expressed suggest that Agesilaos is seeking confirmation through sacrifice for a conclusion that he had already reached, after his few cavalry had been worsted the day before (*Hell*. III.iv.14).

However, when omens came thick and fast it was better to conclude a campaign than to continue. Such was the case with Agesipolis' campaign against the Argives. Strategically, it was sound policy to eliminate the threat to one's rear before attempting an invasion of Attica or Boeotia and Agesipolis undertook the usual border sacrifices. After completion, he went, first, to Olympia and then to Delphi to seek justification for his impending campaign, on the grounds that the Argives were conveniently moving the period of a holy truce to suit themselves and to secure their safety from attack (*Hell.* IV.vii.2). Having achieved the gods' approval, Agesipolis invaded by way of Nemea and was met by heralds, who claimed a holy truce (*Hell.* IV.vii.3). Here Xenophon implies that this was the habitual tactical practice of the Argives. 'And when the Argives realized that they would not be able to hinder the invasion, they sent, *as they were wont to do*, two heralds, garlanded, pleading a holy truce' (author's italics). The Argives seem to have given up this 'holy' tactic, there-after, as is reported by Xenophon when the Spartans called the ban against them in 387 BC (*Hell.* V.i.29).

Rejecting the plea, Agesipolis advanced towards Argos and, on the first evening, after libations had been made following the meal, an earthquake occurred, causing the whole camp to raise a chant of supplication to Poseidon (*Hell.* IV.vii.4). The army expected to be withdrawn and disbanded, as had been the case when Agis had invaded Elis (399 BC), but Agesipolis persuaded his men that the god was showing them his approval. Having made sacrifices to Poseidon, he sought to outdo the achievements of Agesilaos' previous invasion, and herein may lie the cause of the gods disapproval, in Xenophon's opinion. Tactically, he was only partially successful, for he was without his Cretan archers, who were on another mission to Nauplion. He, therefore, could not take advantage of the fact that Boeotian cavalry had been shut out of the city and would have been sitting targets. Lightning then killed several of his men in their camp and, with the intention of fortifying a garrison to secure future access to the land of the Argives, he made sacrifice only to find incomplete livers in the sacrificial victims. At this juncture, Agesipolis decided to withdraw the army and disband it.

Signs from the heavens, however, could be of great import and, by com-parison, the coincidence of lightning and thunder after the exhortation of Archidamos to his men prior to the Tearless Battle (368 BC) was a tremendous boost to morale, happening as it did where a sanctuary and statue of Herakles stood near the command position on the right wing (*Hell.* VII.i.31).

All this is very informative. It shows the careful preparations made prior to a campaign, and the commander's personal involvement in the religious preparations. Given that Agesipolis travelled personally to both Olympia and Delphi, and in that order, the time involved was considerable. We have no evidence for the route taken but if it had been overland on horseback, a minimum of two days would be necessary to reach Olympia, and that would be an optimistic estimate. From Olympia to Delphi would require as much again. Returning from Delphi to Sparta, over the Gulf of Corinth, would have taken at least a day and a half. Had he gone by sea, from a port in the Gulf of Corinth, he might have reached Olympia within thirty hours, given fair sailing, and from there, Delphi in a similar time. Given the time at the sanctuaries for the ceremonials, the journey could not have been completed in much less than a week. Xenophon's comment that this was a surprise invasion does not ring true (*Hell.* IV.vii.7).

The striking feature here is that Xenophon makes it clear, beyond any doubt, that Agesipolis travelled in person to both Olympia and Delphi. No mention is made of the Pythioi, those sacred envoys appointed by the two kings, whose duty it was to consult the oracle at Delphi on behalf of the kings (*Herod.* VI.57). One must question the reason why Agesipolis did not use his appointed Delphic envoy on this occasion, when, to have done so, would have much shortened the time scale, and why he chose to go to Olympia first. Perhaps Agesipolis wished to avoid a possible conflict in responses. By questioning both oracles himself, and seeking that of Apollo to agree with the answer given first by that of Zeus at Olympia, he cleverly used the seniority of the latter to exert compliance from Delphi. This would not be irreverence.

The Spartans were accustomed to make sacrifice immediately prior to engaging the enemy. The victim was usually a goat, as at the Nemea, an offering to Artemis Agrotera, the goddess who safeguarded the well-being and *tyche* (good fortune) of those involved in hunting. At the Nemea, with both armies on the move, the sacrifice was made so close to enemy lines that it was almost a gesture of contempt for the opposition, or it was done in full view of the enemy to indicate a greater show of piety. The reported distance between the lines at the time of sacrifice was 600 feet (*stadion*) and must, under the circumstances, have been a hasty operation (*Hell.* IV.ii.20), unless both lines halted. Obviously, the Spartan line would have had to slow its forward progress for the sacrifice, but if the opposing line continued, it would need at most only two and a quarter minutes to reach the Spartan line, had the latter remained immobile, which it would not. On the basis that a hoplite would cover an average of 250 feet per minute at normal pace and, at the double for the final phase of the onset, as much as 400 feet per minute, and, given that the Spartans may have wished to add impetus to their charge by moving at the double on completion of the sacrifice, it can be assumed that at a clear signal or order, the line came to a momentary halt for the quick dispatch of the victim before, at a further order, their charge was made.[18] The killing of a led goat, by plunging a knife through its throat, would take only about thirty seconds, as it does today for a sheep, prior to the Greek Easter celebrations. However, this is cutting matters rather fine, and stands as a testament to the discipline of the Spartans, and of the confidence of their commander Aristodemos. On the other hand, a slowing, or even a momentary halt for the sacrifice, could well have been the opportunity for hoplites to change their spear grip, so that the charge could be made with the front rows of the phalanx holding their spears above their heads instead of the lower carrying position.

While it is easy to point to examples of ritual observance and piety, parti-cularly from the Spartans, it would be wrong to avoid mention of those actions which are technically impious. A series of related impieties is described by Xenophon, but not directly condemned by him as such. Perhaps the changes in behaviour which affected not only traditional tactical considerations, but also traditional mores, led him merely to report, without comment, on matters which a century before would have been regarded as outrages. Or perhaps the fact that they are related in connection with those he holds in lesser regard is significant. The capture of the sanctuary of Olympia by the Arkadians (*Hell.* VII.iv.14) and the use by the Arkadian leaders of the sacred treasury to pay troops (*Hell.* VII.iv.33) almost pale into insignificance when set against the battle which was waged in the sacred precinct between the Arkadians and their allies, and the Eleians (*Hell.* VII.iv.30–31).[19] Even the temple roofs, including that of Zeus, were used as positions for missile throwers. In like manner, a hole was broken through the roof of a temple of Artemis, and Stasippos and his followers within were subject to attack from above, the missiles being the roof tiles (*Hell.* VI.v.9). Compare these acts of impiety within sanctuaries with the recognition by Agesilaos of a temple being a secure place of refuge after Koroneia (see above). Xenophon makes it clear that, even in pain from wounds, Agesilaos allowed the armed Theban survivors, who had taken refuge after Koroneia in the temple of Athena Itonia, to depart in safety, such was his respect for the goddess (*Hell.* IV.iii.20; Plut. *Ages.* 19).

The commander's attitude to religious observance is therefore regarded as critical to the maintenance of high morale and discipline. Agesilaos' example of piety, in leading by example while at Ephesos, and in dedicating his garlands after exercise to Artemis, is typical of the best that would be expected of a leader (*Hell.* III.iv.18).

Finally, Xenophon himself points to the capture of the Theban akropolis by the Spartans (383 BC) as being an act of impiety, following their pledge that all city states should be independent (*Hell.* V.iv.1). He further develops his argument to give this as a reason why the Spartans, hitherto invincible, were defeated by the very people they subjugated.

Xenophon's opinion, that the Spartan Assembly brought the misfortune of Leuktra upon themselves by not honouring their oath to disband their forces, is made very clear. The suggestion of Prothoos (*Hell.* VI.iv.2) to do so was disregarded by the Spartan Assembly, no doubt urged on by Agesilaos. The opportunity to deal once and for all with the Thebans led the Lakedaemonians to ignore the accepted code of piety on the grounds of a technicality. Had they adopted the pious route, as suggested by Prothoos, the Thebans would have had to face a combined force of allies, made up of the signatories to the agreement, that all Greek cities should be independent. However, this would have deprived the Spartans of the opportunity to crush the Thebans themselves. As it was, the Thebans still controlled the cities of Boeotia and did not disband their army. Xenophon makes it clear that the Spartans were being led on by fate (*Hell.* VI.iv.3) and that in the battle itself, fortune was on the side of the Thebans (*Hell.* VI.iv.8). Xenophon clearly believed that the Spartans brought the calamity upon themselves through impiety. He reports that the Thebans were buoyed up by a variety of omens, such as an oracle which predicted that the Spartans would be defeated at the spot where a monument to the virgins stood (*Hell.* VI.iv.7). Such a monument stood conveniently adjacent to the prospective battle area. This was followed by news that all the temples in Thebes were opening of their own volition, and that their priestesses were predicting victory for Thebes. In addition, the arms of Herakles had disappeared, suggesting that the demigod himself was to support the Theban side.

With such news coming to the Theban army it is no surprise that its morale was lifted. However, Xenophon, although not gainsaying the possibility, reports that it had been suggested that the Theban leaders had engineered these signs (*Hell.* VI.iv.7) to enhance the resilience of their soldiery.[20]

Morale, Training and Discipline

'He will win whose army is animated by the same spirit throughout all its ranks' (Sun Tzu III.17).

'The consummate leader cultivates the moral law, and strictly adheres to method and discipline; thus it is in his power to control success' (Sun Tzu IV.16).

In the writings of Xenophon no character is given a more rounded treatment than that of Agesilaos. The view of tradition is best summed up by Plutarch (Plut. *Ages*. 15) who described him as a great king and general, but regarded him even more highly as a friend and intimate. It is not surprising, therefore, to find cogent examples of the essential elements required of any great commander being cited within the description of his actions.

For both personal and tactical reasons, his care for the humanity within his charge was seen to be unimpeachable. The option of winning the opposition to his side by persuasion and fair dealing was his preferred route. The knowledge that it was difficult to sustain armed forces in enemy territory if the civil population was terrorised showed commonsense, and appeared to stem from an innate respect for his fellow men. It was only when faced with an intransigent opposition that he showed no compunction in seeking to crush his enemies. Loyalty to friends, reverence of the gods and unquestioning obedience to the laws of his country made him a man to be admired. Only one question can be raised against this view and that is in respect to his unremitting hostility to Thebes. This led him, on more than one occasion, to act in an uncharacteristic manner, quite at odds with his usual even-handed approach. This, initially inexplicable attitude, may be explained as stemming from resentment. His immediate withdrawal from Asia in response to the ephors' edict was laudable. The cause for his recall from a campaign which promised not only to break the power of Persia once and for all, but to bring Agesilaos unparalleled glory, was Thebes. The very vehemence of his unnecessary frontal attack on the Theban phalanx, in the secondary phase of Koroneia, showed a desire for revenge against those who had acted in an untimely manner for the greater good of Greece, and who had robbed him of the opportunity to be listed with the heroes.

On campaign in Asia, he encouraged his men to treat their prisoners well and took into care those unsold children who had been abandoned by merchants (Xen. *Ages*. I.21) later organising their safe settlement, as he did with those prisoners who were too old to be taken with the army. After he had raised his new cavalry arm, he instituted a training schedule for the whole army at Ephesos, offering prizes for all sections who improved both their physical fitness and their proficiency at arms (*Hell*. III.iv.16; Xen. *Ages*. I.25). Leading by example, the prime virtue of any commander, he shared in the training and led

131

the daily procession of his men to dedicate their garlands to Artemis. Xeno-phon notes the three virtues in this, of reverence to the gods, training and obedience, as fundamentals for good morale (Xen. *Ages.* I.27; *Hell.* III.iv.18). As it was the custom of the Persians and their Asiatic allies to shield their bodies from the sun with their clothing, Agesilaos had those prisoners captured by patrols paraded for sale naked, so that his men could see the paleness of their skin and their less well conditioned bodies through a lack of regular physical exercise (Xen. *Ages.* I.28; *Hell.* III.iv.19; Plut. *Ages.* 9). It seems obvious that Agesilaos must have been selective in those he ordered to be put on view in this manner, and it is likely that the naked prisoners were members of the ruling class. Nonetheless, any fears of the enemy held by his men evaporated at the sight of what, to them, appeared to be womanly traits.

The commander who kept his men in a state of readiness, in good physical condition, sustained a competitive spirit and did all he could to ensure their safety, could guarantee high morale. Iphikrates, like Agesilaos, is singled out by Xenophon for praise on these matters on his relief expedition to Kerkyra. His decision to row for much of the journey around the Peloponnese was taken with a view not only to achieve an earlier arrival than would be possible by sail alone, but also to improve the physical fitness of his men (*Hell.* VI.ii.27). Sail was used to rest the men when there was a good breeze and when there was not, and speed was of the essence, he had a rota by which the men rowed and rested in turn (*Hell.* VI.ii.28). For midday and evening meals, he would have the fleet draw up in line, parallel to the shore, to race to the landfall. The prize for being the first to land was the ease with which the crew could gather water, have longer to sit at rest and eat their meal. Those who were last found themselves greatly hurried in all that they had to do before re-embarking (*Hell.* VI.ii.28). The attention to security was meticulous. The setting of watches suggests a possible new practice for the period. Xenophon indicates that Iphikrates made the usual dispositions for those watches on land. However, while watches from ships on the seaward side of an encampment would be usual, it is the manner in which Iphikrates arranged these which is given particular mention. Rather than a deck watch, he had the masts hoisted so that lookouts could be placed at their tops, thus affording a wider view over a larger area (*Hell.* VI.ii.29). By day, manoeuvres were practised to a series of signals, so that the fleet could move from column to battle line effectively (*Hell.* VI.ii.30). The implication of the time of such practice shows that these were visual signals. When encamped on shore no fires were permitted in camp, but were kept burning in front of his position, so that an enemy approach could be seen

(*Hell.* VI.ii.29). More often than not, re-embarkation took place after the evening meal, before any enemy forces arrived, encamping as they were on enemy territory (*Hell.* VI.ii.29–30). By so doing, Iphikrates' men spent more time on the water and thus arrived more quickly at the appointed destination (*Hell.* VI.ii.32). Such care and attention to the safety, training, discipline and well being of his men is the mark of a good commander.[21]

Sustaining morale was an imperative and when Agesilaos was faced with the news of Peisander's death and defeat (394 BC) prior to the battle of Koroneia, he chose to obfuscate the truth, and let it be known that there had been a resounding victory (*Hell.* IV.iii.12). Such dissembling was not unique, for Eteonikos sought to sustain the morale of his troops by ordering the boat, which had brought news of the Athenian sea victory at Arginousai, to sail out of the harbour and return garlanded, as if in celebration of a Spartan victory (*Hell.* I.vi.36). Similarly, good news needed to be shared as soon as possible. Agesilaos was quick to send news, via Derkylidas, of the Spartan success at the Nemea, to those cities which had supplied troops for the return to Greece (*Hell.* IV.iii.2–3). A testament to the quality of morale in the army of Agesilaos is to be found in Xenophon immediately prior to the battle of Koroneia (Xen. *Ages.* II.7–8). Proof that such morale was the product of constant thoughtfulness for the needs of his men is to be found at *Hell.* IV.v.3–4, where Agesilaos sends ten men with fire to the regiment occupying the heights near Piraion in adverse weather conditions.

An understanding of human nature lies at the core of successful strategy. Agesilaos rebutted the Achaean criticism of his campaigning method in Akarnania which seemed limited in its first year. 'I shall again lead an expedition hither next summer; and the more these people sow, the more they will desire peace.' This was a clear case of a strategy designed to sap the morale of the enemy (*Hell.* IV.vi.13). The measure of his success (*Hell.* IV.vii.1) is borne out by the suing for peace by the Akarnanians in the following year, 388 BC.

Agesilaos' brother, Teleutias, was obviously a well loved commander. His return home, after defeating the Athenians at Aegina, is a testament to his relationship with his men, his departure being given the celebratory salutation of handshakes and garlands (*Hell.* V.i.3–4). His return as admiral, after some ineffective actions by intervening commanders, was greeted with great enthusiasm by the forces, who willingly followed him, despite the fact that he had no money at the time to pay them for their services (*Hell.* V.i.13–14). Such was the confidence which the men placed in the leadership of Teleutias, that he was able to persuade them to play the pirate in an audacious attack on Piraeus, disabling warships there and towing loaded merchantmen away to Aegina. The goods from these last were sold to provide payment for the men, along with other booty acquired from captured vessels at Sounion (*Hell.* V.i.20–24) (For further detail see also under 'Tactics' below.)

Lysander's death, which greatly damaged Spartan confidence, is inexplicable from the evidence (*Hell.* III.v.19; Plut. *Lys.* 28). Whether through arrogance or misinformation concerning the number of Thebans within the city of the Haliartians, his advance to the walls of the city proved his undoing. The aftermath, however, is significant in terms of morale. Having been the most successful commander the Spartans had produced to date, his death had a deleterious effect on the Spartan spirit. It is evident in sources that every conceivable excuse was put forward not to engage the enemy in battle, when Pausanias, at the head of another Spartan army, arrived on the scene (*Hell.* III.v.23). Plutarch, however, indicates (Plut. *Lys.* 29) that the older Spartans were against a truce and clamoured for a battle. Whatever the background, Pausanias was charged but fled before his trial.

Obviously, men could place their trust in a commander who looked after their safety and needs and who was successful, but this has to be viewed in the context of the strategy of the state he served and the evidence of personal ambition which sometimes ran counter to state policy. A successful commander cannot always be termed a truly good commander. The case of Lysander is the prime example. Rather than hand over a settled command structure to Kallikratidas at the end of his term of authority, it seems very obvious that Lysander resented the command transfer and deliberately engineered a series of major problems for his successor. His refusal to hand over the fleet to Kallikratidas, as requested, at Miletos (*Hell.* I.vi.2) was followed by Kallikratidas' discovery that the support from those men who were Lysander's friends was minimal and that they sought to undermine his authority. Further, they broadcast a rumour around the regional allies that the replacement of Lysander was a strategic error on the behalf of the Lakedaimonians which could only result in disaster (*Hell.* I.vi.4). The success of Kallikratidas in his leadership, to the time of his death at Arginousai, is a testament to his tenacity. The defeat for the Spartan fleet at that battle was followed by the act of concealment by Eteonikos, referred to above, in order to sustain the high level of morale of the Spartan forces.[22]

The importance of trust and respect of men for their commander is best exemplified by the negative example of Mnasippos in his campaign in Kerkyra. The wholehearted support of mercenary troops was an absolute essential to a commander of these times, and the withholding of two months pay from those serving under him could not have enhanced their loyalty (*Hell.* VI.ii.16). The point is made that he had the money to do so, but had not honoured the obligation (*Hell.* VI.ii.16). What he intended to do with the money is not pursued. Xenophon also makes the point that discipline was, unsurprisingly, not as good as would be expected. The Spartan guard posts had become less scrupulously manned, and this had been observed by the Kerkyraians (*Hell.* VI.ii.17). They, reinforced by the force of 600 Athenian peltasts who had arrived a few months earlier, made an attack on the troops scattered around the countryside. In his attempt to organise a counterattack, Mnasippos found grievances laid against him by the leaders of the mercenaries. These officers told Mnasippos that their men were reluctant to follow orders because of a lack of provisions. Mnasippos' answer to this problem was to physically attack two of the officers, one with his spear-butt, the other with a staff (*Hell.* VI.ii.18– 19). In the action which followed, it is obvious, from Xenophon's description, that the morale of Mnasippos' professionals had slipped to a point at which a rout was inevitable.[23]

Following the defeat of the Mantineians in 385 BC, after their refusal to take down their city walls, it is striking that Xenophon should make special mention of the orderly release of the sixty populist leaders, as a matter of good discipline. At the request of Pausanias, the exiled king, his son Agesipolis, allowed these men to depart the city in relative safety, on a road lined on both sides by his hoplites. Xenophon comments that, even though the Spartans hated them, they did not attack them as they departed. The arrangement was obviously the matter of a direct order from the commander, Agesipolis, and the fact that this order was followed is cited as an example of exemplary discipline (*Hell.* V.ii.6). At this stage one must question the relative degrees by which discipline was measured at this time. If Xenophon chose to make this substantive point in relation to the best disciplined army of his time, it must surely indicate that, whereas discipline on the field was unquestioned, a certain laxity was not uncommon following a victory, surely a problem for the less able commander.

The key to success in command, therefore, lies with discipline. A discipline which is seen to be fair, firm and serving the interests of the army community in all aspects of welfare. These being in place, it is also the key to excellent morale. Therefore the confidence placed by the army in a commander had to be won and, once won, retained. The Spartan failure at Leuktra can be signalled as early as 378 BC, when Agesilaos was preferred to Kleombrotos as commander against the Thebans on the grounds of a lack of confidence in the latter (*Hell.* V.iv.35). It was only a matter of accident that Kleombrotos was in command of the army in Phokis at the time when action was demanded against Thebes. Indecision promotes a lack of confidence and Kleombrotos seems to have been imbued with a reluctance to take decisive action. The censure of his friends, who warned him that if he allowed the Thebans to escape without a battle he would face trial in Sparta, and listed his shortcomings hitherto, shows that as a commander he was not leading but being pushed from behind (*Hell.* VI.iv.5). In such circumstances the main body of the army could not remain unaffected. One can presume that the track record of successes against the Thebans led the army to believe that they could win the match without a captain. Another illuminating comment made by Xenophon suggests that the king commenced his opening move in the battle without clear orders being given, and exemplifies the character of his style of command (*Hell.* VI.iv.13) and the expectations of his men: 'Now when Kleombrotos began to lead his army against the enemy, in the first place, before the troops under him so much as perceived that he was advancing . . .'.

Lack of discipline caused the death of Thrasyboulos who had proved himself an able commander up to the point at which he required money to pay his men. The initial method of collection was by plundering those cities who resisted allying themselves to his cause. When it came to those cities who paid their dues without action being taken against them, the pickings for the men were, obviously, less than hitherto. In the case of the Aspendians, who had already paid their requested amount, to be subject to acts of plunder by Thrasyboulos' men thereafter, led them to make a night attack on his camp in which he was killed (*Hell.* IV.viii.30). An obvious example of indiscipline, when not wholly under the control of the commander in matters unrelated to direct action. However, Xenophon makes specific mention of the morale and discipline of those serving under Epameinondas, prior to the second battle of Mantineia (*Hell.* VII.v.19–20). Despite having suffered serious setbacks, a shortage of provisions and marches night and day without respite, Xenophon expresses admiration for the fact that the men were in good heart, still well disciplined and very eager to come to battle.

The careful preparations of Kyros the Younger were put at risk by the very secrecy of his true intent. In keeping his ultimate aim to himself, until his army had penetrated deeply into Persian territory, he risked a mutiny and the abandonment of his plan. Only by meeting the mercenaries' demands for higher pay was he able to secure their continued support (*Anab.* I.iv.13). A calculated risk, but one which shows that the men initially accused their generals of misleading them from the outset (*Anab.* I.iv.12). It displayed the danger to loyalty and discipline to which even a hint of mistrust in a commander could lead. Thereafter, the fragility of inter-relationships became more acute and the worst of them are covered in Xenophon's narrative, namely, the near battle between Menon and Klearchos' troops (*Anab.* I.v.13) and the treachery of Orontas (*Anab.* I.vi.3–4). Loyalty was maintained by further promises of reward (*Anab.* I.vii.6-8) but it is evident from Xenophon's description that discipline became progressively lax (*Anab.* I.vii.20) until, at the report of the king's approach, the whole army seemed unprepared and in considerable confusion (*Anab.* I.viii.1–4). Immediately prior to the battle itself, there was clearly a difference of opinion between Kyros and Klearchos, and the commander-in-chief eventually deferred to the latter. (See also under 'Tactics' below.)

Following Kounaxa, on the initial march supposedly away from the Persian army, Klearchos, on discovering himself to be in the vicinity of the enemy, chose not to deploy his troops for battle, knowing them to be tired and hungry (*Anab.* II.ii.16). Later, he showed leadership by example, at those times when bridge-building was necessary, by chastising anyone whom he deemed to be slacking, and by taking part himself in the hard labour (*Anab.* II.iii.11–12).

Finally, an army operates well when it is well provisioned. Perhaps the most impressive aspect of the warfare of this period is the high standard of commissariat. Although, in the case of Spartan commanders, this was not directly under their control, they had to decide on the locations for a market and achieve them on the march, no mean matter of judgement.

On the March and in Camp

'We are not fit to lead an army on the march unless we are familiar with the face of the country – its mountains and forests, its pitfalls and precipices, its marshes and swamps.' Sun Tzu VII.13.

The order of march can be seen to have been determined by topography and the prevailing military conditions as perceived by the commander. By necessity, reference to marches has been made in other sections. Here will be given the reasons which would lead a commander to make a march, the conditions of the route, the formation selected and any other illuminating features. Xenophon often omits details which would have been informative, but is useful in highlighting a tactical consideration in conjunction with a march, or a place of encampment. Thus, we have only the distances given of each stage of Kyros the Younger's march to the interior, but a greatly differing treatment of those of the return. In a sense, Xenophon's approach to reporting marching and camping is wholly tactical and is a good indicator of these skills of command.

More information is available concerning manoeuvres on the march for the Spartans than for the armies of other city states. This is possibly because of the existence of the Constitution of the Lakedaemonians, but more probably due to the fact that whoever wrote it would not have done so had it not been plainly obvious that Sparta differed in some practices from her contemporaries. In the preparation for an expedition from Sparta all equipment required for the march was assembled, together with carts and baggage animals for its portage. The necessary craftsmen were engaged, following the levy of infantry and cavalry (*Lak.Pol.* XI.2). If an enemy unexpectedly appeared when marching in column, the order to deploy to the left was given and a battle line quickly formed. If the enemy appeared to the rear the file countermarched so that the younger men were at the front of the formation as was normal (*Lak.Pol.* XI.8). In this way the first ten or fifteen age classes from manhood could charge any attacking skirmishers. The question of the possible disadvantage of having officers on the left of a formation, in view of the custom for the command position usually to be on the right, is discounted on the grounds that an outflanking movement by the enemy would be less likely to succeed (*Lak.Pol.* XI.9). If it were deemed better to have the company commander on the right, the army counter-marched by rank (*Lak.Pol.* XI.9). Similarly, attacks on either flank were quickly dissipated by wheeling the *lochos*.

The Spartans eschewed a rectangular camp design, preferring a circular form, except when their rear was protected by hill, wall or river (*Lak.Pol.* XII.1). Sentries were posted facing inwards to the armament store for the purpose of ensuring security from sympathisers of the enemy (*Lak.Pol.* XII.2). The cavalry was given the task of observing the enemy from positions of vantage and, at night, the Skiritai, a people from the borders of Lakedaimon who operated as a skirmishing light infantry, operated as observers outside the lines (*Lak.Pol.* XII.3). An important point is made that camp was frequently moved to cause discomfort to the enemy and to aid allies (*Lak.Pol.* XII.5). The king decided where a camp was to be made (*Lak.Pol.* XIII.10) and led the order of the march, preceded only by the Skiritai. When an enemy appeared, the king wheeled his regiment to the right and placed himself between flanking regiments (*Lak.Pol.* XIII.6).

The Thebans, however, in their first invasion of Lakedaimon following the battle of Leuktra, set up a barricade of felled trees in front of their encampments. This fulfilled two aims. The first to improve the defences of their camps and the second to contribute to the depredation of enemy territory, although Xenophon does not allude to the latter point at *Hell.* VI.v.30.

Following the action at Kounaxa the problem of a route for withdrawal from the heartland of Persia bedevilled the Greeks.The correct choice of a line of march was imperative. Ariaios proposed to make the return march by a different route from that which was taken on their inland journey, for the reason that the army had already consumed available provisions on that route (*Anab.* II.ii.11). The thinking behind his planning for the first stages of the march was sound. To cover as much ground as possible initially, so as to put two or three days between themselves and a pursuing force, thus leaving the enemy with the insuperable problems of deciding whether to pursue with a force which could overtake, but which would be too small to cause problems, or to follow with an effectively large force which would be too slow to achieve contact. In both cases supplies would prove difficult for those in pursuit, following, as they would, an army which would have already taken what was available (*Anab.* II.ii.11–12). As it was, the route taken led them within a day's march (whether by accident or by the design of Ariaios) towards the Great King's encampment, instead of away from the enemy.

The distance covered in a limited time was often critical to the success of operations, as Alexander was later to prove. No less effective, however, was Agesilaos. Having lulled the Akarnanians into a false sense of security by the slowness of his advance of no more than one and a third miles per day, destroying their crops as he went (*Hell.* IV.vi.5), he made a march of 160 stadia, nearly nineteen miles, in a single day, to arrive at the place where the bulk of their cattle was grazing in what the Akarnanians presumed was complete safety (*Hell.* IV.vi.6). Agesilaos' return from Asia through Thrace is noted for its celerity (Xen. *Ages.* II.1) but receives no mention in the *Hellenika*. Marching in battle order, and at full readiness to engage, was a crucial decision for a commander. It seems a commonsense arrangement, when exposed to the harrying of cavalry or light infantry, and within enemy territory, even prior to contact being made. Provided the commander retained the initiative and did not relax his vigilance, his men would be safe. A good example of this is the march through Thessaly by Agesilaos (see below).

Two examples serve to show that carelessness in the order of march, and complacency in the acceptance of immediate intelligence, brought disaster upon commanders. The first is when Kyros the Younger, who had maintained a battle line formation in his approach to the area evacuated by his brother at the trench (*Anab.* I.vii.14), proceeded thereafter with the greater part of his army in disorderly column, their weapons being carried on wagons (*Anab.* I.vii.20). He had little time to deploy when the enemy advanced, sub-commanders, e.g., Klearchos, did as they thought best rather than follow Kyros' orders. The second example is when Anaxibios took at face value the reported position of Iphikrates (*Hell.* IV.viii.36) and did not take the due care expected of any commander when an enemy was within the same region. His army proceeded in a long column and was successfully attacked by peltasts. The place of the attack was well chosen on a gradient, much of which was within a narrow path, so that the van, which had already reached the plain, was unable to return uphill quickly enough to give relief. The rout which followed caused almost 300 fatalities, and proved the great effectiveness of well trained peltasts, when used in an advantageous location.[24] This action was successful, not merely because it was a well judged ambush, but also, probably, because Anaxibios' scouting arrangements were poor.

The march from Poteidaia to Olynthos was made in battle order by Teleutias. It would have been helpful had Xenophon indicated the specific troop positions. Teleutias showed good tactical sense and did little or no damage on his approach. This to achieve easy access and withdrawal for his formation, reserving the matter of cutting trees to serve as impedimenta to any who followed (*Hell.* V.ii.39).

Xenophon does give the order of march in his description of Agesilaos' trek through Thessaly. The question remains, however, whether he did so because he was present on that occasion, or whether the formation of a hollow square, with cavalry to the front and rear, was unusual. The former seems the more probable and exemplifies the problem which many scholars seem unwilling to accept. Unless he had seen it, or had trustworthy witness, Xenophon omitted that of which he was unsure.

Similarly, an order of march is shown in the *Anabasis* (*Anab.* II.ii.4–5). Klearchos defines the column as being vanguard, probably in battle line, followed by baggage animals adjacent to the river bank, flanked on their other side by hoplites. It goes without saying that there would have been a rear-guard. A normal procedure for a defensive formation would have been the baggage train within a screen of hoplites.[25] Klearchos used the advantage of the river to protect one flank, while having the advantage of all his troops to the landward side. What is even more significant was the arrangement of signals by which the formation was to be organised. The normal call for going to rest was to signal packing in preparation for departure. The second signal was for loading pack animals and the third to start the march. The signal was made on the κέρας (keras – see the closing section of Part Three), the instrument for night time calls.

At the stopping points, Klearchos maintained his men under arms and in battle line (*Anab.* II.ii.8). Scouts were well deployed (*Anab.* II.ii.15) and the army proceeded usually in line of battle (*Anab.* II.iii.10). Later, at *Anab.* II.iv.25, Klearchos marched past an army going to the support of the Great King, and employed a device for making the army look bigger, presumably as a defensive ploy. He led them two abreast, halting the vanguard from time to time. This had a ripple effect throughout the column, thus making the passing much longer in duration and impressing the likely opposition.

The aftermath of Leuktra saw Agesilaos struggling to abide by the King's Peace, while at the same time seeking to maintain control over the cities to the north of Sparta. Mantineia's decision to build walls, factionalism in Tegea and a movement to unite all Arkadia, led Sparta to make an expedition against the Arkadians. On his march, Agesilaos captured Eutaia, but purchased the requirements for his troops from the inhabitants, restoring to its owners any booty which had been taken. Having gained goodwill by such conduct, he continued on his march into Mantineian territory, where he laid waste to crops and made camp to the west of the city near the foot of the mountains. The following day, the camp was moved to a point less than two miles from Mantineia, where it was learned that a force of Arkadians, coming from Tegea, was on its way to join with the Mantineians. Mindful of the safety of his men, and because of the very proximity of the city, Agesilaos refused to attack this force in case he was attacked himself, in flank and rear, by the Mantineians (*Hell.* VI.v.16). The Phleiasian cavalry, together with Orchomenian peltasts, joined Agesilaos after their successful night march past Mantineia and, with the combined forces, he pushed on into enemy territory. At this point, his usual scrupulous attention to detail seems to have left him, for his place of encampment was made within a valley, the exit of which was very restrictive for deployment (στενοῦ – narrow) (*Hell.* VI.v.18). This is a surprising lapse for Agesilaos who normally read topography well. It may well be that his march did not reach its intended destination prior to nightfall, and that he was obliged to encamp in this risky location (*Hell.* VI.v.17). The following morning saw the Mantineians gathered in force in the mountains to the rear of what would have been his retreating column. He sought to fold back his rear behind the van. He presented a line of battle facing the mountains, being, in the usual command position, on the right wing and nearer the exit to the valley. Had the whole army faced to the right and an attempt been made by Agesilaos to lead it out of the valley, his rear would have been endangered. Accordingly, he ordered the hoplites at the rear (his left as they faced the enemy) to right face and march, line by line, behind the phalanx until such time that the length of line was much diminished and the depth of the phalanx was doubled to eighteen or twenty shields. In this formation he led the phalanx out into the plain where the line was extended once more.[26] This manoeuvre, the ἀναστροφή (anastrophe) demonstrates the precision and order within Spartan armies when marching. Even on the battlefield, wheeling and countermarching took place as battle was joined. The very confidence in the successful outcome of such manoeuvres led to success at the Nemea and Koroneia, but had disastrous results at Leuktra and Kerkyra (*Hell.* VI.ii.21–22). The timing of orders, as always, was crucial to give space and time for a manoeuvre to be successfully completed and further discussion on this issue for Leuktra is given later. If a manoeuvre took more than one movement to complete, the time during which self defence was ineffectual was lengthened. More than one manoeuvre when under attack could prove disastrous and, when conducted near an enemy stronghold, foolhardy. Such was the problem at Kerkyra in 373 BC. Whoever gave the order to double the depth of the phalanx with the idea of gaining greater security caused the subsequent rout and the death of his commander-in-chief Mnasippos (*Hell.* VI.ii.21–23). Similarly, the well intentioned attempt of Archidamos to capture the hill overlooking the Arkadian position at Kromnos found him engaging, while still in column. Tactically sound in intention, but lacking in forethought on matters of topography.

Agesilaos was earlier caught encamped in a less than secure position (*Hell.* IV.vi.7) on a mountainside. He was dislodged by missile fire from Akarnanian peltasts on the ridge and forced to relocate on the plain. It is likely that Agesilaos had men posted on the ridge, but that they had been forced to withdraw by superior forces, when the considerable forces of Akarnanians, participating in the action of the following day, are taken into consideration. No mention, however, is made of this in the text, and it is possible that he had made an error.[27] The Thebans also surprised the Lakedaimonians at their defence point of the Oneion mountain range by a well timed night march (*Hell.* VII.i.15–16). Undertaking a night march, particularly in mountainous country, where the ground is uneven, was an extremely difficult operation to complete with surprise and success. Xenophon notes that the starting time for the march of about three and a half miles was calculated so that the time of arrival would coincide with the end of the night watch, and the arousal of their enemy from sleep.[28] This shows a good knowledge of topography, of the capabilities of the men to be involved and intelligence of the enemy's defensive arrangements. Similarly, Epameinondas' overnight strike at Sparta, dealt with below under 'Tactics', indicated an increased care in planning, as did the selection and co-ordination of the four invasion routes into Lakedaimon by him and his allies.[29]

The lateness of Gylis' march through Lokris, also dealt with under 'Tactics', demonstrates the crucial importance of reaching the intended place of encampment during daylight.

Secrecy, Spies, non-combative Deception and Intelligence

Obviously the gathering of reliable intelligence can lead a commander to lay plans for a subsequent successful action against enemy forces. Following his escape from Sardis (*Hell.* I.i.10), Alkibiades joined the Athenians, who had received news that Mindaros, with sixty ships, was about to sail against them at Sestos. It appears clear that Mindaros was unaware of the Athenian withdrawal, for Alkibiades arranged that the ships should return to Sestos while he took the overland route to join them, possibly to gather intelligence more easily. Alkibiades was on the point of putting to sea in order to engage, when his fleet was reinforced by an additional forty vessels. With the enlarged force of eighty-six ships Alkibiades proceeded first to Parion, and next, by sailing at night, to Prokonnesos, where he learned that Pharnabazos, with his army, had joined Mindaros at Kyzikos. So that the size of his forces would not be known to the enemy, Alkibiades took control of every sailing vessel in the harbour, to retain the element of surprise (*Hell.* I.i.15). Weather conditions were with him in that, on setting sail across the strait to Kyzikos in heavy rain (*Hell.* I.i.16), he was in position, between the enemy fleet and their shore base, when the skies cleared. The surprise, engendered by the unexpected size of the Athenian fleet, led the Peloponnesian fleet to race away and make for the shore. After an outflanking movement by Alkibiades who, with twenty shiploads of men, sailed around the two fleets to beach further along the shore, the land engagement brought the death of Mindaros, the capture of all the enemy ships except those of the Syracusans, and the subsequent much needed collection of tithes from ships sailing through the Bosphoros (see also *Diod.* XIII.50.1–3 for an alternative account). Opportunism was successful on the back of knowledge of the enemy's position and likely intention, the concealment of the size of available forces and a concealed approach near to the battle position. The account of Kyzikos above and that of Aigospotamoi following illustrate Xenophon's attitude to the gathering of intelligence even if they may not be historically accurate.[30]

For four days Lysander (405 BC) appeared to prepare for battle against the Athenian fleet of 180 vessels, only to refuse to engage (*Hell.* II.i.24). From sunrise to near sunset each day, the Athenians sailed up to the harbour entrance of Lampsakos in the hope of drawing Lysander into battle and bringing relief to the town of their ally. On their return near to Aigospotamoi, as sunset was approaching, the Athenians were followed on Lysander's order by the fastest of his ships, so that the disembarking troops could be observed and reported upon. Such was the care that Lysander took for the security of his forces that they were not permitted to disembark until the reports of the spy ships had been received (*Hell.* II.i.24). Whereas the forces of Lysander were able safely to derive their provisions from the city itself in the safety of its harbour, the Athenian encampment was some four and a half miles from Sestos, and their men had been observed, over the four days, to become more and more relaxed and scattered in the collection of their needs (*Hell.* II.1.27). The eventual action brought rewards for the systematic intelligence gathering of Lysander.

Alkibiades, who, for the last two years had been out of favour with Athens, had seen the Athenian position from his stronghold on the Chersonese and judged, correctly, that their supply lines were tenuous. His suggestion to the Athenian commanders that they move to the safe anchorage of Sestos itself was met with scorn (*Hell.* II.i.26; Plut. *Lys.* 10; Plut. *Alk.* 36). On the fifth day, Lysander arranged for the scouting ships to display on high a shield at the midpoint of their return, to signal that the enemy had disembarked and dispersed. At that point, Lysander launched his attack, and only Konon with nine ships escaped, all others being captured on the beach by the Peloponnesians (see *Diod.* XIII.106.1–7 for a different and less plausible account of the battle).

Intelligence gathering was routine. However, its interpretation depended on the quality and accuracy of the information accumulated, and the skill of those who received it. A good example is that of Tissaphernes' recognition that Kyros was preparing for something much bigger than a punitive expedition against the Pisidians. This conclusion, passed on to the Great King, led on to the more obvious conclusion that an attempt was to be made on the throne (*Anab.* I.ii.4–5). The actions, following an interpretation of intelligence, depended on the objectivity of the assessor and his willingness to share his views with those who had to execute those actions. The case of Kyros the Younger illuminates the problem. Having achieved his initial objectives, in keeping the build-up of his forces secret, and advancing deep into his brother's territory before his true intention became obvious, his judgement became increasingly faulty. The discovery of Orontas' treachery was fortunate and had nothing to do with spies or intelligence gathering. It may have jolted his confidence, for his judgement thereafter was not so sure-footed. Shortly after reviewing his troops, deserters appeared from whom information of his brother's army was gleaned (*Anab.* I.vii.2). Other information must have been passed, but this does not appear in the evidence. That information was given directly to Kyros, who, like his namesake in Xenophon's fiction, may have been the sole assessor of its merit. The analysis of the abandoned defensive trench and the tracks may well have been entirely his, even though it is obvious from the text that he shared his decision: 'Kyros and *the rest* concluded that he had given up the idea of fighting' (*Anab.* I.vii.19).

At the meeting of commanders to discuss battle plans, no mention is made of whether Kyros shared his intelligence, or merely gave his reading of it. Xenophon is particular to make mention of what appears to be a small but obvious matter. Kyros states that his brother's troops will make their advance with great shouting and noise (*Anab.* I.vii.4), a wholly innocuous point, except when taken with the actual circumstances of the battle itself. Here (*Anab.* I.viii.11), Xenophon goes out of his way to point out Kyros' error when the Persian advance was described as being utterly silent and in good order. The very lack of other information in terms of Kyros' intelligence structure suggests that he did not share such knowledge with others. His unpreparedness shows that either his judgement was faulty, or that he had been fed disinformation.

By comparison, open discussion prevailed among the Greeks in the aftermath of Kounaxa. There is a marked increase in the amount of information and intelligence reported in the text. Messages are passed between the separated forces of Klearchos and Araios (*Anab.* II.i.3–5; II.ii.1–2). The tone of the Great King's demands changes from surrender to a request for a truce (*Anab.* II.iii.1–2). Irrigation trenches filled with water, at a time regarded as being inappropriate by Klearchos, urged caution (*Anab.* II.iii.13). A lessening in trust between Araios and the Greeks is evident (*Anab.* II.iv.1–5) on the grounds of suspected collaboration, a situation which worsened when fraternisation was seen between the troops of Tissaphernes and Ariaios (*Anab.* II.iv.9–11). The message from Araios, encamped alongside Tissaphernes, which warned the Greeks that the Persians intended to attack them during the night and also to destroy a bridge over the Tigris, was evaluated and presumed false (*Anab.* II.iv.15–22). Information about the area in question was sought and found to indicate that it could be one in which a permanent defensive position could be established (*Anab.* II.iv.21–22). Suspicions proliferated, and an attempt to stop them was made by Tissaphernes (*Anab.* II.v.1–26) promising to give the names of those who were involved in subterfuge. At the meeting which followed, the Greek generals were captured and subsequently executed. All these matters were the subject of scrutiny by the commanders and only at the last fence was Klearchos incorrect in his evaluations.

Perhaps the most significant section in the text which shows the extent of open discussion is the second book of the *Anabasis* (*Anab.* II.iv.2–7) which enumerates the worries of the Greeks and the evaluation of their present circumstances by Klearchos, based as they were on security and the welfare of the men, i.e., provisions, the lack of cavalry and the uncertainty concerning the terrain they would have to cross.

When marching north to take action against the Olynthians, Phoibidas encamped his army very close to Thebes, indeed near the gymnasium (*Hell.* V.ii.25). There, he was reported to have been approached by Leontiades, one of the chief civic leaders, who offered to pass into his hands the Theban akropolis, the Kadmeia. The reason for this amazing offer is suggested as being factionalism between the parties of Ismenias and Leontiades. It is difficult to accept the successful capture of the Kadmeia as related in Xenophon as pure opportunism. A march such as Phoibidas was making could not be delayed unless other considerations were in hand. His brother had been dispatched post haste, to bring relief to the cities being endangered by the Olynthians (*Hell.* V.ii.24). It had been assumed necessary to take immediate action (*Hell.* V.ii.23) and with only 2,000 men with him, and those being emancipated helots, perioikoi and the skirmishing Skiritae, Eudamidas could only fight a defensive war until his brother arrived with the main force. The vote to supply a contingent to the Spartan forces, in line with the original agreement among the allies, had been voted down by the Thebans (*Hell.* V.ii.27). Four years earlier, 387 BC, Agesilaos had been thwarted in having an excuse for invading Thebes, when the Theban ambassadors returned with the approval of the citizenry for the terms set out by the King of Persia that all cities should be independent. Their return had been speedy enough to nullify the mobilisation Agesilaos had called immediately on their refusal and departure. Xenophon is very clear that

Agesilaos was moved by hatred of the Thebans (*Hell.* V.i.33) a sentiment endorsed in the Corinthian war (Plut. *Ages.* 22).

The timing and ease with which the Kadmeia was taken required more planning time than opportunism permitted. The feigned departure of the Spartans northward and their recall to be led unimpeded to the citadel, at a time when the men of Thebes were in session at the Boule, in a building in the market place rather than their usual place of assembly, the Kadmeia, the streets empty in the heat of the day and the women conveniently celebrating the festival of the Thesmophoria in the Kadmeia itself, display too many threads coming conveniently together to suggest accident (*Hell.* V.ii.29). Although no direct mention is made, the point that the womenfolk were in the position of hostages perhaps helps to explain the ready acquiescence of the Thebans. Phoibidas was brought to trial, but was strongly defended by Agesilaos for an action which had brought Thebes firmly under the control of Sparta and placed the pro-Spartan faction in power. From the outset the overt duty of Phoibidas was to have marched with all speed to deliver to his brother Eudamidas the balance of the forces he required to prosecute the war against the Olynthians. Given the evidence in Xenophon, there can be little doubt that this plan had been of some time standing and had been hatched between Agesilaos and the pro-Spartan faction in Thebes, with Phoibidas merely acting as the instrument of policy. However, in the account of the capture and subsequent liberation of the Kadmeia in Diodoros, Phoibidas' action was not officially sanctioned even if Agesilaos had suggested it.[31]

The recapture of control at Thebes was, likewise, the product of deception. It too was timed to coincide with a festival, that of Aphrodite, the occasion when the serving polemarchs ended their term of office. The plot was the product of a meeting in Athens between Melon, an exiled Theban, and Phillidas, secretary to the polemarchs, who had business there. At the duly appointed time, Melon, with six others, entered Thebes, armed only with daggers, at the time when people were returning from their work in the fields (*Hell.* V.iv.3). They spent that night and the following day concealed in the house of a man called Charon, until they were brought by Phillidas to the place where the celebration of the polemarchs was to be staged. Phillidas had agreed to supply women for Archias and Philippos, a matter on which Xenophon clearly shows his disapproval. 'And they – for they were that sort of men – expected to spend the night very pleasantly' (*Hell.* V.iv.4).

The ladies of the night were replaced by three of Melon's men disguised as women, with the remainder as their attendants. They joined the party after

147

Phillidas had seen to it that the servants had withdrawn. Upon being seated, the conspirators revealed themselves and killed their targets (*Hell.* V.iv.4–7).

Another, more likely, story is that the seven merely arrived as if they were celebrating and carried out the assassinations. From there, they went to the house of Leontiades and killed him. Thereafter, Phillidas with two of the seven went to the prison, where he duped the guardian there, claiming he was bringing a prisoner from the polemarchs. Having dispatched the prison keeper and armed the released prisoners, they all went down to the Amphion where they proclaimed the freedom from tyranny. An uneasy night followed, but next day saw the able-bodied men of the city joining them and news was sent to the Athenian forces on the borders. These were obviously in position, ready to move in support of the coup (*Hell.* V.iv.9) and it would appear from their involvement that the matter was one of Athenian policy. The Spartan commander had sent for help to Plataea but such succour was worsted by the Theban cavalry. The resulting withdrawal of the Spartan forces from the Kadmeia under truce was honoured by the Thebans, but was followed by what must have been a bloodbath, in which whole families of the faction which had supported the pro-Spartan group, perished (*Hell.* V.iv.12).

Such an involved plot, in which two Athenian commanders were implicated, leading substantial forces, points to a much wider interest in securing the freedom of Thebes (*Hell.* V.iv.9). However, self interest prevailed and the Athenians, on noting the Spartan show of power in their subsequent invasion of Theban territory under Kleombrotos, sought to distance themselves from the plot, by indicting both generals and putting one to death, the other having the wit to absent himself from the trial (*Hell.* V.iv.19). It is interesting that it was at this time, 379 BC, that Agesilaos invoked the tradition for himself that no person needed to undertake military duty outside their own country after having completing forty years service. This was the reason for Kleombrotos' first campaign, one which shows the increasing extension of the campaigning season into winter. Considering Agesilaos' commands, one must assume that this declaration was political, particularly when viewed in the light of following events.

In the following year it is implied by Xenophon that the Thebans bribed the Spartan commander at Thespiai, Sphodrias, to make an incursion into Attica (*Hell.* V.iv.20). Plutarch suggests that the Thebans persuaded Sphodrias through flattery (Plut. *Ages.* 24). Their purported hope was to alienate the Athenians from the Lakedaimonians. Suspicion of Athenian involvement in the affair of the Kadmeia must have been prevalent, and one must question the assumption that the subsequent action of Sphodrias was the product of a Theban bribe. A strong possibility is that this was a facet of Spartan policy, albeit as a matter of subterfuge. When the attempt to capture Peiraeus failed, embarrassment was caused to the Spartan ambassadors at Athens (*Hell.* V.iv.22). It appears, in the light of Sphodrias' subsequent acquittal *in absentia* that he may have been following orders when he led the abortive march on Peiraeus. How an experienced officer believed he could successfully make a march of about sixty miles over difficult terrain in one night defies explanation. Had it been only a matter of money, Sphodrias could have siphoned off some of the funds which Kleombrotos had left him to hire mercenaries (*Hell.* V.iv.15). Thus the point of a Theban bribe diminishes. He did not present himself for trial and, without giving detail of his whereabouts, Xenophon notes that he did not obey the ephors' command that he should return (*Hell.* V.iv.24). How Sphodrias had the reported conversation with his son Kleonymos, unless the latter was part of the group carrying the ephors' order of recall, or that he was with him and came to Sparta to plead his cause, is difficult to conceive.

Xenophon goes to great lengths (*Hell.* V.iv.25–33) to show Agesilaos' part in seeking his acquittal, but is strangely silent on the matter in his life of Agesilaos. The foregoing, although not directly concerned with command in the field, perhaps points to frictions which occurred between State strategy and tactical action, and Agesilaos was concerned with both. What is most significant in this area of Xenophon's account is the critical comment on the leadership of Kleombrotos, whose forces wondered whether or not they were actually at war with the Thebans, such little damage having been done (*Hell.* V.iv.16). An apt preparation for the Leuktra debacle.

Agesilaos proved to be a master of deception on campaign and fed misinformation to Tissaphernes. He sent messages to cities in Karia to make ready supplies to be purchased by his forces *en route*. This convinced Tissaphernes that this was to be the campaign area, particularly as Agesilaos was deficient in cavalry. However, by going in the opposite direction towards Phrygia, Agesilaos picked up the reinforcements he had requested from the northern cities and collected significant booty from the cities which fell to him (*Hell.* III.iv.11–12; Xen. *Ages.* I.15–16; Plut. *Ages.* 9). Having succeeded with this ruse, Agesilaos achieved a double bluff, when he let it be known that the army would move towards Sardis. Tissaphernes thought that this was another ruse and that his true intention was to invade Karia on this occasion, and established his forces accordingly. This time Agesilaos did as he had announced and, in so doing, was allowed three trouble free days to resupply the army (*Hell.*

III.iv.20–21; Xen. *Ages.* I.29; Plut. *Ages.* 10). Such deceptions and mis-information show Agesilaos as an astute reader of the minds of his adversaries, and as a commander who had the capacity to retain the initiative so vital in warfare. The result of making Tissaphernes seem inept and never being in the place he should be, led to him being charged and beheaded for treachery (*Hell.* III.iv.25; Plut. *Ages.* 10; Xen. *Ages.* I.35 merely reports the blame of the Great King and the replacement Commanders).

The campaign of 377 BC saw Agesilaos employ a similar tactic against the Thebans. In duping his opposition, Agesilaos used the same ploy of giving out misinformation concerning his prospective line of march. Having reached the friendly environs of Plataea, Agesilaos ordered that provisioning for the army would take place at Thespiai. The Thebans swallowed the bait and sent a large part of their forces to guard the pass from Thespiai into their territory (*Hell.* V.iv.48) at which point Agesilaos struck directly north east, passing the unguarded defensive palisade, and destroying, unhindered, the crops in this fertile plain south and east of Thebes. He had achieved his objective by making a forced march, covering in one day the distance of a normal two day march (*Hell.* V.iv.49). (For the following action, see below under 'Tactics'.)

Epameinondas secured a brilliant deception at the second battle of Manti-neia. Initially, he gave his adversaries the impression that he was about to offer battle by forming his line in battle order (*Hell.* VII.v.21) but then led his line to the west towards the mountains and not north towards the enemy. On arrival at the foot of the range the front of the line halted and turned right to face the enemy, grounding their arms as if in preparation to encamp when dismissed. The remainder of the line continued on its march westwards until the left wing achieved the desired depth, by virtue of company after company coming to a halt behind the original line, at which point the attack was ordered behind the shock cavalry attack. All this at a time when his adversaries, expecting the Thebans to encamp, had relaxed their vigil, and were on the point of standing down themselves.

Tactics

The set battle piece to be expected prior to the fourth century was usually one of two opposing lines each seeking to match the other in the length of line, and hoping to achieve an overlap on the right flank by which the enemy might be attacked in flank. The customary self preserving edging to the shield side which occurred in the preliminary advance often achieved this overlap accidentally, for one or both of the opposing armies. The basic frontal bloody clash of shield on shield, thrust and counterthrust, heave and counter push, was almost ritualised. In such a world discipline and the ability to manoeuvre made the Spartans the masters of all. However, it is obvious that Theban commanders, even before Epameinondas, had been deliberately experimenting with the depth and close order of the phalanx (twenty five deep at Delion, *Thuc.* 4.93.4; more than the sixteen agreed with the allies at the Nemea, *Hell.* IV.ii.18, for the agreement, *Hell.* IV.ii.13). Further, at the Nemea, it has been persuasively noted that the Boeotians matched the Spartans in a similar marching manoeuvre on the opposite wing to achieve an overlap.[32] Two things are clear. Other city states were learning from the Spartan example and, as has been noted above, were undertaking training and producing specialist forces. Possibly one of the most significant statements by Xenophon is to be found at *Hell.* IV.iv.14, which gives notice that the Greeks ceased to rely on a citizen army, reserving it for garrison duty only, while relying on mercenaries to prosecute any war. This had repercussions for any commander, adding the need for finance, for the payment of troops, into his planning at the time of the Corinthian War.

The good commander was he who read the prevailing conditions correctly and made the most of his opportunities. Indeed opportunism, courage and the certitude that it was easier to make a surprise attack on a larger fleet at anchor than engage a lesser in the open sea, persuaded Teleutias to undertake his highly successful and disruptive attack on Peiraeus, and later, on all who sailed in the waters between Aigina and Attica (*Hell.* V.i.20–24). (See also above under 'Morale'.) The attack was made at night on virtually unmanned warships at anchor, at a time when he presumed, correctly, that the Athenians were off their guard. Having neutralised the available Athenian warships, he was left free to make the most of his opportunity to pillage as he wished, both at sea, and on the seaboard of Attica. He was so successful that he was able to wipe out the arrears owed to his men, and to give them a month's pay in advance. His sequencing of action, and the highly effective use of limited resources, is to be admired. In modern terms he achieved two of the three designated maritime roles: *sea denial* (preventing an enemy from using the area of operation); *power projection* (using a naval force to neutralise shore positions and resources held there) and for a time secured the other, *sea control*.[33]

The actions of the polemarch Praxitas display the features of a commander who made the most of his opportunities without putting his men to inordinate risk. Given the chance to make entry within the walls leading from Corinth to

Lechaion, he was extremely careful to have the entry point thoroughly scouted by one of his trusted followers. This, despite the fact that he knew and trusted both collaborating Corinthians (*Hell.* IV.iv.7). Once through the wall, Praxitas had his men erect a defensive palisade and trench. In the engagement which followed next day, Praxitas was selective in the times of hoplite commital. First, in relief of the Sicyonians, his approach to the Argive rear caused these last to take flight even before contact. Their return from the seaward side towards the city took them between the eastern wall and the Spartans, thus presenting their shieldless side. The progress of the Argives was further impeded by the exiled Corinthians returning from the city after being victorious over the mercenary force under Iphikrates. In such circumstances, the advance of the Spartan infantry against an enemy, initially caught in disorder on the undefended side, then trapped against the wall, led to probably the greatest carnage of the Corinthian War. Thereafter the Boeotian garrison in the port was annihilated. Praxitas then had sections of the walls taken down to permit the easy passage of an army and protected the approaches in both directions by establishing garrisons at Sidos, Krommyon and at Epieikeia.

By contrast, delay in implementing an agreed plan can lead to its obvious benefits being lost. Having approved the plan to engage the Spartans in their own territory, rather than allow them to enlarge their forces as they marched north prior to the Nemea, the allies wasted valuable time debating the depth of their battle line and leadership issues. When they finally came to some form of agreement, the Spartans had already reached the Corinthian Gulf and had been joined by the Tegeates and Mantineians. Timolaos' plan (*Hell.* IV.ii.11–12) could have been decisive, if it had been acted upon immediately, but by the time of the battle the Spartans had, in addition to the aforementioned, received Eleians, Triphylians, Akrorians, Lasionians, Sikyonians, Epidaurians, Troizenians, Hermionians, Halians, Marganians, Letrinians and Amphidolians (*Hell.* IV.ii.16). These contingents enlarged the Spartan led army by approximately fourteen thousand men. Such was the outcome of leadership by committee.

A commander had to be in complete control of his forces if his intentions were to be fully carried out. A salutary example of a brave and normally competent commander who failed at the final fence was Kyros the Younger. Given that disciplinary problems arose (see above under 'Morale'), the laxity which prevailed in the final stages of the advance into the interior must be blamed for the unpreparedness of the army, clearly evident in Xenophon's description (*Anab.* I.viii.1–4). The major faults are self evident. The careful advance with the whole army in line of battle (*Anab.* I.vii.14) was abandoned once it had passed the defensive trench dug by the Great King and, with no adversary making an appearance, the march continued with only a small force in the vanguard maintaining battle formation. At such a time greater vigilance would have been expected and a readiness for battle wholly sustained, rather than the description of the advance given by Xenophon being the case.

> And so on the following day Kyros proceeded more carelessly; and on the third day he was making the march seated in his chariot and with only a small body of troops drawn up in line in front of him, while the greater part of the army was proceeding in disorder and many of the soldiers' arms and accoutrements were being carried in the wagons and on pack animals. (*Anab.* I.vii.20)

Further, the surprise and unnecessary confusion caused by the appearance of Pategyas, one of Kyros' staff officers, bringing news of the proximity of the Persian army, suggests that scouting arrangements were poor. Kyros' intention to attack the command point in force was thwarted by Klearchos' unwillingness to move his right wing away from the river to be in a position to confront the enemy's centre (*Anab.* I.viii.13). Klearchos was aware of the great overlap enjoyed by the enemy line. He feared being attacked on both flanks if he left the protection which the river afforded his right. It appears from the text that Klearchos was not wholly clear in his response to Kyros' request, and possibly led Kyros to believe that his order was about to be followed: '... he told Kyros, in reply, that he was taking care to make everything go well' (*Anab.* I.viii.13). Whether this was an intentional attempt to mislead, and avoid an argument, is difficult to ascertain.

Kyros' earlier exhortation to the Greeks not to be dismayed at the clamour of a prospective Persian advance (*Anab.* I.vii.4) proved misleading, for their actual advance was orderly, slow and in absolute silence (*Anab.* I.viii.11). During that very advance, Kyros' army was still in the process of establishing its battle line (*Anab.* I.viii.14). In the battle itself, the Greeks were victorious on the right wing, while the Great King's centre and almost unopposed right won their portions of the field. Kyros was killed in his abortive and hopelessly heroic attack on the Persian command point and the Persians went on to pillage the Greek camp. At that stage, both sides thought themselves to be wholly victorious. Here, Xenophon's comment that Koroneia was unlike any other battle of his time (*Hell.* IV.iii.16) must be refuted, if it was only the manoeuvres to which he referred. What followed at Kounaxa was virtually a prelude to Koroneia in that both armies now faced each other in battle line from the opposite direction of their first action. The fact that the Persians broke and ran before being fully engaged was fortuitous.

All this smacks of a gradually fragmented command structure but, more importantly, if the description of the days preceding the battle are examined from the point of view of Persian strategy, they can be more than suggestively informative. Kyros' assessment of when his brother would offer battle was incorrect. He had knowledge of the Great King's available forces prior to his arrival at what Xenophon described as a defensive trench (*Anab*. I.vii.16), and the tracks of a great number of men and horses there persuaded him that his brother had withdrawn from this position. That trench dug to a width of about thirty feet and a depth of eighteen feet must have been impressive, stretching as it did nearly forty miles to the Median defensive wall according to Xenophon, although he claims he did not know this last point until later (*Anab*. II.iv.12). The fact that only a small path of some seven yards in width separated the end of the trench from the river Euphrates should have given Kyros pause for thought. It is one thing to assume the abandonment of a position as being a retreat and quite another to lead an army into an area from which one's own withdrawal would be compromised. Kyros rewarded his soothsayer Silanos for having predicted that the Great King would not offer battle within ten days and now, having arrived at the trench on the eleventh day, assumed that he would not fight at all. Behind that assumption, and the persuasive evidence of the Persian withdrawal, lay a clear strategy of dissimulation. Although it cannot, on the evidence available, be firmly placed in the section dealing with Deception, it seems clear, given the time scale of later events, that this was a well prepared plan of action on the part of Artaxerxes. Kyros had repeatedly expected to come to battle (*Anab*. I.vii.1 and 14) following the discovery of Orontas' treachery. In the absence of any resistance he allowed himself to be lulled into a sense of false security and increasing unpreparedness (see above under 'Morale'). He was brought to battle at a time and place of his enemy's choosing, with the result that the victorious Greeks found that they had not been able to eat for a whole day (*Anab*. I.x.19). 'Deception seeks to manipulate perceptions and expectations in order to mislead the enemy into acting in a way prejudicial to his interests.'[34]

'Thus the highest form of generalship is to balk the enemy's plans' (Sun Tzu III.3) and 'Therefore the skilful leader subdues the enemy's troops without any fighting' (Sun Tzu III.6) seems to find an echo at *Hell*. III.v.1, where Tithraustes effectively put an end to Agesilaos' Asian campaign by offering Thebes, Corinth and Argos money to make war on Sparta, leading to the latter's recall (*Hell.* IV.ii.1–8). Thus, until the King's Peace, Persian money kept the Greeks occupied in hostilities among themselves, largely orchestrated by Pharnabazos (more money to the allies to sustain the war against Sparta, *Hell.* IV.viii.8; money to the Athenians to help rebuild the Long Walls and to maintain the fleet, *Hell.* IV.viii.9). So, from being in a position whereby the empire was endangered, the Persians had removed the threat and eventually brought Sparta to the point where she sued for terms with the Great King.

In almost identical passages (*Hell.* IV.iii.19; Xen. *Ages.* II.11–12) Xenophon points to the risk taken by Agesilaos at Koroneia. Rather than adopting the usual practice in such circumstances of taking the returning Thebans in the shieldless flank as they passed and pursuing them thereafter, he chose to countermarch his forces again to meet the Thebans head on.[35] His reason for doing so need not be debated here, but the outcome proved conclusively to the Thebans that the Spartan line could be resisted and indeed broken if close order was maintained. Whether the heightened adrenaline and desperation of their situation led the Thebans to achieve their partial success is irrelevant. The Theban tradition, as exemplified by Plutarch, categorically states that the Thebans could not be broken and that the Spartans were obliged to open their ranks to allow them through. The pursuit and attack from the flank did not succeed in producing a rout (Plut. *Ages.* 18). However, from the point of view of one who was present, Xenophon does not make any allusion to a deliberate opening of ranks by the Spartans. Rather he makes it clear that some Thebans were forced or 'fell through' the Spartan line given the weight of their dense formation. In other words they broke through the Spartan ranks. 'Finally, some of the Thebans broke through and reached Mount Helikon' (*Hell.* IV.iii.19).

Xenophon does not criticise Agesilaos directly for adopting his tactic of confrontation, but makes comment that there was a safer course which could have been followed. It seems to have been common knowledge throughout the entire ancient world, that it is best to leave an enemy an opportunity for escape. 'When you surround an army leave an outlet free. Do not press a desperate foe too hard' (Sun Tzu VII.36). Xenophon, himself, in an effort to dislodge an enemy force from a hill, ensured that his men did not wholly surround the position, but left a way of retreat which the enemy eventually took (*Anab.* IV.ii.11–12).

There is a hint here that Xenophon felt that Agesilaos was moved by more than tactical considerations. He is more openly critical of the king's brother, Teleutias (*Hell.* V.iii.7), when, on seeing the success of the Olynthian cavalry against his peltasts at the river crossing, he was so enraged that he led his army too hastily in support and too close to the city walls, resulting in a reverse for the Spartans and the loss of his own life (*Hell.* V.iii.6).[36]

A similar but accidental scenario is described, wherein desperation among enemy forces led to an unexpected outcome (*Hell.* V.iv.42–46). The passage contains examples of good practice and clear sighted command, but demonstrates clearly the necessity of avoiding any possibility of placing an enemy in desperate straits without recourse to withdrawal, and of the necessity to conduct a disciplined and well supported pursuit. Phoibidas, as governor at Thespiai, had laid waste much of the land around Thebes and induced the Thebans to send their whole army against him. On the march they were obviously so severely harassed by Phoibidas' peltasts that the advance was abandoned and a hasty retreat ordered. This retreat became more disorderly with Phoibidas' unrelenting peltast pressure and, in the hope of provoking a rout, he ordered the Thespian hoplites to follow in battle order. It seems obvious that the Theban retreat was not wholly over the same ground as their advance, otherwise their cavalry, possibly covering the rear of the withdrawal, would not have been faced with an impassable declivity which forced it to turn in the face of the pursuing peltasts. The peltasts, not being a match for cavalry unless on higher ground or in considerable number, are noted as being few at this point. Perhaps the pursuit had led to disparate groups not wholly in contact one with the other. Had Phoibidas ensured close support for his peltasts the outcome would have been very different. Whatever the case, some of that few took to their heels, and those who stood to fight, including Phoibidas, were killed. The result of this short cavalry action, brought about by desperation, was the headlong flight of the peltasts, then the mercenaries on the death of the commander and finally the Thespian hoplites.[37]

In similar vein, the Tearless Battle could well be described as an action taken by men driven by desperation, for Archidamos had already refused battle and withdrawn to a safe position, when the Arkadians and Argives had come to the relief of the Parrhasians. It is clear, from Xenophon's account, that they intended to deny the Spartan forces any opportunity to return to Sparta unhindered (*Hell.* VII.i.29). As it was, the Syracusan contingent under Kissidas, which had left the main body of the Spartan army because the term of its duty was completed, had been impeded on its journey to Sparta by the Messenians. Archidamos, in coming to its relief, was faced with the Arkadian and Argive army, and would appear to have had no other choice but to offer battle. The tactics of the commanders of the Arkadian and Argive forces had been sound. It was their misfortune that they had not completed their march to a point where a position could have been secured giving the Spartans no chance of a safe return. They were not to know that the Syracusans would leave the main body, or that Archidamos would come to their support and must have been surprised to find the enemy much closer to them than expected. The combination of this surprise and its effect on the morale of the Arkadians and Argives, together with the obvious desperation felt by the Spartan citizen troops, led to what must have been a rout. Xenophon notes that in the pursuit, the Celts, light armed troops and the cavalry, in all probability Syracusan, were prominent in causing the majority of the casualties (*Hell.* VII.i.31).[38]

Peltasts or light armed troops take on significant importance within this period. The circumstances of their successes usually depended on quicker manoeuvrability, surprise, attacks from higher ground with missiles, attacks on the shieldless side and the relentless pursuit of retreating hoplites. The clear recognition of one or more of these necessary components gave a commander a clear definition of their role in combat. The attempted taking of Corinth by the Thebans and allies (369 BC) met with a surprising rebuttal (*Hell.* VII.i.18–19). Described as advancing at the double in an attempt to force their way through the gates, the Thebans, and notably the Sacred Band in the van, were met by a force of peltasts, very close to the walls, who had made a sally and thereafter established themselves on tombs and other high points from where they poured javelins and projectiles into the Theban ranks. Casualties among the Thebans were considerable in this action and in the short pursuit following their retreat. Again the commander is not identified, but the planning and control of this engagement exemplifies all that is best in the handling of peltasts. In particular their sudden appearance when the Thebans were only four *plethra*, 400 feet from the walls, their immediate occupation of high points and the limited pursuit of less than half a mile, three or four *stadia*, shows firm discipline.

Commanders sometimes chose to use the younger, and obviously more mobile, of their hoplites, in a pursuit or attack. As has already been noted of Agesilaos in his attack on the Theban cavalry (*Hell.* V.iv.40), his cavalry was intermingled with his younger hoplites. Similarly, against the Persians, he employed his youngest 'ten years' who formed the front ranks of the phalanx to attack the enemy cavalry at close quarters, in conjunction with his force of peltasts (*Hell.* III.iv.23; Xen. *Ages.* I.31). It should be noted that there were two arms, one in support of the other, in the incidents cited, which makes it all the more tactically significant when comparing the success on these occasions to the disastrous unsupported use of the first ten year classes by the Spartan polemarch at Lechaion (*Hell.* IV.v.14). Iphikrates' order that his peltasts should retire before any Spartan hoplites came near them proved effective. When the Spartans gave up pursuit of the peltasts before approaching too near Kallias' supporting hoplite line, and turned to return to their own line, Iphikrates caused his peltasts to resume their attack by throwing javelins at the Spartans' rear and also their unshielded side by running along the flank. What is significant is that the polemarch did not learn anything from his initial action, but increased the year classes to fifteen in order to continue the fruitless pursuits (*Hell.* IV.v.16). So the Spartan casualties mounted and even the arrival of their cavalry did not help matters. Rather than run down the peltasts the cavalry kept pace with their hoplites both in attack and retreat, a manouvre which led inevitably to further losses. While it can be recognised that Agesilaos was making imaginative use of his forces, it is obvious that the polemarch was a man accustomed to the usual, in terms of combat, and did not have the capacity to deal with the unusual.

Enemies occupying a higher position on hills provoked problems for a commander when on the march, where his first duty was to safeguard the well-being of his men. Agesilaos, in his campaign of 389 BC, against the Akarnanians, had been forced to move his initial camp from the mountainside to the plain by the continuous fusillade from peltasts and slingers (*Hell.* IV.vi.7). The following day the mountains on both sides of the pass, through which Agesilaos wished to proceed, were bristling with enemy forces. Such was the effect of these missile attacks that the Spartan army was unable to proceed. Attempts at pursuit against those attackers on the Spartan right proved fruitless presumably because of the severity of the gradient. What followed showed a commander who read the topography well and who came to a decision as to the best way to deploy his available troops to redeem a difficult situation. His decision to attack the enemy on the Spartan left was made because the gradient, on this side of the valley, was amenable to a pursuit of cavalry and hoplites (*Hell.* IV.vi.9). It should be noted once more that we have here two intersupporting arms making a pursuit, with the remainder of the phalanx following to give support, in terms of morale and security, and to exploit further any success they might achieve. The first fifteen year classes of hoplites together with the cavalry made for a successful pursuit, sustaining casualties, as they approached the ridge, from the Akarnanian phalanx and their supporting peltasts drawn up in battle line. The Spartan pursuit was obviously successfully pressed further and allowed the following phalanx to engage with devastating effect. In a hoplite battle and pursuit, casualties of three hundred or so can be regarded as catastrophic for the defeated. It is no wonder that the depredations committed by the Spartan army thereafter on the economic basis of Akarnania were serious. The Achaians, on whose behalf Agesilaos had undertaken this campaign, were not of the same mind (*Hell.* IV.vi.13). However, they were persuaded by the promise that he would return once more to destroy the Akarnanian crops, and that people too, realising his intention, concluded a peace. Here we have an example of a commander showing flexibility in the use of his forces, tuning his decisions to the prevailing conditions and pursuing an ultimate goal.

Another example of economic warfare, which concerns the holding of high ground and the reading of topography, occurs within Agesilaos' campaign against Thebes in 377 BC. Having laid waste to a considerable portion of Theban territory, Agesilaos was faced by the Theban army, strongly positioned outside their stockade on a ridge, with a difficult approach to their deployment. Surmising correctly that the city of Thebes was virtually undefended, Agesilaos refused battle at this point and turned his line of march towards the city (*Hell.* V.iv.50). This manoeuvre caused the Thebans to set off in an attempt to reach the city first, obviously along the ridge (*Hell.* V.iv.52). There can be no doubt that the Thebans were worsted by sorties to their flanks as they passed by the Spartans, despite losses within the Spartan forces. The ground over which such sorties took place was not onerous and casualties obviously favoured the Spartans. In refusing battle and persuading the Thebans to retire from a secure position and conducting attacks upon them as they retired towards their city, Agesilaos continued to hold the initiative, the prerequisite for any commander.

The position taken by Thrasyboulos in his attack on the forces in control of the Peiraeus (404 BC), was higher than that of his enemies and, in consequence, the plan as outlined was to disrupt the opposing ranks by missiles (*Hell.* II.iv.15–16) thereby counteracting the disparity in numbers. Successful actions could be achieved by smaller forces if the ground they held was to their advantage.

After Koroneia, with Agesilaos absent at Delphi, command of the forces fell to Gylis, a polemarch. Following a successful pillaging of Lokris, the Spartan force was beset by missile-throwing Lokrians on the heights to their unshielded side. The Lokrians were obviously highly successful in their action and avoided contact in the repeated pursuits made by the Spartans. Eighteen Spartiatai were killed, including Gylis, as they, the rearguard of the forces, groped their way over rough ground towards the camp (*Hell.* IV.3.23). Gylis had obviously made several errors. The first, in not having full knowledge of the topography through which he was to travel. The second, in not having prearranged a force by which expected attacks from high positions could be nullified, so that the main body could be protected. The third, in not having taken control of the high ground himself. The fourth, in making his march to the place of encampment much too late and in darkness.

It is customary to find the person acting as *strategos* being one of the architects of state strategy. It is this intertwining of policy making and the execution of that policy in the field which can bring lasting results when that person is unchanged. In Epameinondas and Pelopidas we have the examples of men who, more often than not, held the post of Boeotarch over a number of successive years. This was often not the case elsewhere and accounts for the policy vacillations encountered. In Sparta the ephors and kings were arguably the policy makers. Continuity of command, at times of a strong personality, could be reasonably assured by that personality's influence on the assembly. Agesilaos, often being given the unenviable credit of being the 'teacher' of Pelopidas and Epameinondas, refined the art of economic warfare which, to be wholly successful, had to be carried out for more than one campaigning season. His successive expeditions against the Akarnanians threatened their economy and his motivation is clearly stated (*Hell.* IV.vi.13). Similarly, his repeated excursions into Boeotia, and in particular to the land around Thebes for the same reasons, demonstrated the strategy. It has been argued that Theban strategy during the 370s was defensive and aimed to avoid a pitched battle, but this argument is not convincing.[39] While seeking to limit the destruction caused by Agesilaos' foragers with defensive palisades, the Thebans had enough men in the field to take the initiative of coming to battle, had they manoeuvred the Spartan army into a position favourable to themselves. That they were unable to do so is proof of Agesilaos' skill in keeping them in a reactive role. In other words, he retained the initiative which is the prime concern of every good commander.[40]

Given the clear example of repeated despoliation to bring economic hardship on opponents, one should not be surprised that Epameinondas, in his successive invasions of Lakedaimon, sought to do the same. However, this would be to belittle Epameinondas' greatest achievement. Despoliation could be serious but the situation could be retrieved within a year, if it was not repetitious or of a more permanent nature. Epameinondas' wresting of the control of Messenia from Sparta proved to be the death knell of Spartan predominance, striking as it did at the very heart of the Spartan economy and of the social structure which depended upon it. This, therefore, should be regarded as his greatest achievement. In preparation for doing this, Epameinondas had detached strategic members from the Spartan alliance who had been important to the manpower of their armies, thus limiting their future effectiveness. In so doing, he had also created a ring of containment around Spartan influence by detaching those allies who had sent support to Sparta during the first Theban invasion. The only remaining allies of Sparta were Corinth and Phleious.[41]

Following 370 BC, Epameinondas achieved the total encirclement of Sparta and established walled and defensible cities at Mantineia, Tegea, Megalopolis and Messene. Herein lay the problem which Sparta was never to overcome, despite its counterattack of 368 BC. It is during this period that Agesilaos adopted a defensive strategy, despite the events of 368 BC, in recognition of these developments. A comparison to the attitude of command at this point shows that Agesilaos recognised immediately the necessity to move from the offensive to the defensive under the conditions which were presented to him. However, in the case of Epameinondas we only see an offensive commander. There is no evidence which shows any significant involvement in Theban affairs prior to Leuktra, except at his representation of Theban interests in the Council of Athenian allies in 375 BC. Whether he approved or disapproved of the Theban stance in the 370s is not known. Certainly there is a change in Theban attitude just prior to the battle itself, and that change was not easily achieved, depending as it did on the casting vote of the last Boeotarch who joined Epameinondas. However, the Theban success at Leuktra was the beginning of an attritional period unparalleled in Greek history.

To achieve such a result required repeated successful action in the field and it is as well to analyse how this was achieved. First and foremost must be the continuity of command, which was almost wholly unbroken from Leuktra on. Next was the training of the citizen body into a force of confident veterans under a command upon which they could wholly rely. Finally, there were commanders who were quick to adopt and develop tactics which proved beneficial, and who obviously considered the tactics which were likely to be adopted against them. It is unfortunate that Xenophon makes no mention of Tegyra, but then, neither does he note any of Pelopidas' activities in the north. However, it is this engagement in 375 BC which, with the unforgotten lesson of the success of hoplites in depth and very close order at Koroneia 394 BC, lies at the heart of Theban tactics thereafter. At Koroneia, in the second phase of the battle, the Thebans, on their return from the Spartan camp, found themselves arraigned on the left of the field against the Spartan right for the first time. This disposition meant that they were fighting against the command point of their opposition and the fact that, despite considerable loss of life (*Diod.* IX.84.2: more than 600 men), they broke the Spartan line proved a significant lesson. Given that Theban tradition would make much of Tegyra, it is not surprising that Plutarch should enjoy recounting the exploit of Pelopidas.[42] It is fair to say that his description of the engagement offers an insight into the tactics employed and, because of their unusual nature, there is more reason to believe the tradition from which they sprang (Plut. *Pelop.* 17). Although the details are not wholly clear it would appear that, having brought his cavalry from the rear, he ordered them to charge the enemy line, which itself was unsupported by cavalry, and followed with the Sacred Band in close order to attack further the same point as the cavalry contact. Here, where fighting is reported to have been extremely fierce, both Spartan polemarchs were killed. This suggests a highly unusual arrangement where one polemarch was on the right of his *mora* and the other on the left of his, unless they had placed themselves at the expected point of attack, i.e., the centre. It is credible that Pelopidas did make his attack on the centre considering the description of what followed. The Spartans are reported to have opened their ranks to allow the Thebans to pass through to escape. In view of Koroneia this is debatable, particularly as this is suggested as having being after the deaths of the polemarchs. Despite the fact that Spartan armies had an officer class which permeated through the ranks and command would now have devolved to the *lochagoi*, this was an order which could not easily have been put into effect particularly if the fighting was concentrating around the point where the polemarchs had fallen. It seems more likely that the Spartan line was broken.[43] Whatever the circumstance, the more important issue is that Pelopidas and his men did not pass through the Spartan ranks to the rear but used the breach which had been made to attack the Spartans in flank. In so doing, a heavily outnumbered force of hoplites supported by cavalry defeated its unsupported opposition of heavy infantry.

So much that follows at Leuktra and at the Second Battle of Mantineia becomes clear when set against the combined lessons of Koroneia and Tegyra. An attack directed at the command point, initiated by a cavalry action, followed by the infantry phalanx in extreme depth and very close order almost in column, achieving a breach in the enemy line from which attacks could be made against the exposed flanks of the corridor, particularly the unshielded side, proved unstoppable.

Although it has been pointed out that Teleutias took command on the left on one occasion, the usual command position was on the right wing for the Greeks and at the centre for the Persians. It is significant therefore that Epameinondas, in his two set battles, should choose to take command on the left of his army and attack the command position of the opposition, employing his cavalry in a softening up position which his hoplites could exploit. It is obvious, at Second Mantineia, that those forces who were destroyed as they made their way to the (Theban) right of the battlefield, had continued the pursuit of the disintegrated and fleeing enemy line and had come up against the Athenian phalanx and cavalry still in formation. These Boeotian peltasts and *hamhippoi* did not have the support of their hoplites or cavalry. These last had abandoned any thought of following up their initial victory on the loss of their general. While Mantineia was the product of a ruse, Leuktra can be explained as being the recognition of opposition habit. The leading to the right in order to achieve an outflanking movement, which had been a successful tactic of the Spartans down to the Nemea, was almost too predictable and could be used against them. The oblique approach from the left in massive depth with a trailing, unengaged, but threatening right, proved an unstoppable formula for its time.[44] 'Do not repeat the tactics which have gained you one victory, but let your methods be regulated by the infinite variety of circumstances' (Sun Tzu VI.28).

Tactically, after the initial phase of the battle, the Nemea raises a variety of questions which have been explained as the result of poor discipline.[45] This seems only part of the answer. Opportunities were lost by commanders of both hoplites and cavalry to disrupt the victorious progress of the Spartans by attempted attacks on their flank. However, the fundamental key to Epameinondas' success in battle lay in his knowledge that his cavalry would be superior to that of the Spartan forces. Had he not been so secure, he would not have been able to lead the very deep phalanx obliquely to the left without the danger of the unshielded flank being exposed to cavalry attack. Presumably the order to attack was made when he was sure that the Spartan cavalry was being worsted at Leuktra.

Obviously to military historians one attraction would have been the pitting of the two ablest commanders of the period, one against the other, in battle, namely Agesilaos and Epameinondas. Unfortunately, this has led to some kite flying[46] which cannot be supported by the existing evidence and this necessitates a digression which deals with the last campaign of Epameinondas.

The question of the command for those opposed to the Thebans was possibly the arrangement made in 369 BC (*Hell.* VII.i.14) whereby each of the allies held the position by rotation for a period of five days.[47] Certainly, the time had passed when Sparta automatically commanded the land forces in which she fought and, if command was rotational, which was unlikely, the forces of the state in whose territory any engagement was to be fought may well have been given the position on the right. A further related question concerns the size and position of the Spartan forces at the battle itself. It is as well now to continue the digression and to rehearse some of the issues which would have led to a limited Spartan committment in the Second battle of Mantineia and the absence from the battle of Agesilaos.

Epameinondas had waited in vain at Tegea for additional support while the opposing forces were becoming more formidable. His opportunity for positive action came with the news that Agesilaos was marching north to join the allies. In a bold stroke, leaving a garrison at Tegea, Epameinondas marched south on Sparta. In the attack on the unwalled city which followed, and which found Agesilaos back in time for its defence, the description of the action centres around the actions of Archidamos. With missile throwers manning the roof-tops dissuading Epameinondas from entering the city on a rising gradient (*Hell.* VII.v.11), Archidamos led an attack obviously from another point, uphill, with less than a hundred Spartiates. They dislodged a formidable force of Thebans from their more advantageous position and it can be concluded that the attack was made before the Thebans had fully completed their deployment. The main Theban casualties were sustained by the leading ranks (*Hell.* VII.v.13) and it is implied by the reference to a Spartan pursuit that the Theban line was broken. Further losses were probably avoided by a successful Theban regrouping and the fact that the Spartan force was too small to press home a complete rout of their enemy. Unquestionably the action was successful. A victory trophy was set up on the site (*Hell.* VII.v.13) and, by claiming his dead under a truce, Epameinondas conceded defeat. The attack on Sparta may not have been successful in terms of capturing the city, but it saw Agesilaos with his forces back in the heartland of Lakonia.

There is no doubt that the Spartans were present at Mantineia. It is highly likely that, whatever the size of the contingent present, it would be close to the right of the army in which it served (Plut. *Ages.* 35.1–2; *Diod.* XV.85.2; *Paus.* VIII.9.6–7) if only by virtue of the quality of such a force. It is clear that the cavalry, mercenaries and three lochoi had gone on ahead to join the allied forces, and that Agesilaos was marching to join them, when news of Epameinondas' lightning march on Sparta reached him at Pellene (*Hell.* VII.v.10).[48] Having returned for the defence of Sparta, it is highly unlikely that, in the aftermath of this second trauma for the Spartan populace, they would be willing to allow the remaining forces to march immediately north through enemy-held territory to join their allies. If anything, Epameinondas' strike at Sparta served to keep the nine lochoi and Agesilaos at home for its defence and may well have been made for that very purpose. While it is evident that although Epameinondas required some significant success (*Hell.* VII.v.9) he was careful to avoid any action in which his enemy had the advantage of terrain. Similarly, it was in his interest to ensure that no junction of enemy forces was completed. In particular, it would be in his interest to ensure that Agesilaos was unlikely to be in command of any united opposing forces (*Pol.* IX.8.2 and 6: despite Polybius' claim that the full Spartan army under Agesilaos was present at Mantinieia). For a commander of Agesilaos' experience to march to a position north of the enemy position in relation to Sparta at that time would have been tactically inept, and, in such circumstances, almost unthinkable. He was better placed to threaten his enemy's rear, if occasion arose, by staying where he was and calming the Spartan populace by his presence. This last point is important. The population of Lakedaimon had enjoyed virtually total security until Leuktra. Since then stress, anxiety, all the insecurities known hitherto only to others, had beset the Lakedaimonians. Over a period of eight years the world had become a very different place for them.[49]

The exact location of the Second Battle of Mantinea (362 BC) is unknown. However, knowledge of the topography of the area together with the very few geographical details Xenophon gives permits a considered suggestion when taken with a description of the action. The plain of Mantinea and Tegea is extremely flat. At that dry time of the year the dust made by an army on the march must have been considerable. Reading dust formations would have been a common military skill (Sun Tzu IX.23). It is likely that the forces which were opposed to Epameinondas had taken up a position south of Mantinea near the narrowest point of the plain. Epameinondas' initial preparations had persuaded them that he was about to offer battle (*Hell.* VII.v.21). Moving north from the environs of Tegea he had established his battle line. His army did not, however, proceed directly towards the enemy, but moved obliquely in column to the west, skirting the foothills of the Menalon range thus convincing his enemy that there would not be an engagement that day (*Hell.* VII.v.21). This manoeuvre brought his troops to a position in the area of modern Merkovouni, or Skopi, adjacent to a rise of 3,500 feet. In describing the early line of march Xenophon uses the plural 'mountains', whereas he has the Thebans arrive at the 'mountain' (*Hell.* VII.v.22) and the location given above is the most likely place to fit the description.

What followed was an ingenious deception which ensured that Epameinondas' enemy could not avoid contact. As the leading ranks of his battle line arrived at the foot of the steep incline he had them right face and ground arms, suggesting the common practice of preparing to make camp (*Hell.* VII.v.22). Those following in column continued their march rank by rank unseen by the opposition behind their front and, in turn, right faced and grounded their arms, thus increasing the left flank considerably. By this time his enemies had interpreted the activity as indeed that of making camp, had relaxed their vigil and had in turn started making preparations for their own encampment. At this juncture Epameinondas launched his surprise massed attack from the left wing on an unprepared enemy (*Hell.* VII.v.22).

Xenophon makes specific comparison of the opposing cavalry arms (see also earlier for the Theban formation). Epameinondas' cavalry was supported by and intermingled with peltasts, while those of the Arkadians had formed up in the normal Greek manner, six deep like a phalanx unsupported by infantry. There is no doubt that Xenophon agreed with the practice adopted by Epameinondas (*Hipp.* V.13; VIII.9).

The Theban left broke through the unprepared enemy right wing and a rout could have ensued had not Epameinondas been killed and the pursuit abandoned in consequence. Xenophon contradicts himself when he states that the whole enemy army fled (*Hell.* VII.v.24). Earlier he had noted that Epameinondas had tactically excluded the Athenian forces stationed on the left wing from any initial action by placing cavalry, presumably Thessalian, and hoplites in such a position as to endanger their rear and flank had they attempted to come to the aid of their beleaguered allies (*Hell.* VII.v.24). Another example of a trailing and threatening right. Indeed, it was this force of Athenians which mopped up the hitherto victorious Theban peltasts as they made contact in their progress across the battlefield. Thus the failure to follow up the initial victory on the Theban left was offset by the victory of the Athenians in their part of the field.

Perhaps it is an indictment of the Theban command structure that the death of its commander on the brink of an assured and complete victory led to the stalemate in which both sides claimed victory (*Hell.* VII.v.26–27).

With the tactical discussion which has preceded this point, it is possible to address the issue of Leuktra. Infinite caution must be taken when attempting to reconstruct the manoeuvres of this battle. Contemporary evidence (by

Xenophon) of the actual engagement itself is minimal and that of later writers hold too many discrepancies (see Diodorus), or are possibly coloured by practices of later times not in vogue at the time of the battle itself (see Plutarch).

Epameinondas may have personally made a conscious decision to attack the Spartan command position by taking station on the left, but the choice of such a deployment prompts the question whether the presence of reluctant and coerced allies made this a necessity. The danger was that the Spartan right would have destroyed the Boeotian left and then, having wheeled, rolled up the remainder of the line by taking the Thebans in flank. It was to avoid this outcome which led Epameinondas to adopt his new command position. The lessons of Koroneia and Tegyra had taught the Theban commanders that they could not only withstand a Spartan assault if they maintained density and formation, but also effect a breakthrough of the Spartan line if they assumed close order by contracting their formation (συσπειραθέντες – 'massed together' as at Koroneia) (Hell. IV.iii.18; for Tegyra see also Plut. Pelop. XVII.2).

Xenophon's description of the action itself leaves many questions unanswered. His neglect may have arisen from a natural distaste to dwell long on the misfortunes of his adoptive state, or he actually tells us all that he can be sure of, considering the confusion of the action itself. His avoidance of even giving mention of the Theban commander is significant when taken alongside the list of notable Spartiates who lost their lives (Hell. VI.iv.14).

The account itself shows the propitious beginnings of Kleombrotos' campaign and his imaginative line of march from Phokis over difficult country to outflank the Theban position and to surprise and capture the twelve Theban triremes at Kreusis, in an opportune attack, before moving north to make camp at Leuktra. This new route to Boeotia avoided a repetition of his failure to pass Kithairon some five years earlier (Hell. VI.iv.5) where the impeding of his advance to the Theban plain in this campaign (Hell. VI.iv.7) by the direct route, and his avoidance of contact, served to do little to enhance his reputation as a decisive commander (Hell. VI.iv.5). Epameinondas had set up a strong defensive position at Koroneia between Mt. Helikon and Lake Kopais and would not have expected Kleombrotos to cross Helikon.[50] By taking this more circuitous route, Kleombrotos lost any element of surprise and allowed the Thebans time to take up a defensive position in the hope that the arrival of contingents from the more distant Boeotian cities would secure their position further. At this juncture, and at a new location, an immediate engagement would seem to have been heavily in the Spartan interest.

167

It is interesting to note references in Xenophon's account to the obvious psychology at work on both sides. Kleombrotos' apparent reluctance to engage an army of inferior number led some of the officers on his own side to question his commitment (*Hell.* VI.iv.5). This, and the desire to avoid another failure, possibly led to the unexpected overeagerness which brought about the questionable deployment criticised by Xenophon (see later).

The Theban leaders, too, were concerned that Boeotian cities might revolt (*Hell.* VI.iv.6) and that, if Thebes itself was put in a state of siege, they themselves would be unpopular and possibly exiled once more. Xenophon makes the point that, rather than face exile, they would prefer to die fighting (*Hell.* VI.iv.6) and desperate men are more formidable than ordinary men (Sun Tzu V11.36 '... leave a way of escape and do not press a desperate enemy too hard'). In this state of mind they would be heartened by the report of the oracle concerning the virgins, the report of their priestesses predicting victory for the Thebans and the news that Herakles himself was armed and coming to their aid (see earlier under 'Piety').

It is as well to emphasise the distinctive and all embracing role played by religious practice and belief in the day to day affairs of the Greeks.[51] As has been noted earlier in the specific section on 'Piety', Xenophon's writings are peppered with references to religious observances and his own pious attitude. Indeed, his own viewpoint of the battle is that the Spartan assembly brought the misfortune upon themselves by not honouring their oath to disband their forces first.

The morale of the Thebans was high, bolstered by the series of favourable omens coming to them. Xenophon may well be correct in his suggestion that such news was a ploy (*Hell.* VI.iv.7). If this was the case, it was an agreed policy of command and Epameinondas must take some, or all, of the credit.[52] The controlled and filtered 'good news' to troops appears systematic and well planned, in line with a necessary propaganda programme orchestrated by the Theban command. No direct evidence exists to support this view other than Xenophon's belief that it was a ruse, and his studied avoidance to name the Theban command indicates the likelihood that this was an exercise in misinformation designed to boost morale. Such was the confidence on the one hand, and the eagerness to refute criticism on the other, that the command of both sides decided to come to battle (*Hell.* VI.iv.9).

The people who sold supplies to the Theban army, and those allied contingents unwilling to remain and fight, had attempted to withdraw from the impending conflict. They were herded back to the Theban camp by a mixed force of peltasts and cavalry (*Hell.* VI.iv.9), presumably from the Spartan allies and mercenaries on the left wing, making the Theban forces larger than they would otherwise have been, and increasing the number of 'desperate' men within the forces opposed to the Spartans.

As to the battle itself, the few indications given by Xenophon show the possible outline planning of the opposing commanders. The Spartan phalanx was arranged in *enomotiai* three abreast, giving a density of twelve men. Presumably the aim was to outflank the enemy by making a longer battle line. However, the Thebans had adjusted their phalanx, opposite the station of the Spartan king, to a depth of fifty men, a formidable and unstoppable weight (*Hell.* VI.iv.12). Epameinondas obviously hoped that, given a breakthrough at the point of command, the rest of the Lakedaimonian army would be demoralised. This also implies tactical discussions between Pelopidas and Epameinondas prior to the battle, and consideration being given to lessons from experience.

It is at this juncture that questions arise. Xenophon states categorically that Kleombrotos advanced towards the enemy before troops under his own command knew what was happening (*Hell.* VI.iv.13), an obvious breakdown in communications. He also makes it clear that the Spartan cavalry had been placed in front of the phalanx (*Hell.* VI.iv.10), giving as the reason for doing so that the area between the armies was a plain. Xenophon states the facts baldly, and gives no other explanation for this deployment, possibly because he did not know of one. The Theban cavalry was also placed in front of their phalanx, either in response to the Spartan deployment, or as a preconceived ploy to cover the manoeuvre which led to the deepening of their phalanx. The latter is the more probable. Having condemned the quality of the Spartan cavalry, Xenophon leaves the reader with the problem of understanding why Kleombrotos placed a force he expected to be ineffectual in front of, and impeding, his phalanx. Was it simply an act of inept command? He could not hope that his cavalry would be successful against the much more experienced Theban horse. Or was it in response to the deployment of the Theban cavalry? Which force was deployed first? The terrain is largely unchanged and it is a good area for the infantry manoeuvres of the period; it was obviously chosen for this reason. Or was it that the placing of the cavalry force in front of the phalanx was planned so that the dust, raised by their movements, would conceal some countermarch, deepening of the line or manoeuvre, that Kleombrotos and Epameinondas wished to make? The latter seems the more credible, and it would appear that, in what followed, either Kleombrotos'

169

timing of the manoeuvre was at fault, or, more probably, that Epameinondas second guessed what was happening and ordered an immediate advance while Kleombrotos was in mid-manoeuvre. The Spartan horse had, not unexpectedly, been routed by the Theban cavalry and were now being pursued by the advancing Theban hoplites. The Theban cavalry, presumably, had retired to the wing to allow the advance of their infantry, which had quickly moved forward, enjoying the same cover of the dust clouds by which Kleombrotos had hoped to cover his lead to the right. To add to the confusion, the fleeing Spartan horse impeded and disrupted its own hoplite lines making it more difficult for the Spartan phalanx to withstand the massed advance of the Theban hoplites. The fact that part of it did, long enough to carry the mortally wounded king from the battle, indicates a spirited resistance (*Hell.* VI.iv.13). However, the list of senior officers (*Hell.* VI.iv.14) and the numbers of Lakedaemonians and, particularly, Spartiates killed in the battle (*Hell.* VI.iv.15) indicates a catastrophic defeat for the Spartans.

The pride of the Spartans led to delay admission of defeat (*Hell.* VI.iv.15) but the reality of the reluctance of the allies to continue the fight led them to accept the bleak facts of the occasion (*Hell.* VI.iv.15). If Xenophon was the only source for reconstructing the battle we would have to accept the following scenario. Kleombrotos, adopting a similar battle plan as that which had brought success at Nemea and Koroneia, led to the right behind the dust of the cavalry screen. Before the successive contingents of the phalanx could follow his lead, the defeated Spartan horse became entangled with the front ranks of his phalanx. In the disruption which followed, the immediate attack of Epameinondas drove a wedge between those under Kleombrotos, who had moved off unimpeded and those whose progress had been stopped by the retreating cavalry. This is the very point at which Xenophon ceases to be of any direct help. His narrative denies us the detail to pursue anything other than a considered guess as to what had happened.

However, by taking the likely manoeuvres indicated at the outset of the battle by Xenophon together with the broad sweep of Plutarch's account, a likely description of the remainder of the battle can be formulated. Before Kleombrotos, now cut off from the left of his phalanx by the Theban mass, had time to complete his manoeuvre to outflank the Theban line, the Sacred Band under Pelopidas detached itself from the main Theban formation 'at the double' and pinned him down. The remaining Spartans were faced with a dilemma. If they moved across the field to support their king, they would expose their flank and rear to attack from the Boeotian right wing which had thus far been withheld from action. The Spartans and allies on the left were probably mere onlookers of the disaster befalling their king, as the greater part of two *morai*, containing a high proportion of Spartiatai, including the Hippeis, was decimated.

If we accept the word of Plutarch and his source, Pelopidas cannot have been held in reserve as has often been suggested (Plut. *Pelop.* XXIII.2). The days of reserves had not yet fully arrived as an accepted practice. This was an opportunist attack led by Pelopidas from the place of the Sacred Band at the front of, or to the left of, the Theban phalanx as the 'cutting edge'. They came on 'at the double' implying that their speed of attack was quicker than that of the main Theban phalanx. He could only have seen his opportunity at relatively close quarters because of the dust screen, and his forces must have been ahead of the main Theban phalanx for him to take it. In conclusion, in the planning for action, Epameinondas had seen the initial Spartan deployment and had noted the cavalry screen placed by Kleombrotos in front of his phalanx. Having no doubt that his cavalry would easily worst the Spartan horse, his deployment on a narrow front in significant depth was obviously planned to effect a breakthrough, dividing the Spartan phalanx and isolating Kleombrotos from the remainder of his forces. In expectation of an attempted repetition of the manoeuvres of Nemea and Koroneia, his plans were well founded. In the same reference of Plutarch above, the Theban phalanx is described as 'edging to the left'. The natural tendency of phalangites was to edge to the right, in order to protect the unshielded side. This move to the left must have been ordered.

Working back from the depth of deployment for both sides, we can easily see that the Theban front was, in comparison to that of the Spartan, extremely short. Given that the Thebans probably had more hoplites in their phalanx than the Spartans, despite the fact that the Spartan army as a whole outnumbered the Boeotians, it is possible that the main Theban phalanx of possibly five thousand or so men, despite the losses at Nemea, presented a front of a hundred men. The Spartans can only have had about four and a half thousand at most in their phalanx, but at twelve deep would present a front of 375 men, an immediate outflanking if it was allowed to develop. The fact that it was not allowed to develop is the major contribution to tactics by Epameinondas. With a front of only a hundred men it may well be possible that this was extended by placing the Sacred Band to the left of the Theban phalanx, rather than in front. Even so, this would still leave the Spartan forces with an overlap.[53] Certainly, the Band would be in an even better position to pin down the lead to the right which Kleombrotos undoubtedly made early in the battle, and this is what he must have done, while Epameinondas, with the phalanx, bore down on the mêlée created by the entanglement of the Lakedaemonian cavalry with their own line. Further, Epameinondas, in putting his main striking force unusually on the left of his army, could present the protection of his shield side to the isolated extreme right wing of the Spartans following the breakthrough of their line, before turning to take them in flank. His great contribution to the art of command was that he realised that by taking the initiative and sustaining it in an immediate attack on an enemy's command point, he could nullify any early deployment the opposition might wish to make, and deny the opposing commander any opportunity to restore the balance by cutting off his lines of communication with the rest of his army. The concept of an attack in depth, on what the enemy might count as their strongest point, had arrived, as well as the practice of purposefully disrupting communications on the field itself. The only unresolved question is where the Sacred Band was stationed. As a 'cutting edge' to the phalanx, in advance to the phalanx, or as a wing to the phalanx? It was certainly not used as a reserve force. Plutarch (Plut. *Pelop.* XXIII) suggests that Pelopidas detached himself and his men from the main body and made his attack at the time when Kleombrotos was in mid-manoeuvre, with a line unprepared for an assault, and disrupted by his ineffectual cavalry.

Spartan losses were grievous. The Hippeis, the cream of Spartiates, were virtually annihilated, together with at least another 700 men. As it was, the remainder of the Spartan phalanx, together with the allies, fell back without engaging, threatened as it was by the Boeotian right. The fact of their non-engagement was possibly one of the reasons for many Lakedaemonians not wishing to concede defeat in an engagement in which they had no participation.

Set battles were few in this century, and therein lies the key to the development in the tactical use of cavalry and peltasts, in particular, in defensive and offensive operations. In battle, two basic forms of tactic can be discerned. First was the traditional hoplite encounter, wherein the heaving and pushing sought to create a break in the opposition's line which could be exploited. The Spartans developed from this the tactic of using the natural drift to the right of the phalanx, into a tactical leading march to the right, whereby an outflanking of the enemy line was achieved, as at the Nemea, and which led to the rolling up of the enemy's line. Second was an attack in depth on the enemy's command position, using cavalry as the 'softening' up agent for hoplites to exploit. Rather than waiting for a break in the opposition's line the tactic was to create

172

the break, and having done so, to exploit the corridor created. In Theban tactics we see the refining of this principle from Tegyra through Leuktra to Mantineia.

The evidence shows that the successful commander was the thinking commander. Ritualised warring had gone. As the annual season for campaigning extended to year-round activity, tactics and methodology distinguished the good from both the indifferent and the totally unimaginative. No longer was it enough to rely on heavy infantry in tight formation only, with scant use being given to the cavalry, or to the hitherto socially inferior skirmishers, slingers and peltasts. If anything, the period under discussion in this section has shown the vulnerability of hoplites to those very arms which had been deemed less important, particularly when under good leadership. The successful commander was he who could deploy all arms with success, and who kept his enemy in doubt of his intentions. Xenophon leaves his reader in no doubt of his own choice, or of the good reasons for them.

End Notes

1. Buckler, *The Theban Hegemony*, Appendix 2. Although the whole text is admirable in its treatment of the political content it displays a distinct anti-Spartan flavour which is epitomised in the appendix and somewhat unfairly criticises Xenophon for his omissions.

2. Within forty years of the second Mantineia, Aristotle makes comment that, as long as the Spartans were the only people who devoted themselves to rigorous training, they were successful in war. With training becoming the norm elsewhere, they were now beaten in both war and in games (Politics 1338b).

3. Hornblower, *The Greek World 479–323 BC*, p.157.

4. Wheeler, E.L., 'The General as Hoplite', in Hanson, (ed), *Hoplites*, pp.153–4.

5. My thanks to Joanne Thompson, an expert horsewoman, with extensive knowledge of the horse's temperament and of the problems of riding without saddle or stirrups.

6. Anderson, *Military Theory*, pp.118–20. There are two contrasting versions of this action, but that of Xenophon is to be preferred on the grounds that he may well have been at the battle, and, if not actually there, would have gleaned

accurate information from either Agesilaos himself or from his circle (*Hell.* III.iv.20–24; *Ages.* I.28–32; for alternative version *Oxyr.* XI.(vi); *Diod.* XIV.80; for cavalry supported by infantry *Hell.* III.iv.24; Xen. *Ages.* I.32; see also Plut. *Ages.* X.3).

Some interesting observations are made on the discrepancies in the various accounts of Agesilaos' battle with Tissaphernes, in Shipley, *Plutarch's Life of Agesilaos* (Oxford, 1997), pp.156ff and, particularly, pp.165–9.

7. Spence, *The Cavalry of Classical Greece* (Clarendon Press, Oxford, 1995), pp.101–2.

8. Lazenby, *Spartan Army*, p.155, argues decisively that the Boeotians fielded only their own cavalry at Leuktra and did not have the physical presence of Jason of Pherae to bolster their numbers.

9. For cavalry formations see references in Spence, *The Cavalry*, p.25 and n.113, to Arrian Taktike XVI. 1–5, and Asklepiodotos VII.2; see also p.178 and n.57 in reference to Asklepiodotos VII.5–9. Also Marsden, *The Campaign of Gaugamela*, pp.68–98.

One problem is that Xenophon also uses the word ἔμβολον (*Hell.* VII.v.24) for the massed hoplites on the left wing. His description of the manner in which the *lochoi* were moved to that wing (VII.V.22) indicates that he was seeking to increase massively the depth of his phalanx, the shape of which would have been a deep rectangular block. However it becomes part of the *emvolon* when considered as being directly behind the cavalry and peltast 'wedge'. Epameinondas creates the wedge formation by the junction of the disparate arms one behind the other. A.M. Devine must clearly be incorrect in his suggested formations 'Embolon: A Study', *Pheonix*, (1983), 37, pp.201–17.

10. Spence, *The Cavalry*, p.117.

11. On the matter of laying crops waste, the points made by Hanson, *Warfare and Agriculture in Classical Greece*, pp.50–74 are persuasive but misleading. It is a pity that more scholars have not challenged some of the points he makes. Apart from the hill terraces, much of the cultivated land was in the small plains through which any force, marching in battle order rather than in column, could wreak havoc. Chopping down or attempting to burn olive trees, or stripping out vines, is totally unnecessary. Any fruit bearing tree can have its product destroyed at any time of the year. A single man with a six foot pole, about the length of a hoplite spear, can strip out the blossom, the setting fruit,

half grown fruit or even mature fruit, from the branches in a very short time. To destroy part of a crop is to reduce or eliminate the season's surplus at the very least, or bring about a severe shortfall in production. Repeated depredations can lead to total crop failure. Denying access to cultivated land to those who must tend it leads to neglect which encourages virulent weeds to take over. This can diminish former productivity by as much as three years following a single season's neglect. Grain and vegetable plants are particularly susceptible to damage at any time (ask any British farmer). Replacing herds of livestock would be a much bigger problem for the long term. A single season's damage was serious and we are now in a period where the campaigning season gradually lengthened to the whole year. More than one could be disastrous. Finally, if the practice had not been worth while on both terraces and plains, the Greeks would not have indulged themselves. Unfortunately, J. Keegan, *A History of Warfare* (Pimlico, 1994), p.245, has been persuaded by Hanson. Even a visit to modern agricultural Greece would modify those views. The tactical and strategic aims of 'economic warfare' are discussed further in Appendix 3.

12. Spence, *The Cavalry*, p.103.

13. See also Pritchett, *The Greek State at War*, vol. IV, pp.204–6. A difference in perception is noted in sources. Xenophon says that it was the failure to pick up the survivors, whereas Diodoros states that it was a failure to pick up the dead (XIII.100.1–3) which provoked the problem. See also Xenophon *Hellenika* I–II.3.10, edited by Krentz on 1. 6. 35ff and Kagan, *The Fall of the Athenian Empire*, p.354. A significant attitude to the retrieval of the dead is noted in Thucydides IV.44.5–6. A herald is sent by the Athenians to retrieve two bodies under truce and in so doing could be held to have conceded defeat in the battle of Solygeia 425 BC. See also Plutarch, *Nikias* VI.4–7 and P. Vaughn, 'The Identification and Retrieval of the Hoplite Dead' in Hanson, *Hoplites*.

14. See Pritchett, *War*, vol. IV, pp.238–9.

15. Note that there is a suggestion of a class struggle ('*beltistoi*').

16. See Lazenby, *The Spartan Army*, pp.16–18, 42–3, and Hamilton, *Agesilaos and the Failure of Spartan Hegemony*, pp.76–8 for a discussion on the sub-classes in Sparta.

The *neodamodeis* are alluded to in *Thuc*. V.34.1 in the year 421 BC (see also Lazenby, *Spartan Army*, p.14) but *Thuc*. V.67.1 suggests that they may have been in existence in 424 BC.

17. See also Zaidman and Pantel, *Religion in the Ancient Greek City*, pp.100–1.

18. An excellent description of sacrifice immediately prior to battle is given in Michael. H. Jameson's article, 'Sacrifice Before Battle,' in *Hoplites* (ed. Hanson), pp.204–5.
The pace at which the final phase of a Spartan advance was made obviously varied with circumstance. At First Mantineia the advance was measured and in step to the *aulos*. The adverb βραδέως 'slowly' is used. At the Nemea ἡγοῦντο ἐπὶ τοὺς ἐναντίους indicates that the Spartans 'led' the charge and may have been faster-moving and earlier to engage than the remainder of the line of allies. In this case 'at the double ' would not be amiss.

19. Barry, 'Roof Tiles and Urban Violence in the Ancient World', pp.55–74. See also *Hell.* VI.5.9.

20. Buckler in *The Theban Hegemony* gives Epameinondas the credit for using the omens to his advantage prior to Leuktra. See p.62 and also note 23, p.290.

21. See Anderson, *Military Theory*, pp.55–7.

22. Gray, *The Character of Xenophon's Hellenica*. I am not persuaded by Prof. Gray's alternative interpretation which seems idealised and far removed from the machinations of human nature. See pp.22–4 and pp. 82–3. A more cogent approach is made in Cartledge, *Agesilaos and the Crisis of Sparta*, 1987, p.190.

23. See Anderson, *Military Theory*, pp.55–6. I am informed by Prof. J.F. Lazenby of a lecture by S. Hornblower in which it was argued that the use of the commander's staff, βακτηρία, to chastise subordinates was characteristic of Spartan officers. The question is largely one of degree and Xenophon's particular report of the issue seems to infer brutality rather than expected disciplinary measures. See also *Thuc.* VIII.84.2., and Xen. *Anab.* II.iii.11.

24. Anderson, *Military Theory*, pp128–9.

25. Compare the Macedonian practice introduced by Phillip II wherein each man carries his needs and wagons are for siege implements and large items only. See also Keegan, *The Mask of Command*, p.65.

26. It is difficult to be absolutely sure whether this was a single or a repeated *anastrophe* which edged the army closer and closer to the valley exit. The Loeb edition may be incorrect in note 1, p.200, where it states that 'the enemy are

gathering upon the hills on one *side* of the valley' unless that side happened to be initially to the rear of Agesilaos' army. Obviously in executing the manoeuvre Agesilaos presents his line to the enemy. See also Lazenby, *Spartan Army*, p.27.

27. Anderson, *Military Theory*, p.66.

28. See also Buckler, *Theban Hegemony*, p.95.

29. Buckler, *Theban Hegemony*, p.78.

30. See Krentz, *Hellenika* I–II.3.10.

31. See Hamilton, *Agesilaos and the failure of the Spartan hegemony*, pp.141–9 for Phoibidas, and pp.167–74 for Sphodrias.

32. See Lazenby, *Spartan Army*, pp.138–43 for a persuasive account of the manouvres at the Nemea.

33. 0555, Army Doctrine Vol. I.

34. 0448, Army Doctrine Vol. I.

35. Lazenby, *Spartan Army*, p.26.

36. See also Sun Tzu VIII.12.2 & 12.3.

37. Anderson, *Military Theory*, pp.126–7.

38. For the Tearless Battle compare Buckler, *Theban Hegemony*, pp.106–7.

39. See Buckler, *Theban Hegemony*, p62.

40. 0439, Army Doctrine.

41. Buckler, *Theban Hegemony*, p.101.

42. See Anderson, *Military Theory*, p.162 for a rational and balanced view of Xenophon's omission.

43. (*Thuc*.V.66.3). See Anderson, *Military Theory*, p 71, for the organisation of Spartan Command structure, but more importantly Part One of Lazenby, *The Spartan Army*.

44. The deepening of the phalanx was tactical and could not have been the deployment of a strategic reserve as suggested in Cawkwell, 'Epameinondas and Thebes', p.261 and Hornblower, *The Greek World*, p.160.

45. Anderson, *Military Theory*, pp.148–9.

46. Buckler, *Theban Hegemony*, states that Agesilaos was in command at Mantineia *contra* Anderson and Lazenby. He does so without any clear evidence. He states: 'The full Spartan contingent was still led by Agesilaos, the real commander of these forces, although Xenophon in deference to the old king mercifully omits all mention of him'. His anti-Spartan bias also leads him further to say, p.218: 'The cavalry also returned to its own phalanx, riding through the herd of fleeing Spartans and allowing them to escape unharmed', a comment further unsupported by sources and giving the impression that only the Spartans were on the right. This flavour of comment is in line with other anti-Xenophon statements such as that in note 44, p.208: 'nor would it be unusual for Xenophon to suppress knowledge of it.'
   It is likely that the Mantineians, in whose territory the engagement took place, were on the right with the three *lochoi* of the Spartans adjacent, the Elians, Acheans and, on the left wing, the Athenians. See also Cartledge, *Agesilaos and the Crisis of Sparta*, p.235.

47. Buckler, *Theban Hegemony*, p.90.

48. 'Pellene' (πελλήνη) in the text of *Hell.* VII.v.10. is surely Pellana, the Doric form of Pellene. Pellene was a small town to the west of Sikyon, whereas Pellana was a perioecic town north of Sparta. Polybios IX.viii.2 states that Agesilaos was already at Mantineia when he heard of Epameinondas' march on Sparta. Xenophon's account seems the more probable.

49. 'Generalship shows itself in preventing the concentration of the enemy's forces. He overawes his opponents and their allies are prevented from joining against him' Sun Tzu XI.54. 'Thus, the highest form of generalship is to balk the enemy's plans. The next best is to prevent the junction of the enemy's forces. The next in order is to attack the enemy's army in the field' Sun Tzu III.3.

50. Buckler, *Theban Hegemony*, pp.55–61.

51. Zaidman and Pantel, *Religion in the Ancient Greek City*, Chapters 1 and 2.

52. Buckler, *Theban Hegemony*, p.62.

53. See Lazenby, *The Spartan Army*, pp.152-6 where a convincing argument is presented concerning the figures and deployment of both the Spartan and Theban battle lines. The explanation of Spartan losses is particularly cogent given Xenophon's evidence. One minor quibble, however, is that the suggested

Theban front of eighty, relying as it does on a presumed total of 4,000 Theban hoplites, does not fit comfortably with the notion of the Sacred Band making up the first three ranks of the Phalanx. Given that this elite corps was at full strength, three ranks of 100 men would satisfy the scenario only if the total number in the Theban phalanx was around 5,000, a not inconceivable number, against the figure of 4,480 plus the 300 *hippeis* for the Spartans.

PART THREE

THE IDEAL COMMANDER

In his fantasy novella about the education and life of Kyros the Great Xenophon outlines all the attributes he would wish an ideal commander to possess. In so doing his own theories on strategy and tactics are made clear.

The *Kyropaideia* and the *Cavalry Commander* are the two works which set out in a systematic manner Xenophon's views on the role of a commander. The former deals with the wider responsibilities expected of a commander-in-chief and his subordinate officers, and places these as essentials to be put in place before the final piece of the jigsaw – action in the field – can be contemplated. The latter details the responsibilities expected of a commander of horse. In the *Kyropaideia* Xenophon pictures the ideal ruler building the ideal state based on Spartan training and education mixed with limited Athenian influences. As an Athenian exile held in high regard by the Spartans, he admired much of his adoptive state's practices. He is, however, quick to point out deficiencies where he sees them, particularly in military matters, and these will be highlighted throughout.

Detachment from direct action is an asset to a commander-in-chief who can thereby receive and send messages, deploy and redeploy forces and react to the changing circumstances of an unfolding engagement while maintaining an overview of the whole. This facility was largely unavailable to commanders within the period of this study who fought within the forces they led. 'Leading from the front' was the order of the day or, if not literally from the front, very near it. Once battle was joined, they could do little to change the initial plan to which the army was committed save at opportune moments of pause within a conflict. In the *Kyropaideia* it is noted that Kyros climbs one of his moveable towers to have a better view of the field of battle (*Kyr.* VII.i.39). In certain circumstances the commander also combined his duties as a leader of men with that of priestly duties and in this Kyros is defined in the *Kyropaideia* in a manner modelled on Spartan kingship. The training for command is inter-linked with the available forces at the commander's disposal, the traditions of their deployment in action either as a unit or in combination, together with a capacity in the commander himself to learn from experience and observation. In Kyros' case we observe the selection of those units to fulfil preconceived roles in his building of an army. This displays Xenophon's own deliberations following direct personal involvement in action or his reflections on the actions of others, particularly those of his hero Agesilaos. Xenophon's monograph on Agesilaos can be taken as the kernel of actuality in the background of the *Kyropaideia*. His opinion was already partly formed. The model for his ideal king was already known to him. He lists the virtues of the good king in his encomium, and in the repetitious summary (Xen. *Ages*. XI), labours the characteristics which he found so admirable in his hero. Xenophon's writings reflect and hint at the changes which were to lead the Greek mode of warfare away from the ritualistic hoplite engagement to one which found important roles for combatants other than heavy infantrymen.

The first half of the fourth century saw subtle changes in the conduct of Greek warfare. These mainly concern the use of cavalry, light armed infantry and mercenaries. Although uncommon, the designation of certain forces as a reserve appeared and was given a definitive role (*Anab*. VI.v.9). The possibilities presenting themselves in the use of mixed forces exercised the minds of commanders particularly when opposing non-Greek adversaries. Lessons were generally quickly learned and, as a result, treatises on military theory appeared (*Aeneas Tacticus*), and teachers of tactics and drill offered their services, e.g., Phalinos, held in high regard by Tissaphernes as an expert in tactics and in the handling of heavy infantry (*Anab*. II.i.7). Warfare for Greeks ceased to be an affair conducted by amateurs as more and more city states undertook serious training for their men and organised specialist corps at public expense. This aspect is dealt with in more detail in the opening pages of Part Two.

Xenophon's writings prove to be a fertile area from which contemporary ideas and examples of practice can be culled. Personal involvement in some of the actions described make his accounts invaluable even if we regret the lack of essential detail at times. With the exception of the fantasy novel *Kyropaideia*, his accounts are essentially essays or memoirs. The *Kyropaideia* itself is a mine of good practice for any commander of the period to study and follow, and details what Xenophon believes to be the essentials to be considered by any in a position of command over others.

He obviously regarded cavalry as underused and potentially more important. He was quick to regret the lack of quality in the Spartan cavalry at Leuktra (*Hell*. VI.iv.10–11) and to revel in the success of the Athenian cavalry prior to the second battle of Mantineia (*Hell*. VII.v.15–16). His own experience gave him examples of its successful use to support his views, notably the action of the allied cavalry from the Asian Aegean littoral which was with Agesilaos on his march south through Thessaly prior to Koroneia (*Hell.* IV.iii.6–9). The fact that later Spartan commanders did not learn from this must have been irksome to Xenophon.

The differing attitudes within Greece to the use of cavalry at this time were the direct products of political and cultural traditions influenced by topography. The huge plain of Thessaly was a natural horse breeding area and riding proficiency was held in high regard resulting in the strongest cavalry force in Greece. To a lesser extent the Theban and Boeotian lowlands lent themselves to cavalry manoeuvres and their citizen cavalry contingents were usually competent, particularly when stiffened by Thessalians. Athens too had learned the effective use of cavalry against Spartan foraging parties in the Peloponnesian War and those who owned horses were proud to serve as cavalrymen. Sparta, however, with its hoplite mess society, eschewed the idea of their better men being used in any capacity other than as heavy infantrymen within the phalanx. This attitude obviously had an effect on the quality of both the cavalry and light infantry they employed. Those who owned horses put them at the disposal of the weaker and less able combatants within the Spartan armies (*Hell.* VI.iv.11). Its very conservatism made it slow to address such lessons in the use of cavalry as had been presented successfully in Thessaly by Agesilaos, and ineptly by the polemarch and hipparch at Lechaion.[1] In this last engagement a striking lesson in the use of light infantry by Iphikrates seems also to have been ignored. Further, Boeotian cavalry action against Spartans at Tegyra and Leuktra brought only a slow realisation that a more capable cavalry arm was an essential (see Part Two for Spartan use of Syracusan cavalry). It is no surprise therefore that Xenophon, the Athenian, living the greater part of his life among Spartans, should perceive the developing advantages of an effective cavalry arm and give his fairy tale hero Kyros his first taste of battle in the van of a cavalry action (*Kyr.* I.iv.20–22) or that the boyhood preparation for war emanated from hunting (*Kyr.* I.ii.10–11).

Xenophon's opinion that hunting was an integral part of a young man's experience prior to war is reaffirmed in his essay on that subject (*Kyn.* I.18) and at length within Book XII of that monograph, though not all hunting was conducted on horseback. His most direct statement from that source (*Kyn.* XII.7–8) makes it clear that the character building involved in the enterprise of hunting provides for the best soldiers and generals. It can be surmised that his views on cavalry were rehearsed regularly with his Spartan friends and it is appropriate that those expressed or implied in his writings should be discussed at this point in terms of what a commander must know to raise, train, equip and use tactically such a force.

Accepting that Xenophon had a predilection for the cavalry arm, having almost certainly served in the Athenian cavalry in his youth, possibly under Alkibiades or Thrasyllos in Asia Minor in 408 BC, and that he foresaw developments which were to prove particularly effective in the Hellenistic period, it is informative to review his treatment of this subject within the *Kyropaideia* and in his other writings.[2] Kyros learned more from experience than from direct instruction, in direct contrast to most Spartan commanders. However, Kyros' empiricism was the product of Xenophon's observation and experience. He also reflects Xenophon's view of the relative importance of cavalry *vis-à-vis* infantry when he instructs the officers of the newly constituted cavalry to select one of their comrades to take over the command of their infantry units (*Kyr.* IV.v.58). This would have been anathema to his Spartan friends.

Cavalry

There is an interesting balance to the description of an army given early in the *Kyropaideia* (*Kyr.* I.vi.10) when Kyros' father implies equal importance in the value of infantry and cavalry. The importance of having cavalry is stressed by Kyros in his statement that, without this arm, no defeat of enemy forces can be safely followed up by troops only effective at close quarters (*Kyr.* IV.iii.5), i.e., heavy infantry. This is almost an echo of Xenophon's own experience (*Anab.* III.iii.8–10). Kyros then moves on to a qualitative level (*Kyr.* IV.iii.7) in wishing to have his own Persian cavalry at least of the standard of the Medes and Hyrcanians, and proposes to create such a force (*Kyr.* IV.iii.8) with protective armour, thrusting and throwing spears. From that point, like all commanders who must take responsibility for the arming, training and provisioning of their men, he develops the argument further by suggesting that, unlike boys in training, the battle skills have already been learned by infantrymen and it is only the skill of horsemanship which needs to be acquired. Horses are already available in Kyros' camp (*Kyr.* IV.iii.9) just as they were for Xenophon himself when he proposed forming a cavalry unit (*Anab.* III.iii.19). If for any reason an action has to be fought in the early stages of their training before this skill is wholly mastered, it would be easy to dismount and revert to infantry practice, declares Kyros (*Kyr.* IV.iii.14). Here, there is possibly an echo of the action of Pasimachos and his dismounted volunteers (*Hell*. IV.iv.10) against the Argives in 390 BC. Again, reference is made to the option of dismounting to conduct an action as infantry (*Kyr*. IV.v.49) implying the advantage of the quicker mobility of mounted forces and the futility of a cavalry force engaging disciplined heavy infantry in battle formation, although this is to be disputed later.

The steady build-up of the cavalry arm continues throughout the account as more and more horses become available (*Kyr*. IV.v.46; V.iv.32; VI.i.26) until a force of 10,000 is realised. After Thymbrara the subjugation of Phrygia, Kappadokia and the Arabians bring additional armour for 40,000 Persian cavalry, and horses in sufficient numbers to satisfy both them and all the allied forces (*Kyr*. VII.iv.16). The description of the procession (*Kyr*. VIII.iii.15–18) numbering 44,000 cavalry, plus undisclosed numbers of additional cavalry forces of the Medes, Armenians, Hyrcanians, Cadusians and Sacians, is no doubt intended to impress the reader in terms of those numbers but also to underline the importance which Xenophon attached to this arm. Finally, at the end of his conquests Kyros is reported by Xenophon to have 120,000 cavalry, a quarter of the number of his footsoldiers (*Kyr*. VIII.vi.19).

Although not directly stated, the question initially to be asked is whether Xenophon is suggesting a significant and flexible force capable of operating as cavalry or heavy infantry as circumstances dictated. Certainly the description of the protective armour of the horses (*Kyr*. VI.iv.1) and the indication that the cavalry is to be used in hand to hand fighting (*Kyr*. VI.iv.16) implies a form of early heavy cavalry modelled on that of the contemporary Persian which was not actually employed in that mode. There are, however, slightly contradictory statements not least in terms of protective armour and the question of the use of the javelin or heavy spear.

The horse itself was to have protection for upper legs, chest and head (*Kyr*. VI.iv.1) and a form of quilted cover over its back which deeply overlapped the sides, giving further protection to the belly (*Peri. Hipp*. XII.8). Such quilting would serve to give the horseman additional grip with the legs in the absence of stirrups. The rider in Xenophon's discourse on horsemanship was to wear a breastplate which also covered the neck and gave mobility to the javelin arm, and a Boeotian style helmet. His throwing arm was covered by a form of greave on the forearm and by skin or metal plates on the inside upper arm which became exposed when lifted for action (*Peri. Hipp*. XII.6). The left arm was protected from shoulder to fingertip by a form of gauntlet (*Peri. Hipp*. XII.5). However, in the *Kyropaideia*, no mention is made of the left arm guard used by cavalrymen and normally expected of cavalry in both Greece and Persia at the time. Rather, the reference to the shields of the cavalry (*Kyr.* V.ii.1) suggests a slightly later development which appeared in Macedonian cavalry where the rider was armed with a shield and a long spear, but whose horse and person was less armoured.

With such protection, in addition to body armour, close engagement with infantry became a realistic possibility for cavalry. The only difference being, that instead of the long spear, one recommendation is made of javelins for use as missiles and for thrusting at close quarters. Xenophon's own preference for javelins of the shorter Persian style over the spear was because the former were stronger and the latter awkward to control (*Peri. Hipp.* XII.12). However (*Kyr.* VI.ii.16), Xenophon has Kyros encouraging his men in the face of some loss of morale by listing the advantages their own army has over its potential enemy, one of which is that the cavalry has given up the bow and the javelin as weapons and is now armed with a single heavy spear with the intention of fighting at close quarters with spear and sword. His officers are similarly equipped (*Kyr.* VII.i.2). This being the case, the allusion to the enemy infantry having difficulties withstanding a cavalry charge (wherein steel is driven by the weight of the horses in the later Macedonian manner) becomes a distinct possibility (*Kyr.* VI.iv.18).

Practice in javelin throwing and close combat with blunted weapons is given detailed treatment (*Peri. Hipp.* VIII.10-11). In war the discharge of a javelin as a missile is recommended to be from long range, the rider rising from his seat by using his thighs, turning his left side[3] to the enemy, and using the forward movement of the horse to give impetus to the throw, releasing his weapon with the point higher than the horizontal plane. The distance gave the rider time to turn in safety and take the remaining javelin from his other hand (*Peri. Hipp.* XII.13). The second javelin could then be used as a further missile or for close quarter thrusting when, hopefully, the enemy line had broken.

Clearly there are tactical options here for a commander to consider and, that commander, in exhorting his men to practice, should lead by example (*Hipp.* I.21). At Thymbrara in the opening action Kyros attacks the enemy flank, personally leading the cavalry, and the fighting is conducted at close quarters (*Kyr.* VII.i.26). However it is noted that in the first battle with the Assyrians, and prior to his building up of the cavalry force, Kyros leads the charge with the infantry and is on foot (*Kyr.* III.iii.62–63). Further, Xenophon states (*Kyr.* VIII.viii.22) that Kyros arms both men and horses with breastplates, stops fighting in terms of skirmishes and introduces hand to hand fighting. This is a portent of the Macedonian method of cavalry use. Indeed, Xenophon under-lines his distinct preference for cavalry when he declares through Kyros that the Persian cavalry was the most efficient section of the army at Thymbrara (*Kyr.* VII.i.46).

An attendant is appointed to each horseman to carry his shield and *kopis* (*Kyr.* V.ii.1) – a curved sword with a single cutting edge employed in a slashing style, the design coming from Iberia and preferred by Xenophon to the straight sword (*Peri. Hipp.* XII.11). On the march these attendants or squires are placed within the column between van and rear and ordered not to change their position.

Other duties expected of the cavalry outside direct engagement are to safeguard systematically the advance of the infantrymen, ensure that provisions are procured for the army from the area of advance and to collect booty (*Kyr.* III.iii.23).

In battle at Thymbrara, Kyros opens his attack leading the cavalry against the enemy flank and, in combination with the heavy infantry which follows him, engages in hand to hand fighting (*Kyr.* VII.i.26). In the ensuing flight of the enemy, it is the cavalry which is active in mopping up the stragglers seeking refuge from both the chariots and mounted militia (*Kyr.* VII.i.28), a clear example of the combined operations of hitherto disparate sections of an army. In the fight against the Egyptian phalanx, Kyros takes them in the rear having ridden round them supported by infantry. It is worth noting that even Xenophon does not allow his imaginary hero to indulge in a charge on the Egyptian phalanx. Instead he orders Chrysantas, a cavalry commander, to attack the surrounded Egyptians from a safe distance using missiles (*Kyr.* VII.i.39). There appears to be slight ambivalence here. If the cavalry was to charge a phalanx it would have to use the long heavy spear alluded to earlier, but the order was to use missiles, implying javelins. We are still not wholly clear which offensive weapon Xenophon seeks to have his imaginary hero adopt for his cavalry, and one can only conjecture that the 'squires' may have carried the spares. Perhaps this was the essence of a mid-fourth century debate which was finally resolved at Chaironeia. Perhaps Xenophon was suggesting both light and heavy cavalry units, although he did not directly state this to be the case (see below under 'On the March'). Indeed, there was no need to attack a surrounded enemy frontally: it was sufficient to pour missiles into the mass from a safe distance. The description of what followed was almost a rehearsal of what ensued at the battle of Carrhae in 53 BC (see Plutarch *Life of Crassus,* XXIV) although with a happier outcome for those who were surrounded. Here

Xenophon's first hand knowledge of the Persian preference for conducting warfare at long range is demonstrated to good effect. However, at Carrhae a camel corps was employed to bring up further supplies of missiles so that the assault could be continuous.

Xenophon has Kyros form a camel corps with two archers on each beast (*Kyr.* VI.ii.8), obviously with a similar tactical intention of distant warfare, but alters the focus for the employment of camels to that of disturbing the cavalry of the opposition (*Kyr.* VI.ii.18) in the same manner that horses were later distressed by elephants until trained out of the reaction. Indeed, his later comments imply a social condemnation of the use of camels, almost as an afterthought (*Kyr.* VII.i.48–49) and, thereafter in his tale, they are given, in his changed opinion, a more appropriate role as pack animals.

Pursuing the topic of cavalry in relation to the training of a commander, it is seen that many of the attributes and responsibilities alluded to in Xenophon's *Cavalry Commander* are those which should already be present within, or be followed by, the commander of any force, large or small, such as piety (*Hipp.* I.1; V.14; IX.8); leading by example and taking pride in the appointment (*Hipp.* I.25; III.13); having natural intelligence (*Hipp.* VII.1) and sound judgement (*Hipp.* VII.5); the capacity to take decisions (*Hipp.* VIII.21; IX.1–2) and those attributes which, if not innate, can be acquired through experience such as maintaining the discipline of men, provisioning of adequate equipment, e.g., horses (*Hipp.* I.3–4; VIII.4); armour for the men (*Hipp.* I.6); knowledge of terrain (*Hipp.* IV.6; VIII.9); the ability to use deception successfully (*Hipp.* V.2–3; V.5–7; V.9–12; VII.13; VIII.18); knowledge of the capabilities of the forces under command (*Hipp.* V.1; VIII.11–14; VIII.21); the setting up of a successful chain of command (*Hipp.* I.8; II.2–3 and 5–7; IV.9); the maintenance of security (*Hipp.* IV.4–5 and 7–10) and knowledge of the enemy (*Hipp.* IV.7 and 16; VII.8). These together with the all important issue of sustaining morale (*Hipp.* I.26; VI.2–6; VIII.22) are the basic elements which Xenophon viewed as being important to any in a position of command. However it is in the exercise of that command that his comments on tactics prove illuminating, involving as they do the items listed above. (See 'Tactics' below.)

Piety

Xenophon is careful to make it absolutely clear that Kyros plans with the approval of the gods (*Kyr.* I.v.14). The nature of his conversation with his father on the importance of omens (*Kyr.* I.vi.1–6) shows him from the outset to be a pious man ready to take his father's advice (*Kyr.* I.vi.44). Through this mouthpiece, Xenophon makes clear the prime importance of first gaining the approval for any action from the gods.[4] The sacrifice he makes prior to his attack on the Armenians (*Kyr.* II.iv.18–19) is made before Kyaxares (his uncle and co-commander) set off for his attacking position and the result is not known until after his departure. Kyros presumably leaves himself uncommitted to action depending on the outcome of the sacrifice. This outcome might not be immediately favourable and in such circumstances no action could be taken until further sacrifice resulted in a satisfactory portent. Such a problem faced Pausanias at Plataia (*Herod.* 9.61–2) when a succession of sacrifices was made before the gods appeared to approve of action, during which time the Spartans suffered casualties.

It can be argued that the commander made a considered tactical decision but required divine endorsement for his course of action. If he failed in battle, other reasons for that failure must be sought. It would be interesting to catalogue those failures in view of the fact that, in the ancient world, opposing commanders would both make sacrifice and after the battle only one could claim that the gods were on his side.[5] Needless to say, Kyros always seems to have the gods' support at the first sacrifice. He has already assumed the role of the familiar Spartan priest king (*Kyr.* III.iii.34) when he wears a garland as a crown and makes sacrifice on behalf of all assembled.

Prior to his invasion of Assyria Kyros indulges in a 'catch all' ceremony in which sacrifices are made, first to the king of the gods, Zeus, then to the remaining gods of the pantheon, with following prayers being offered to the local 'heroes' or demigods for support (*Kyr.* III.iii.21–22). This illuminates what must have been the fairly common practice of Xenophon's time. It is to be regarded as good practice much in the same way that in certain modern liturgies God is first exhorted individually, then in terms of the Holy Trinity, with additional prayers being said through the agency of the Virgin Mary and the dedication saints of the local church, or those associated with the content of the subject matter of the prayers. The presence of army chaplains is no accident in the modern army although they operate under the aegis of the commander and perform a surrogate role in attempting to satisfy the psychological needs of the common soldier.

Personal and direct prayers are made when Kyros prays to Zeus that he can be worthy of the faithfulness that the Medes show to him (*Kyr.* V.i.29). His establishment of a college of magi and his personal example to his peers and subordinates suggest that belief must be reflected through one's actions in life (*Kyr.* VIII.1.23 *et segue*). He also exhorts his men to pray to the gods (*Kyr.* VI.iv.19) while he and his subordinate commanders are involved in sacrifice. Such a sacrifice seems to have taken some time and implies elaborate ceremonial, for servants bring breakfast to them, part of which is offered to the gods (*Kyr.* VII.i.1). The prime purpose may have been religious but in practical terms for the commander such rites reinforced a sense of community within an army and focused attention on him.[6] Essentially the commander's piety and his involvement of the men in his army in ceremonial sacrifices was good for morale.

Morale, Training and Discipline

Xenophon viewed good morale as of prime importance and saw discipline as a foundation on which to build. Just as observance of ritual brought about self-discipline, so the shared imposed discipline of drill and tactical training brought about a sense of well-being and confidence both to the individual and to the group within which that individual served.

However, this had to be done largely through caring and kind words (*Kyr.* II.iv.10; *Hipp.* VI.1–3). In any endeavour he believed that a shared evaluation of the enemy with the army, and an endorsement of the capabilities of his own forces by a commander, would give heart to his men. Thus we see the need on occasion to address the army, as Kyros does at the point of a drop in morale prior to the battle of Thymbrara (*Kyr.* VI.ii.14–20), to reinforce their confidence and display a commander's confidence in his troops. It was essential that the army trusted its commander and he must be careful in what he said to them. If he was not sure of an outcome, he must retain the trust of the men under him by having his opinion aired by others, thereby achieving his end and at the same time maintaining the trust of his followers (*Kyr.* I.vi.19). The commander had to lead by example, enduring the same or more discomfort than his men (*Kyr.* I.vi.25; *Hipp.* I.25) much in the same way that Agesilaos did on campaign (Xen. *Ages.* V.3). In addition, the knowledge that a commander cared for the needs of his men would inculcate loyalty and good feeling (*Kyr.* I.vi.10; I.vi.42; *Hipp.* VI.2–3). That care could be translated to the protection of health. So the location for encamping an army had to be without disease (*Kyr.* I.vi.16; VI.i.23) and Kyros ensured that high quality physicians accompanied him (*Kyr.* I.vi.15). The importance of good health and its

189

maintenance even in peacetime is reinforced by Kyros' establishment of what could almost be described as a National Health Service (*Kyr.* VIII.ii.24–25).

The commander had to plan that sufficient provisions were available for a march. Food, blankets, replacement straps for armour, harness and tools all had to be commissioned. Artisans, such as blacksmiths, sandal and boot makers, carpenters, and the very important engineers who would make good the way ahead, had to be engaged, and necessary inducements given to the accompanying merchants (*Kyr.* VI.ii.25–40).

Eating had to be balanced by exercise, often with the incentive of prizes in order to preserve physical fitness (*Kyr.* I.vi.17–18; *Hipp.* I.26; *Kyr.* II.i.29). Competitive drill and, in modern terms, 'bull' was to be rewarded in the most successful cases (*Kyr.* II.i.22–24) and all rewards are to be given according to merit (*Kyr.* II.ii.20; II.iii.4; III.i.3). There is an even-handedness in all this which is to be admired, but Kyros is aware that jealousy can arise in circumstances when reward or a heightened regard is involved. His antidote for this is to involve the men in action where comradeship is at its best (*Kyr.* III.iii.10). Prior to battle, the rivalry to excel is sharpened by the organisation of a hunt with rewards for the most efficient. Contests are arranged to accompany any sacrifice or festival which may occur (*Kyr.* VI.ii.4–6). The very camp itself is to be organised for the maintenance of morale. Kyros sees that his camp is organised by companies living together thereby promoting comradeship and reliance on one another (*Kyr.* II.i.28) and, more importantly, recognises that by such arrangements, greater cohesion in the battle line will be achieved among trusting friends and intimates (*Kyr.* II.i.27; VI.iv.15). Invitations to dine with the commander are given to those of any rank who prove worthy (*Kyr.* II.i.30).

The imperative which Kyros places on knowing the names of his men is significant (*Kyr.* V.iii.46–50) and suggests a style of command which is not unusual in the modern armies of today, provided that the surname is preceded by the rank. Knowledge of, but not necessarily familiarity with, many of those men serving under him would be usual for a commander of any Greek army. Essentially a citizen levy where most people knew one another and probably had had some part in the appointment for the command of their own army, relationships would be decidedly different from that of the professional armed forces of today which are made up from a much wider community. Greek discipline was founded on the inter-relationships stemming from a close knit community, its ethos, traditions, religious observances and the need to preserve the common good. That commonality of interest served to unify a Greek army and make its members proud to serve and obey instructions without the necessity of the over-riding codes of discipline imposed on the rank and file of modern soldiery. Beyond the confines of the Greek city state the idea of being part of a wider Greek community helped save the southern Balkans from Persian domination in the fifth century despite the fact that most cities Medised.[7] Agesilaos, and Xenophon himself, traded on this concept when in Asia Minor. However, even at the time of Alexander's exploits, the idea of nationhood had not seen fruition and in the *Kyropaideia* the notion of welding disparate nationalities to a common purpose beyond that of merely defeating a common enemy stretches credibility.

The observable elements of morale, courage, self-control, enthusiasm and obedience are to be seen in the attack on the Assyrians (*Kyr.* III.iii.58–64) and at the order to retreat; the discipline arising from the high morale of the men is evident in the swiftness with which they obey and go to their appointed positions (*Kyr.* III.iii.70). Knowing one's position in line or file is further stressed by Xenophon as an essential (*Hipp.* II.8) and the result of not knowing it is emphasised (*Hipp.* II.9).

Xenophon believed that when morale is high action must be sought (*Kyr.* III.iii.14) but when an enemy refuses to fight, an advance right up to their position offering battle with inferior forces will not diminish the morale of that enemy (*Kyr.* III.iii.30). Kyros' decision to march to Babylon in full view of the enemy (*Kyr.* V.ii.31–37) is made on the grounds that to do so will elevate the morale of his own troops and diminish that of the enemy which had already been defeated.

Kyros seeks to improve morale by giving his troops confidence not only in their own abilities, but also in the abilities of their comrades. He does this through a training programme which demonstrates clearly to the men the advantages of physical fitness and the new mode of fighting he wishes them to adopt. Clearly Xenophon believed that discipline and obedience were all-important (*Hipp.* I.24) and that regular arms practice for all, including the commander, was imperative (*Hipp.* I.25).

Kyros goes to the heart of the problem, that of time. He leaves the men no excuse for not training in the new methods by first ensuring that all their personal needs are met and by relieving them of the need to continue practising with bow and spear (*Kyr.* II.i.21). Caring for equipment (bull) is a duty which brings about self-discipline and on a practical level keeps that equipment in a state of readiness and order (*Kyr.* II.i.22). At the same reference all those in command from the leader of five men, to the leaders of a hundred, are to be responsible for seeing that all men under them do their duty. Those forces proving their success see advancement for all ranks as a reward (*Kyr.* II.i.23) and prizes are given for the best disciplined (*Kyr.* II.i.24). No man can come for a meal unless he has had significant exercise (*Kyr.* II.i.29), a ploy to ensure the fitness of the army and to bring about a self-confidence which will be useful in the face of an enemy.

Kyros rewards initiative in training by asking whole units, with their commander, to share his company and evening meal. Such is the captain who introduced a practice whereby half of his men armed with breastplate, shields and clubs fight the other half who rely on missiles picked from the ground. It demonstrated that once the first group had come to close quarters the missile throwers were put to flight and, when the groups exchanged weaponry, the same result occurred (*Kyr.* II.iii.17–18). Proving by example that close quarter combat is highly effective, this system of training is pursued by many other units in the army.

The remainder of Book II is given over to examples of drilling men in different formations from single file to four abreast in marches which include changes of direction bringing the last man in file to the position of leader for the return (*Kyr.* II.iii.21). Examples of manoeuvres are given in the following section and that on 'Tactics'.

On the March and in Camp

The primary concern of a commander is the conservation of his force. Planning for the safety of his men at every turn requires an intelligent man willing to avail himself of all information and opportunities which present themselves to achieve this end. Xenophon shows in both the *Kyropaideia* and the *Cavalry Commander* those matters which need to be considered, the best of tried methods in achieving safe transit through enemy territory and setting up a secure camp. Thus, in using Gobryas as a source of information for the terrain – 'the road is smooth and wide' (*Kyr.* V.iii.36) – and as a guide for the following support force and baggage train, Kyros makes his advance into enemy territory (*Kyr.* V.ii.34–35). There are, however, problems of interpretation. The composition of the advance party he chooses is not wholly clear. He selects the best men and horses provisioned for three days (*Kyr.* V.iii.35) and gives the van to Chrysantas, a cavalry commander. The men with breastplates lead the march because they are the slowest (*Kyr.* V.iii.37) and later, at the same reference, Xenophon mentions light forces. If all are mounted, this implies both heavy and light cavalry and perhaps goes some way to explaining the problem encountered in the arming of the cavalry: heavy cavalry using a long heavy spear or lance and light cavalry using javelins.[8] However, he has infantry ahead (*Kyr.* V.iii.38), followed in turn by camp followers and, thereafter, Persian cavalry ensuring no one fell behind. If his statement (*Kyr.* V.iii.37) that the slowest portion of the force is to lead, i.e., those wearing breastplates, so as not to fall behind had the lighter forces been in the van, it must be assumed that the march is made with some of the men leading their horses and proceeding on foot. This is not a satisfactory scenario unless *Hipp.* IV.1 is taken into account, and the concern for resting both horse and man by alternating riding and walking, is given consideration. Whatever the resolution to this problem may be, it is obvious that Kyros wishes to have his most formidable and best equipped men in the van regardless of the unspecific designation of nationality given. It was customary for an army on the march to have a cavalry screen protecting the infantry, described as following, to be protected both in the van and in the rear, the position given to the Persian cavalry. That apart, the point which Xenophon sought to make is clear. On the march no section is to be allowed to lose contact with their fellows and the cohesion of the whole is to be preserved.

From *Hipp.* IV.2 the argument can be developed further in relation to cavalry on the 'march'. There Xenophon suggests that when a commander is uncertain of the position of the enemy, he should rest regiments of cavalry in turn so that at least a core is retained in readiness for immediate action. For narrow roads the army proceeded in column, but on broad roads such as Kyros was to take, the disposition of a broader front became possible and necessary (*Hipp.* IV.3). The important issue of the delivery of commands is dealt with and the suggestion that these should be given by word of mouth by both file leaders and leaders of half files, rather than by the fairly public means of the herald, ensured concealment of an advance or of an army on the march (*Hipp.* IV.9).[9] However, unless the order was absolutely simple and clear and not liable to misinterpretation in the manner of 'Chinese whispers', success would not be guaranteed. It may well be that such verbal orders were to be given in the manner indicated in the *Anabasis* where the watchword was either passed down the line twice or went from front rank to rear and then returned from the rear to the front rank as a means of checking that all was understood (*Anab.* I.viii.16). Although this may have been a quieter means of delivery than by a herald, it is obvious from the same reference that this was not by any means a silent one.

Of interest is the comment that an advance was less likely to be detected if the orders were not given in writing prior to the event. This implies an eye to security within the forces under command (*Hipp.* IV.9). Again Xenophon suggests that for a quiet and obviously concealed advance the commands should be by word of mouth (*Hipp.* IV.9). All such enterprise is taken with the view of finding and fixing the enemy.[10]

Advancing at night posed some problems. The need to march in silence is stressed (*Kyr.* V.iii.43). Kyros positions himself by the roadside to check on the the progress of the march, and to send messages to those who were lagging behind (*Kyr.* V.iii.53). The inference that the majority are on foot or proceeding at the pace of a marching man is made by the ease with which Kyros can ride up and down the ranks (*Kyr.* V.iii.55) after he has given the order to quicken the pace (*Kyr.* V.iii.54) to Chrysantas in the van. He uses horsemen to deliver the orders (*Kyr.* V.iii.54). Further precautionary measures are taken to secure a safe advance by sending a small force of light infantry ahead of Chrysantas to listen and gather information required to be reported to the officer commanding the van, both parties to be in sight of each other (*Kyr.* V.iii.56). This last point seems dubious unless there was some light from the moon. Advance guards or reconnaissance forces are recommended to be ahead of scouts for the purpose of attack or defence, in the case of discovering enemy forces some distance ahead (*Hipp.* IV.5). This is made with reference to the deployment of the much more mobile cavalry corps, but has a validity for a large mixed force on the move and would give more time to take action to safeguard its security.

A changed order of march is required for daytime. Cavalry are left with the rearguard for protection and the remainder of the cavalry forces is ordered to the van so that if a pursuit is required, Kyros will be in a position to order it, and his forces in a position to meet any attack (*Kyr.* V.iii.57).

Prior to the Battle of Thymbrara Kyros sends patrols and scouts ahead, the latter to the highest points of the country so as to have a better view (*Kyr.* Vi.iii.2). His order of march is different on this occasion because he has the baggage train with him. The preparations for the march are meticulous, with the aim of arriving before the enemy at the place where the provisions for the vast enemy host are being collected (*Kyr.* Vi.ii.23). From this reference to the end of the chapter a detailed list of requirements is given to his men which covers their welfare; twenty days' provisions for an expected fifteen days march, any additional food to be counterbalanced by the loss of an equal weight of blankets; a gradual weaning off the drinking of wine until the body is accustomed to drinking only water; the description of the meats to be taken suggests only those which have been cured in some form or other, certainly the reference to saltiness implies a recognition of the healthy need of this substance in the diet; handmills for grinding grain; medicines for a field hospital; accoutrement replacements and hand tools to keep weapons sharp; wagons to carry the supplies and timber for their own repair and that of the chariots, as well as tools such as shovels and mattocks; pack animals to carry an axe and sickle with their baggage; engineers, smiths, cobblers and supply merchants. Within that list (*Kyr.* VI.ii.27), at the point when he seeks to justify the replacement of wine for water, Kyros reminds his men that when they eat anything boiled it has been prepared with copious quantities of water. Whether or not the recommendation is one of drinking only water which had first been boiled is not clear, but if this is taken to be the case, it is a clear safeguard to health.

An important point is that Kyros makes his first encampment at a short distance from the base camp so that anyone who might have forgotten anything could resolve the deficiency (*Kyr.* VI.iii.1). In this instance Xenophon may be attempting to give an oriental flavour to his novella for the 'short first days march' is considered to be a distinctly oriental practice.

Kyros leads the cavalry in the van behind the patrols and scouts. Where the terrain is flat he has the baggage train move abreast on a wide front behind him so that the phalanx can march in readiness for battle (*Kyr.* VI.iii.2), rather than having the baggage train contained and protected within it. Whether the baggage train would impede the effectiveness of an enemy attack or, more importantly, Kyros' phalanx by this marching order, is conjectural.

When the road narrows, the baggage train is placed within the lines of the phalanx now obviously marching in file, in the formation known to the Greeks as a 'hollow square' (see Parts One and Two for examples). In this order, each company's baggage has its own identifying mark (*Kyr.* VI.iii.4) and travels with its company. It may have been a form of flag, but it did allow men to have access to their requirements without delay. Thereafter the order of march seems to have been forgotten by Xenophon with the sighting of the enemy.

A tactical comparison can be made between the two marches on and past Babylon. With fewer numbers the first approach is made openly, following the first engagement with the Assyrians and the capture of their first and second camps. The reason is one mainly of morale – that a beaten force, when faced by its successful opposition, will deepen in despondency and be reluctant to engage whereas, if left to recover its courage, it will be a greater danger (*Kyr.* V.ii.31–36).

The march is preceded by foraging cavalry, with the main force of infantry and the remainder of the cavalry following presumably in near battle order under Kyros (*Kyr.* V.iii.1). At the same reference an opportunity is taken at this point to give the new Persian cavalry some active campaign practice in riding, by the order that they should join the foraging forces. Quite a number are thrown from their mounts, but others have success and return with booty. At the time of the second march past Babylon, Kyros' forces have grown, and he makes the distinction between the act of marching up to, and that for marching past, the city. The first was in battle order, but the second is a march which entails protecting the baggage train. This means that the march is in long columns with the fighting forces (used as a protection) being diluted (*Kyr.* V.iv.46). It was best therefore to conduct the march some distance from the walls of the city for two reasons; to avoid the chance of a sally by enemy forces at close range (*Kyr.* V.iv.47) and to give the enemy a view of what, to them, would appear to be large forces (*Kyr.* V.iv.48).

The distance from the walls gave time for the marchers to take counter action should a sally be made and made it more difficult for those conducting the sally to do it with the assurance of a safe retreat (*Kyr.* V.iv.49). Kyros further ensures safe passage by arranging that sufficient forces are at hand locally to rebuff any attack.

Light marching order meant being unencumbered by provisions or baggage and this is what is suggested to Kyros by those who wish to come across to his side after his first success against the Assyrians. An unencumbered force would have the facility of overtaking one which had a baggage train forcing it to move at a slower pace (*Kyr.* IV.ii.6).

The organisation of a camp has been dealt with under 'Morale' (*Kyr.* II.i.25) but a more detailed reasoning is behind the arrangements listed (*Kyr.* VIII.v.8).

Kyros' own position is at the centre of the camp, believed to be the most secure position. Circled round him are, first, his most trusted men, then the cavalry and charioteers, in the commonsense knowledge that these forces required additional time to prepare for any engagement (*Kyr.* VIII.v.9). He seeks to avoid the kind of confusion which reigned in the camps of others wherein it was difficult to loose the horses, prepare them for battle, arm and ride through a camp in darkness (*Kyr.* III.iii.27). Targeteers are to the left and right of the cavalry, and archers are to the front and rear of their position (*Kyr.* VIII.v.10). Those armed with large shields encircle the entire force so that a shield wall can be erected in case of attack (*Kyr.* VIII.v.11). These last three groups were to sleep with their arms at the ready (*Kyr.* VIII.v.12).

The 'large shields' pose a problem. Which group has these large shields? It cannot be the Persian commoner infantry who were armed with a small shield at the reorganisation of the army (*Kyr.* II.i.9) in the manner of the peers, and who were forced back by the Egyptian phalanx because of those small shields (*Kyr.* VII.i.34). Nor can it be the newer cavalry contingents, because they are not directly involved in the description of the positioning. No satisfactory solution can be found for this problem other than assuming that Xenophon is thinking of Greek hoplites or has forgotten to mention earlier some forces which possess such shields. Mention is made of hoplites and men armed with large shields protecting the force with a shield wall so that the cavalry could arm safely (*Kyr.* VIII.v.11). Yet, at no time does Xenophon in his treatment of Kyros suggest that hoplites or forces with large shields are present within his army. The only probability of a force with large shields being present at the time of Kyros' assumption of power and reorganisation of the empire was if it came from the Egyptians who chose to stay with Kyros after the battle of Thymbrara and who settled in cities within the interior of the empire (*Kyr.* VII.i.45) or from hoplites from the Greek cities of the Asian littoral.[11] Nonetheless, the picture is clear and makes sound sense as a security measure when viewed with Greek forces in mind, hoplites having large shields capable of protecting much of the body.

The place for encampment when Kyros opposes the Assyrians is concealed from view. That choice is made for psychological reasons more than for the necessity of security which is assured by his method of setting up camp. He seeks to inspire terror in the opposition by a sudden appearance (*Kyr.* III.iii.28). Fires are lit in front of the guards and outposts to give light to the area over which an enemy advance might be made (*Kyr.* III.iii.33) and yet the encamped forces might remain unseen by the enemy (*Kyr.* III.iii.25). Fires are also lit to the rear of the camp in the hope of deceiving the enemy into thinking that the camp lay behind rather than ahead of the fires (see also in Part One, where Xenophon discovered this to be the practice employed by Seuthes). No fires are to be lit within the camp (*Kyr.* III.iii.25). Xenophon even finds a tactical use for outposts in addition to safeguarding their own forces (*Hipp.* IV.10–12). He recommends that they be concealed so as to be safe themselves and to heighten their advantage over an enemy who would be obliged to give support to every advance he might make. They could also be used as a force for ambush if screened by a few readily seen guards in advance of their position and supported by an equally visible second force of guards to their rear. At no time should reliance on information from whatever source dissuade a commander from posting guards in the usual manner (*Hipp.* IV.8).

Secrecy, Spies, non-combative Deception and Intelligence

Operational planning can never be successful, other than by pure accident, unless it is interdependent with some form of intelligence structure. That structure may vary with differing operational needs and a commander must set out his prior requirements for such intelligence gathering so that he can make his plan. The initial outcome may well determine the level and type of force which should be used and that in turn may well alter the type of intelligence requirement. Thereafter, as the plan is developed, there may be a need to amend further those requirements. His officers must know the outcome of such information gathering and any amendments so that, at opportune moments, as sub-commanders, they can take advantage of a developing situation in line with their mission command. Intelligence can be garnered from a wide variety of sources: local populations, prisoners, deserters, spies and observers from one's own forces. There is nothing more profitable in war than deception (*Hipp.* V.9).

Xenophon advocates the use of spies before the outbreak of hostilities and suggests bogus deserters as well as neutrals and merchants who are useful agents because of their ease of movement (*Hipp.* IV.7).

Although not explicitly described as such, and relating more to the control of an empire composed of disparate peoples than to campaigning, Kyros, by his rewards to individuals for any worthwhile information, arranges that he has 'many ears and eyes' on which to rely. Indeed, this was the establishment of a secret service (*Kyr.* VIII.ii.10–12). Throughout the *Kyropaideia*, Kyros regularly consults with his colleague, Kyaxares, and more often with his officers, on important questions throughout the campaign. These discussions are not merely tactical, but often follow on from new information received.

Kyros' question to Kyaxares (*Kyr.* II.i.4) as to his certitude of the number of the enemy and indeed of their coming, is confirmed explicitly from information gathered from people who have come from the area of the enemy and who give the same information. This is followed up by the very pertinent question concerning the fighting methods employed by each subscribing force within the enemy ranks (*Kyr.* II.i.7). The analysis of that information in the light of the disparity in numbers between the armies, leads to the reorganisation and rearming of the Persian forces, which at that time were mainly foot soldiers, and the adoption of hand to hand combat (*Kyr.* II.i.9).

Under the guise of a hunt, Kyros plans with Kyaxares to establish a foothold in Armenia as a base for further action. He is concerned that such a ruse will be believed both by the Armenians and also by those in his own camp (*Kyr.* II.iv.17), obviously with an eye to internal security. Later during the hunt, when Kyaxares and his forces are making their approach, Kyros sends a message secretly to Kyaxares asking him to encamp some distance away from Kyros in order to maintain the deception (*Kyr.* II.iv.21). The officers are only briefed as to the true meaning of their current mission and of the tactics which they will have to pursue, when all forces are in position (*Kyr.* II.iv.22).[12]

On the matter of intelligence collection Kyros is selective in those he wishes to employ.[13] By persuading the Indian envoys to gather information about the enemy whilst at the same time pretending to be on a mission from the King of India to the Assyrians, he effectively promotes deception as well as spying (*Kyr.* VI.ii.2). People in their position were more likely to have access to, and gather, more useful information, than the spies disguised as slaves used by Kyros (*Kyr.* VI.ii.11), whose reports are more in confirmation of information already gathered. The report of the Indians on their return gives Kyros initial news that Croesus has been made commander-in-chief, that huge sums of money are available to him and that Thracians, Kypriots and Egyptians have been hired to join the forces; that all the allies are present together with the Asiatic Greeks. An attempt to form an alliance with the Spartans has been made and the meeting place for the army will be at the River Paktolos where supplies are being collected (*Kyr.* VI.ii.9–11). This is also confirmed by recently taken prisoners.

Rumours can be productive if directed to enemy outposts where, because of their exposed position, limited numbers and distance from the main force, misinformation can be most effective (*Hipp.* VII.13). It is notable that Kyros also uses spies disguised as slaves pretending to be deserters (*Kyr.* VI.ii.11), no doubt for propaganda and dissimulation purposes. The problem here is that Kyros himself could be subjected to similar activities by the enemy and we have no example of any line of enquiry or questioning by which he ascertained the truth of information received from deserters other than by reliance on confirmation from prisoners (*Kyr.* VI.i.25). Most successes in war, and often the greatest, are achieved by deception (*Hipp.* V.11).

Kyros uses Araspas, at the point where he is obligated to Kyros to redeem his good favour, in the position of a spy. He turns the ill repute of Araspas among the Medes and Persians to his advantage by suggesting that Araspas go to the enemy as one who supports their cause, for it is highly likely that they will believe him on the discovery of his bad conduct (*Kyr.* VI.i.39). On his return, Araspas delivers his report on the numbers and plan of the enemy (*Kyr.* VI.iii.18–20). It is on that information that the final plan for the battle is made, together with the information already gathered from prisoners (*Kyr.* VI.iii.6 and 9–11) concerning the identity of the opposing commander, the morale of the troops under him and their distance from Kyros' current position.

Kyros establishes the intelligence architecture as his own, and as the 'clearing house', he has to disseminate the sifted product of the information. He may consult and seek the observations of his officers, but the decision for action finally rests with him. He had no separate intelligence arm which did the 'sifting' for him.

'Operational Art' is the skilful employment of military forces to attain strategic goals through the design, organisation, integration and conduct of campaigns and major operations'.[14] It is at this level that two of the major principles, 'Concentration of Force' and 'Economy of Effort' are given particular emphasis.

Kyros determines both the strategic and tactical planning for the campaign and it is useful to pursue Xenophon's thoughts through Kyros to see if that planning is foolproof for the age in which the planning is outlined.

Tactics

A number of tactical points have already been touched upon in the foregoing sections, particularly in 'On the March and in Camp', and undue repetition of those will not be made here. Rather, an examination of the teaching texts of Xenophon will be made to elucidate points which have not already been covered and which have relevance to Parts One and Two of this volume.

The placement of various sections of the army when in camp has already been noted, and the need for units to be identified by flags or banners so that it could be immediately obvious to the commander that his orders were being carried out. What was not in order must be brought into order (*Kyr.* IV.v.37). With such preparation the first principle of good tactics could be satisfied, i.e., a secure defence. Xenophon emphasises that Kyros, as a tactician, always plans according to the circumstances which obtained at the time (*Kyr.* VIII.v.16), and retains the belief that, quite apart from exercising the normal drill aspects of countermarching and changing formation, it is often good tactics to break up the army into divisions to achieve such objectives as arriving at a location prior to enemy forces (*Kyr.* VIII.v.15).

Perhaps the most telling tactical decision made by Xenophon's imaginary hero is that he elected to have his forces fight at close quarters, hand to hand, unlike his opponents, and had turned his back upon the customary skirmish at a distance (*Kyr.* VIII.viii.22). In Xenophon's terms, this was an understandable position to take as regards infantry, coming as he did from the hoplite tradition, but what was essentially a newer practice was that he required cavalry to do the same.[15] To digress, it is difficult to determine the full effect of the Theban cavalry charge on the Spartan forces at Leuktra. Certainly, the Spartan cavalry was routed and, in collision with their own infantry, caused confusion, but, in stressing their advantage Xenophon does not say anything about a follow up to their initial success against the Spartan hoplites themselves. It could well be that they achieved more success at close quarters against a disorientated adversary than has been reported, prior to the attack of Pelopidas with the Sacred Band and that of Epameinondas with the heavily deepened phalanx, or as is more likely, the Theban cavalry retired to the flank. Again, the writing of the *Kyropaideia* may have been after Second Mantineia where Boeotian cavalry was used unusually as a shock force (see Part Two). Conjectural as this may be, there is no doubt that just as the 'steel at close quarters' unnerved asiatics, so too did the appalling carnage of the Roman method of total warfare at close quarters unnerve the Macedonians in the second century.[16]

To revert to tactics, a wise commander will never take risks (*Hipp.* IV.13), will always attack an enemy's weakness (*Hipp.* IV.14) and will take every opportunity to harass the enemy (*Hipp.* IV.17) particularly when he is on the march. The larger the opposing force, the more likely it is to make blunders, e.g., by scattering to forage or by not maintaining order on the march, at which point it should be attacked (*Hipp.* VII.9). Although relying on intelligence reports, the commander should observe the enemy for any likely mistakes he might make (*Hipp.* IV.16) and be ready to attack (*Hipp.* VII.8). If any advantage is to be gained by attacking the enemy, it should be taken (*Kyr.* I.vi.26) and Kyros' father exhorts him to do so at times when the enemy is in disorder, without arms, i.e., at mealtimes, when asleep and when he, Kyros, is in a strong position unseen by the enemy (*Kyr.* I.vi.35; *Hipp.* VII.12).

In any operation, plans for a safe retreat are important (*Hipp.* VII.10) and the commander needs to be sure that the line of retreat is not impeded by enemy supporting forces (*Hipp.* VII.14). At all times a commander should have knowledge of the terrain (*Hipp*. IV.6), if not from direct personal experience then from those within his army who do possess that knowledge. In attacking a larger force than one's own with cavalry, it must be over ground which is not difficult for horses. Xenophon makes the pertinent point that to fall from the horse in retreat is different from a fall when in pursuit (*Hipp*. VIII.9). The need for reconnaissance, advance guards and scouts have been mentioned above (*Hipp*. IV.5).

As Kyros' force acquires greater and greater numbers of cavalry, so the tactics employed by his army tend to be led more by the thinking in terms of this arm. In turning to the 'Cavalry Commander', plenty of examples of good practice are given, but always in the full knowledge of the capabilities of the mounts themselves *vis-à-vis* the force it was to encounter (*Hipp*. V.1) and this could only be derived from a commander's observation of sham fights (*Hipp*. III.11). Making a large force look small and a small force seem large, concealment and using pre-emptive strikes to deter the enemy from attacking, are recommended (*Hipp*. V.2–3). More flesh was given to Xenophon's argument when he suggested that only at a distance from the enemy would you have both safety and a chance to deceive. Horses crowded together look greater in number but are easily counted when scattered. With grooms intermingled with lances or bogus weapons, the force was bound to look larger than it was, and, if the force was to look smaller, it should be formed in two rows with a gap between each row, that row facing the enemy carrying their spears upright and those behind in concealment (*Hipp*. V.6–7). A similar contemporary deception was suggested by Aeneas the Tactician for guards or patrols of walls and palisades. By marching two or three abreast with the first rank holding their spears against the left shoulder and the others on the right, the appearance is given of a doubling of the force (*Aen. Tact.* 40.6). This last was unlikely to fool anyone and it is to Xenophon's credit that he appears only to deal with realistic suggestions.

Psychology can be used to disturb the enemy's equilibrium. By pretending to be overcautious, the opposition can be tempted into making rash moves or conversely, if regarded by the enemy as being a risk-taker, a commander, by doing nothing and merely making a pretence of possible action, can throw the enemy command into doubt (*Hipp*. V.15).

A commander can also use psychology to improve further the confidence of his men. A very important point is made in the recommendation for the delegation to the ordinary soldier of responsibility to fill the ranks of a file. Once the commander and his officers have chosen the file leaders from those they considered strong, resolute and well motivated, and also the rear rank members of a file from the older and more experienced men, the file leader should choose the man who was to take station behind him. Thereafter, each successive man should do the same from men in whom they have confidence (*Hipp.* II.2–4). This advice would be equally applicable to infantrymen and may have sprung from Xenophon's own direct experience or from his observations on Spartan practice. The fact that he goes into such detail here and in the succeeding section of Book II suggests that it was not common practice and his words (*Hipp.* II.6) confirm it; when Kyros appoints the officers of his newly formed cavalry, he requires them to take responsibility for the appointment of their successors (*Kyr.* IV.v.58). The important issues are confidence and the clear passage of the word of command through the ranks.

The employment of mercenaries is suggested (*Hipp.* IX.3) in the context of cavalry, as a means of inculcating rivalry between them and those serving under the levy. This was directly associated with the means of improving Athenian cavalry, but bears out Xenophon's experience and is applicable as a way of improving discipline in any force by virtue of examples of practice. He follows this with a provocative comment (*Hipp.* IX.4) which is in direct contradiction of *Hell.* VI.iv.11, where he berates the Spartans for the means by which they raised their cavalry forces before the debacle of their involvement at the battle of Leuktra, but is in support of his idol, Agesilaos, who had earlier used cavalry raised from the Asian Aegean littoral in successful actions on his march south through Thessaly prior to Koroneia (Xen. *Ages.* II.5). However, at the time of his writing of the *Cavalry Commander*, Sparta's loss of manpower made reliance on mercenary or freed helot forces a normal practice. It may well be that the Spartan cavalry arm was improved by the necessary practice of hiring mercenary cavalry, but Xenophon's evaluation of its worth is not borne out by the evidence except in the case of Syracusan forces.[17]

Again, the knowledge of terrain is repeatedly emphasised in the tactic of feigned retreat which led enemy forces, through over-confidence, on to unfavourable ground where they would fall into disorder so that an attack might be made (*Kyr.* I.vi.37). The inference of the following section (*Kyr.* I.vi.38) is that every commander must be ready to invent and create new tactics. This last is an important comment within Xenophon's writings because it suggests an open mind, readily amenable to change and always looking for improvements and new ideas. It is endorsed through the mouth of Kyros' father (*Kyr.* I.vi.38) with the analogy to the practices of performer/composer musicians who play the works of others and also create new compositions.

In this vein may fall his suggestion, possibly borrowed from a purported Theban practice, that cavalry with infantry become a formidable force, those on foot being screened from the view of the enemy when within the ranks of the cavalry or to its rear (*Hipp.* V.13). Such infantrymen, he recommends, should be made up of those who were most bitter against the enemy (*Hipp.* IX.7). Obviously such a suggestion must relate only to light infantry possessing greater manoeuvrability and the ability to operate in open order. A deceptive tactic Xenophon outlined for use when cavalry forces on both sides had parity, was to divide the forces into two units, one to follow the other thus disguising the total number of cavalry committed to the action. On close approach to the enemy the rear unit should wheel to come into line just prior to the charge, thus gaining an element of surprise which would give them an advantage (*Hipp.* VIII.17–18). Both divisions should also have infantry in concealment behind them to make the attack even more effective.

The choice of appropriate forces is a skill which no commander can neglect. Xenophon is quite explicit in his advice. When expecting to win, use the whole strength of forces available (*Hipp.* VIII.11); when expecting to lose, use only a small force in attack to cover the retreat of the main body (*Hipp.* VIII.12 and 15–16). However, that small force should be composed of the best men available, those who were physically and mentally fit and who could best extricate themselves from engagement with relative safety. This could be assisted by sham ambuscades to delay further the pursuit of the enemy. Xenophon criticises the Athenian Iphikrates for his use of inappropriately sized forces against the withdrawing Thebans. He committed all his cavalry to an operation over difficult terrain for a large force. Fewer would have sufficed and twenty men would not have been lost (*Hell.* VI.v.52).

Living off the resources of the enemy is essentially a fundamental tactic for survival and, when it can be done, is an ideal formula for success, but is not a good tactic to adopt in allied territory (*Kyr.* III.iii.15). Similarly, a knowledge of the resources of an area is useful in maintaining a constant supply of provisions for an army by the regular employment of foraging expeditions (*Kyr.* VI.i.24). The denial of resources to the enemy is fundamentally important in any campaign, and to reach a supply in advance of the enemy is not only beneficial to one's own forces but is a blow to the morale of the enemy (*Kyr.* VI.ii.23). Thus the advance of Kyros' forces threw the Assyrians off-balance. Similarly, an advance into enemy territory is to take to the offensive and is a positive move (*Kyr.* III.iii.14). The campaign in Armenia sees Kyros living off the land with some success, and using cavalry to gain possession of provisions by means of foraging (*Kyr.* III.iii.23).[18]

Establishing forward positions in strength with a fort is regarded as important when it is well supplied with water (*Kyr.* III.ii.11), just as occupying heights is presumed an advantage, although no mention of the availability of water comes into the argument at this point (*Kyr.* III.ii.4).

Capturing fortified positions already in the hands of the enemy is another matter. Kyros proved fortunate on Gobryas' defection,[19] for when he personally inspects the fortifications he notes their strength and that there is evidence of a plenitude of supplies available to the incumbents (*Kyr.* V.ii.4). Before he is finally persuaded of Gobryas' integrity, he takes the precaution of sending scouts and a portion of his accompanying forces ahead. Even when he enters the fortress the gates have to be left open, thus securing an avenue of retreat in case of treachery (*Kyr.* V.ii.6). The first principle of any commander is his own security and thereby that of his forces.

When on the boundaries between Syria and Media, Kyros' attack is made on the weakest of the three forts (*Kyr.* V.iv.51). Xenophon makes no comment on why this choice of action is made, but by implication suggests that this weakens the resolve of the remainder so that the second is captured by intimidation and the third persuaded to surrender – a suggestion that it is best to tackle that which has the possibility of a quick resolution and so bring the psychological forces into play which can deliver the totality of the objective. It was a well known fact that attacking a strongly fortified position which had a sufficiency of supplies could take months to reduce.

The successful capture of a fort by employing the services of the disaffected Gadatas was the result of the example to him of Kyros' good treatment of Gobryas and the promise of similar treatment for services rendered. Gadatas' involvement in the deception, which led to him being accepted as a helper in the defence of the fort, gave him the means by which he could take control of it from within at the approach of Kyros' forces, and pass it into the latter's hands. Thus the problem of direct assault was avoided once more and is indicative of the preference to avoid siege warfare in the Greek world at that time. It was regarded as better to take a fortified position by ruse or deception rather than by direct assault. With the notable exceptions of the sieges of Plataia 429–7 BC and Delion 424 BC, it was not until the time of Phillip and Alexander that siege warfare came fully to be within the accepted technological compass of Greek armies and this, by virtue of the Syracusan example, was learned in turn from the Carthaginians. Even Aeneas Tacticus' writings were based upon the premise of defence rather than attack.

The capture of Sardis is achieved by tactical deception.[20] Giving every impression to Croesus' men that he is preparing to make an assault on the city walls by the setting up of his engines and preparation of scaling ladders, Kyros sends a small mixed force of Persians and Chaldaeans to climb the steepest approach to the citadel at night. They are guided by a Persian who has knowledge of a route derived from his time as a slave to one of the acropolis guards (*Kyr.* VII.ii.2–3). With its capture the defenders of the city walls leave their posts and Kyros makes an unimpeded entry. The inference is that the strongpoint of the city was not within the walls but was part of the outer defences and, because of the precipitous nature of its natural position, was less well guarded, a factor which should be appreciated by all who hold command.

Babylon proves to be a different problem and its capture is the second climax of Xenophon's epic. It is therefore treated in more detail than actions elsewhere and is instructive not only in tactics and manoeuvre, but also of the attitudes taken to civilian populations by a conquering force of the time. The feat of surrounding the whole city, as would seem to be suggested (*Kyr.* VII.v.1), is a staggering concept even with the vast forces which Kyros now had with him. If the word of Herodotus is to be accepted, and in this case there is no reason to disbelieve him, a circumference of approximately forty miles is too great for a controlled investment of this nature to be made. Lines of communication would be stretched beyond effectiveness, reactions to enemy sorties would be difficult and the manoeuvre described (*Kyr.* VII.v.3–6) impossible for an army of such size and only feasible with a much smaller force. However, as we are dealing with fiction, the mixture of exaggeration and possibility must be accepted and the manoeuvre itself scrutinised.

On completion of his survey of the fortifications, Kyros is given information from a deserter that, because his line appears weak, the Assyrians intend to make a sortie as he withdraws from the proximity of the walls. Thus, for greater security, he seeks by manoeuvre to double his depth and shorten his line.

The solution proposed in Appendix I of the Loeb edition of the *Kyropaideia* is not wholly satisfactory. The assumption that the 'poorest' are light-armed troops is convenient, but is conjectural. The references for the manoeuvre are always to the phalanx and by implication to what were regarded as heavy infantrymen. What Xenophon was describing was a manoeuvre not dissimilar to that used by Agesilaos to extricate his army from a weak position (*Hell.*

VI.v.18–19) and with the same intention of an ordered withdrawal (see Part Two). Nowhere is mention made of light armed troops other than in relation to their position with the cavalry on the wings. This is not to deny the existence of other light infantry, but their place would not be within a phalanx or necessarily stationed behind a phalanx, and Xenophon makes it clear that, on the completion of the *anastrophe*, the depth of line of the phalanx was doubled. Indeed Kyros' order is made to the heavy infantry only, with no mention of auxiliary forces. Men within each phalanx would not take heart from a doubling of their depth unless it was in terms of other heavy infantry and certainly not if two formations of light infantry were sandwiched between them. The mention of the poorest being between the bravest comes from the fact that, with the ranks of the wing phalanxes being reversed on completion of their march, the bravest and most eager are to the front and rear of the new doubled formation, with the competent but less eager and therefore 'poorer' hoplites being within the body. Any argument suggesting that a phalanx would be made up of mixed forces would be counter to the lifting of morale described as resulting from the manoeuvre, and only possible if one group of heavy infantry came into close contact with another. Quite obviously those hoplites 'poorer' than the best could still be good soldiers, and, when placed in the middle of the doubled formation, would be less inclined to lose heart and flee if supported by the calls of more resolute men to their rear. If one pursued the case of which men would be deemed the poorest in Kyros' army, it would be those who had been captured and dispossessed of their weapons and served now as slingers (*Kyr.* VII.iv.14–15), useful in their own terms but held in little regard. However, quite the opposite attitude prevailed in Xenophon's personal experience when, due to a lack of long range missile throwers, Rhodians who were skilled in the art of sling shot were offered special treatment if they volunteered to become slingers (see Part One) (*Anab.* III.iii.16–18). However, in reviewing the battle line for Thymbrara, spearmen and bowmen were placed between the front line and the veteran reserves but for differing reasons, and this may have given the Loeb editor the idea for what would have been an impracticable solution.[21]

Having completed this change in battle line Kyros first retires and then moves off to the right, initially adjacent to the city wall, in a series of very short marches in which he has the army face left towards the city walls from time to time in case of sorties. When clear of effective missile range the march becomes continuous until camp is reached.

The completion of the survey leads Kyros to propose a siege in the knowledge that the fortifications are too strong to assault with any hope of success. With so many in the city the hope is to bring the enemy to surrender through starvation (*Kyr.* VII.v.7). However, Chrysantas points out that the broad river flows through the city and the plan is made to divert its flow (*Kyr.* VII.v.9–26). Huge ditches are dug with the displaced earth being used to create a protective rampart on the Persian side of the ditch. Large towers for observation purposes are built on foundations of palm trees for security, in case the earth wall breaks and the river enters the ditch. The work is completed prior to a Babylonian festival and, with the Assyrians viewing all this activity with contempt, all is ready for the decisive move. This 'contempt' is obviously further encouraged by Kyros' division of the army into twelve parts, each with the responsibility of doing sentry duty for a month of the year. This persuades the Assyrians to believe that he accepts the necessity for a long siege and they, in their knowledge of how well provisioned they are, have no worries. Such is the deception a good commander must foster to divert an enemy from his main purpose.[22] On the night of the festival, with the Assyrians deemed to be drunk, asleep and certainly not under arms, the Persians and allies gain entry to the city via the river bed after the river has been diverted to the ditches.

In case of attack by missiles from roof tops, a problem common to forces attacking cities, materials for torches are taken by Kyros' men to set fire to the houses built of highly combustible materials (*Kyr.* VII.v.22–23). See also under 'Tactics' in the Part One for Xenophon's similar action against the Drilai.

With the city taken, Kyros orders his cavalry to patrol the streets killing any who are found outside and using those who speak Assyrian to issue orders that all should remain indoors. Thus the establishment of control of the civilian population is achieved (*Kyr.* VII.v.31). With the king dead, the Assyrians surrender the citadels to Kyros who issues proclamations for the surrender of all arms. Anyone found with a weapon in their home is to be killed along with all other occupants (*Kyr.* VII.v.34). Kyros placates the gods with gifts (*Kyr.* VII.v.35) and distributes property to those who merit reward. The inhabitants are ordered to continue to work their land and many are apportioned to the army as servants (*Kyr.* VII.v.36). Such was the lot of the conquered populace. The necessity to protect the agricultural product was such an important issue that early on in the war an agreement had been entered into between Kyros and the Assyrian king to avoid damage to farms by either army (*Kyr.* V.iv.24–25). This agreement did not, however, include livestock (*Kyr.* V.iv.28).

Reading from signs what an enemy was doing and acting upon it was important and necessitated an immediate reaction. The large reconnaissance body of Assyrian cavalry, which seems to have had the intention of capturing a Persian lookout point (*Kyr.* VI.iii.12–14), is balked by the sending out of Hystaspes with a cavalry regiment to threaten action in support of the position, with the codicil to his orders that he must not pursue the enemy over unknown terrain. A tell-tale sign of a significant force being in the vicinity is that of clouds of dust rising (*Kyr.* VI.iii.5) and this alerted a commander to danger.[23]

Prior to the battle of Thymbrara, Kyros achieves operational advantage over his enemy and is in a position of moral domination where the enemy, on its own, can neither fight effectively nor escape. He achieves this by *sequencing* a planned series of objectives; the continuous winning over of the loyalty of sectors of the enemy's source of manpower; establishing training programmes in the new mode of combat; building special forces; inculcating a high order of discipline; achieving a position of psychological advantage over the enemy after the first battle; capturing and establishing strongholds within enemy territory; sustaining lines of communication; using the resources of the occupied country to provision his forces. The *tempo*[24] is faultless, but there comes a point in every campaign when a commander must face the possibility of having an *operational pause*[25] because he has reached a *culminating point.*[26]

Kyros reaches his culminating point and an 'involuntary' operational pause, largely because his campaign had exceeded the policy objective of the Grand Strategy: to thwart the Assyrian plan to invade and conquer Media (*Kyr.* I.v.2). He is now at a crossroads; whether to withdraw his forces and return home leaving only garrisons on the borders to ensure security in accordance with that strategic objective, or to pursue the outright conquest of Assyria within terms of a changed strategy. Much of *Kyr.*V.v is devoted to the patching up of the differences between Kyros and his principal ally Kyaraxes which could have threatened a serious breach in the command structure and, *Kyr.* VI.i.6–24, regarding the debate on whether to continue hostilities or disband the forces.[27] The points made in that discussion are pertinent and are made in the context of a meeting of generals: increased security if the alliance is maintained (*Kyr.* VI.i.7); the advantage of waging war within enemy territory using his resources; increased security if the alliance is maintained (*Kyr.* VI.i.10); the disadvantage of allowing an Assyrian recovery (*Kyr.* VI.i.11) and Kyros' summation (*Kyr.* VI.i.12).

With winter approaching and the possible lack of supplies, it was necessary to take the decision to disband the army rather than be forced by circumstances to do so, or to maintain their control of the area by quickly capturing fortified positions and building additional ones themselves to store provisions (*Kyr.*

VI.i.14–16). Siege engines are built and it is implied that it took some time to fulfil the plans. ('Since Kyros realised that a long time would be required for the execution of these designs . . .' *Kyr.* VI.i.23 and 'Thus, then, Kyros was occupied.' *Kyr.* VI.i.25). Presumably the following spring is the point at which Kyros heard from deserters, to be confirmed by prisoners, that the Assyrian king had travelled to Lydia with an abundance of wealth (*Kyr.* VI.i.25). He makes no attempt to share with his forces his conclusion that the Assyrian king has gone to raise another army with this hoard, but leaves them to believe that the king is seeking a place of safety for his wealth through fear (*Kyr.* VI.i.25–26). He embarks on preparations for the coming conflict.

At this point (*Kyr.* VI.i.27–30), and thinking tactically, Kyros forms an additional specialist force of chariots wherein a redesigned vehicle of strong timbers in the form of a turret on a broad wheel base is designed and made. Each of the drivers is provided with armour which covers all but the eyes, and, with long scythes protruding from the wheels, his intention is to have the drivers charge the enemy line with the object of causing a breach and provoking mayhem. Xenophon gave Kyros the credit for the invention of this 'tank' which was the Persian model in Xenophon's own time and which replaced the much flimsier vehicle which had hitherto only been of use in skirmishing. Abradatas, who is to command the chariots, further improves on the original design and has his chariot drawn by eight horses, each pair yoked to one of four poles (*Kyr.* VI.i.50).

Seeing this gives Kyros the idea of having his moveable towers drawn by sixteen oxen yoked to eight poles, thus making it easier for each beast to pull a lesser weight than it would have done when hauling only baggage (*Kyr.* VI.i.54). The towers themselves with their battlements and galleries could carry twenty men, presumably archers and javelineers, and he conceives of them as giving additional protection to his infantry (*Kyr.* VI.i.53) obviously by firing over their heads into the enemy. One of the towers gives him the opportunity to have an elevated view of the battlefield in the actual battle (*Kyr.* VII.i.39), a facility unusual to a commander of Xenophon's time, but indicating the realisation that a commander needed such opportunities to reassess the effectiveness of his deployments.

Some plans in preparation for an engagement have already been dealt with, e.g., that based on the deception of the hunt in the invasion of Armenia (*Kyr.* II.iv.16). In the action against the Chaldaeans the planned feigned flight of the Armenians, now allies of the Persians and Medes, led the pursuing Chaldaeans into hand to hand conflict with the advancing Persians (*Kyr.* III.ii.10) armed as they are with shields, chest armour and the slashing swords issued to the infantry at the reorganisation of the army (*Kyr.* II.i.16). It is after making an evaluation of the quality of his forces (*Kyr.* III.iii.9) that Kyros comes to the decision that he can now move on to the offensive against the Assyrians, and that without delay, but not before he has clearly established the chain of command and method of communicating orders throughout the entire command structure (*Kyr.* III.iii.11–12). An interesting disagreement of the timing of an attack takes place between Kyaraxes and Kyros when preparing for the first battle against the Assyrians (*Kyr.* III.iii.46–47), the nub of which is that the former is eager to attack the enemy as he comes out of camp before its numbers exceed those of the Medes, Persians and allies, while the latter looks to the psychological effect of defeating as many as possible at this opportunity. This would avoid the need to lay plans for another engagement with the Assyrians who would excuse their defeat as one of opportunism against reduced forces, and would therefore suffer no loss of morale.[28]

Both views have merit, but that of Kyros carries greater weight for the following reasons in addition to the two already given above. A decisive victory at this point would have avoided the long term logistics of maintaining an army in theatre in enemy territory. This would have been the first direct experience an Assyrian army would have had of hand to hand conflict, and therefore the best opportunity of inflicting the greatest physical and psychological damage. The balance of greater numbers against a new mode of fighting was in Kyros' favour. Despite this, Kyros is persuaded to attack before he is satisfied that enough of the enemy has emerged from the defences (*Kyr.* III.iii.56).

The action which follows proves his point, but a significant number of the enemy is able to withdraw at night (*Kyr.* IV.i.8). Another disagreement on tactics ensues between the joint commanders and here Kyros must be given support for his desire to instigate a pursuit. He was, at that time, without cavalry of his own and only by persuasion did his uncle reluctantly offer only volunteers in support (*Kyr.* IV.1.21).

Without Kyaxares on this occasion, the enemy is overtaken, and in the overwhelming victory against an unprepared enemy, Kyros derives the full credit from his own forces and allies, but more importantly from the large number of volunteer Medes.

Such were the tensions within a joint command which in this case continues almost up to the final battle. It also persuades Kyros to mould his forces further to become self-sufficient and is behind his decision to form his own cavalry arm

(*Kyr.* IV.iii.7). It can be seen, however, through Xenophon's story, that Kyros gradually assumes the role of supreme commander, adapting, adjusting and never applying exactly the same tactics to similar situations.

The Final Battle

The march, placement of lookouts, their protection and intelligence prior to the Battle of Thymbrara have already been reviewed. The point at which the analysis resumes is at the planning of the line of battle. Here, and in the description of what follows, we find Xenophon theorising on aspects of deployment and tactics in a wholly fictional scenario. In his speculations, echoes of his own experience emerge, some of which are dealt with in Part One, such as the presence of the Egyptians with their long wooden shields (*Anab.* I.viii.9), the open 'tile' or gamma formation adopted by Tissaphernes which may have been, by inversion, the springboard for his description of Croesus' deployment in this imaginary battle (*Anab.* III.iv.14) and the helplessness of unsupported heavy infantry when surrounded by an enemy using missiles and who would not come to close contact (*Anab.* III.iii.8; VI.iii.6–9; VII.viii.18).

Kyros is especially eager to know of the Egyptian formation, recognising that heavy infantry of the hoplite variety will pose him his biggest problem. The report of Araspas suggests a front of four and a half miles for the enemy excluding the Egyptians, a fact that he has been anxious to establish on Kyros' account (*Kyr.* VI.iii.19). Araspas mentions that they cover forty stadia and are drawn up thirty deep. Given the space of three feet for each combatant, four and a half miles seems realistic for this force, but the addition of the Egyptians drawn up a hundred deep with a force of 10,000 men, extends the line almost another three quarters of a mile at least. A front of over five miles was beyond the experience of Greek warfare, but shows that Xenophon was more realistic in terms of Asiatic warfare than his contemporaries. Such a front is more akin to near modern warfare and it denies the immediacy of Kyros' reactions to the moves on the enemy's part, particularly as he takes part in the opening exchanges. Nonetheless, credibility aside, the question to be asked is, does Kyros make his dispositions because of, or in spite of, the enemy's order of battle? Are his plans in this imaginary engagement a reaction to those of his enemy's dispositions or did they have added merit?

Kyros' comment at *Kyr.* VI.iii.20 leads us to suppose that he already has a plan in mind and that he only needs confirmation of the enemy's intentions to adopt it. However, in reality he cannot have had any idea of the enemy's intention of manoeuvre until battle was joined, only his reported intention, and this is where the qualitative nature of intelligence proved its worth. Xenophon is suggesting that by reading the enemy's intentions one can forestall them. This may have been the case when circumstances were more obvious than those in which we are presently engaged, and to read a battle line backed by the obvious opinion that the aim was to outflank Kyros' forces, is stretching credibility. To have knowledge of the disposition of a battle line is important in assembling one's own specialist troops against those that they could operate most successfully but to predict their manoeuvre is almost impossible unless the enemy deals in well-tried, unchanging formulaic practices. The truth of the matter lies in the fact that Kyros is waiting for the opening moves of the battle to be made by the enemy before responding (*Kyr.* VII.i.23).

In his planning Kyros sought, through intelligence, to ascertain the *centre of gravity*[29] within the enemy. Hitherto, that centre of gravity might well have been described as Babylon itself at a strategic level, but, with the appearance of yet another army, it has reverted to operational level and it can be seen that Kyros rightly makes his focus that of neutralising the effect of the Egyptians in the coming engagement. He is looking for *decisive points*[30] at which attacks can be made, leading to a position of ineffectiveness for the Egyptian forces. The length of the opposing front suggests very forcibly that Croesus is seeking to enfold him with his wings and destroy him on the anvil of the Egyptian phalanx in a manner not dissimilar to the Macedonian principle. The answer to this can only come from holding the centre and achieving an early defeat of the enemy's wings and to this end Kyros makes his plans.[31]

His first thought is to have his men in absolute readiness for battle. He ensures that equipment is in good order and that both horses and men are well fed (*Kyr.* VI.iii.21). Kyros is of the opinion that only the front rank of a phalanx can be effective in hand to hand combat, a truism, but denying the inexorable weight given to the formation from the men behind. He orders a formation only twelve deep (*Kyr.* VI.iii.21–23) on the grounds that he will have spearmen in support. This is a category he abolished on the reorganisation of the army, but which makes a surprise reappearance here. Behind them come the archers (*Kyr.* VI.iii.24). Behind these he places the veterans as a reserve, with the light infantry being placed to their rear in support, with further bowmen. The idea is that each unit can be of mutual assistance to the other and that he can bring as many men as possible into immediate contact with the enemy (*Kyr.* VI.iii.24–26). An order is given to encourage those in front and to kill any who attempt retreat (*Kyr.* VI.iii.27). For its time this is a strange formation, but it has a certain logic to it, with those who deal in missiles firing over the heads of their comrades. In addition, he has the moveable towers with the missile throwers positioned immediately behind the rearguard phalanx, with the baggage train placed to their rear (*Kyr.* VI.iii.28–29). Further behind yet, in another rank, come the vehicles carrying the womenfolk to add further density to the formation and to cause any attempted encirclement to make a wider circuit thus thinning the enemy line (*Kyr.* VI.iii.30). Another intention of creating such a deep formation is to give concealment to the forces he has placed behind this last rank in the hope of duping the enemy into an ambush. Two *morai* of infantry and two of cavalry under their *chiliarchs* (cavalry commanders) are stationed there, presumably with the cavalry on each wing (*Kyr.* VI.iii.31–32). The camels are placed under the command of Artagersis, one of the infantry chiliarchs, obviously away from the horse of the cavalry (*Kyr.* VI.iii.33). Finally the chariots are arranged as a screen to the entire force with one hundred in advance of the front line under Abradatas and the remaining two hundred placed in file on both flanks. The horses of this arm are given the protection of side armour (*Kyr.* VI.iv.1). The general appearance of Kyros' host is one of crimson, an obvious echo of the scarlet uniform of the Spartan army.

With these dispositions his plan of attack is made clear (*Kyr.* VI.iv.18). It was his intention to charge the enemy on both flanks, with chariots and cavalry driving home spears using the weight of the horses, thus causing a breach which the supporting, following and enveloping heavy infantry could exploit at close quarters. For the time this was an uncharacteristic use of cavalry, but was being thought of by master tacticians such as Xenophon, Epameinondas and Phillip of Macedon. The spears carried by Kyros' mounted officers had shafts made of cornel wood (*Kyr.* VII.i.2), a material he recommended for a javelin (*Peri. Hipp.* XII.12) while at the same reference he seems to have prefered the javelin to the spear. One can only hope that this ambivalence in choice was finally resolved. The focal point of the command position is given its first obvious reference by the eagle with outspread wings, a detail which has eluded Xenophon's narrative until this point (*Kyr.* VII.i.4).

On the advance, which took a distance of twenty stadia, or about two and a half miles, Kyros halted his forces three times, no doubt to check on its order and to give his battle-ready troops rests in order to conserve their strength (*Kyr.* VII.i.4–5). At this point the enemy is within sight and Croesus brings his centre to a stop so that his wings can execute the manoeuvre for an encirclement, a logical ploy assuming that his centre still has an overlap on each of its new wings. Kyros continues his forward movement (*Kyr.* VII.i.6) with his dense rectangular formation and, by doing so, although not mentioned by Xenophon to whom it may have been obvious, causes the enemy wings to move further away from their own centre in order to avoid early and unprepared contact with Kyros' wings. In other words, Kyros' forward movement causes the enemy wings to seek extra space to finalise their gamma formation in conjunction with their centre, a distance which is crucial to mutual support. That increase in distance is observed and Kyros gives his final orders to each commander as he passes along the line. The advance of Kyros' centre slows (*Kyr.* VII.i.8), no doubt to give a little extra time and to upset Croesus' momentum. With Kyros now on the right wing of the concealed forces at the rear, Croesus signals his wings first to halt and face inwards towards their enemy and then to advance.

The reference to the small tile surrounded by the large is apt (*Kyr.* VII.i.24) but is slightly misleading in the Loeb edition.[32] It deals with the perimeter of a tile shape and neglects depth. The larger Assyrian and allied forces describe three sides of the *outline* of a tile encompassing a much smaller but *solid* Persian tile, the flanks and concealed forces to the rear of which are the engineers of Kyros' victory, as is described below.

Kyros' next order effectively has his previously file ranked chariots face left on the left flank and right on the right flank thus coming into lines respectively facing each of the enemy wings (*Kyr.* VII.i.25). The paean is sung and the battle cry to the god of war Enyalos raised (*Kyr.* VII.i.26). This is the signal for the charge as it had been in Xenophon's own experience (*Anab.* V.ii.14), but without mention of a call from the *salpinx*. The battle opens with Kyros' cavalry attack on the flank of the enemy's left wing which is rolled up by the quick support of the enveloping movement made by the infantry (*Kyr.* VII.i.26). A similar attack is made on the other wing by Artagersis whose use of the camels throws the enemy cavalry, acting as a screen to the flank, into confusion. At the centre Abradatas smashes through the enemy chariot screen but is killed when pressing his attack against the Egyptian phalanx (*Kyr.* VII.i.32). This is the only reference which confirms that the Egyptians are in the centre. Abradatas' death is partly attributed to his only being supported in that charge by his messmates (*Kyr.* VII.i.30), the remainder of the charioteers having gone off in pursuit of the fleeing enemy chariots. Although disruption is caused to a section of the Egyptian phalanx, the main body pushes the Persians back and a comparison is made between the effectiveness of hand to hand fighting in Kyros' manner, with slashing swords against a modified but identifiable hoplite phalanx. The phalanx is winning this meeting hands down, albeit with longer than normal spears and large shields. Was this the kind of thinking which led Phillip of Macedon to make the *sarisa* the normal equipment for his army? With its greater depth, the weight of such a phalanx must inevitably prevail. It is only when the Persians in their backward movement against the inexorable push of the Egyptians come under the protective firepower of the moveable towers that the momentum of the phalanx is slowed (*Kyr.* VII.i.34). The rear ranks of veterans in Kyros' army do not permit any retreat by missile throwers at this juncture. With the rout of both enemy wings the Persian forces which achieved this initial victory are free to attack the flanks and rear of the phalanx (*Kyr.* VII.i.36), until the Egyptians form a circle behind their shields as a protective wall (*Kyr.* VII.i.40). This is Xenophon's plan for security within the camp. The vantage point of the tower for a view of the battle field and the final encirclement and surrender of the Egyptians has been dealt with earlier.

What Kyros recognises is the possibility of dealing with the wings piecemeal while holding the enemy centre and denying it any possibility of giving support to the beleaguered wings. His more compact formation has the capability of mutual support, but the centre of the enemy is too distant from the points of the initial attack to render any help. Kyros brings more of his men into direct contact because of the shallower depth of his line, and in so doing makes the most of his resources, whereas a great number of Croesus' men are initially in a passive role because of their great depth.

On paper Xenophon's gamma formation for Croesus seems a good one until one examines it more closely. Had the three lines advanced inwards there would have come a point when the ends of each wing and those of the centre would have impeded one another. It would have been informative to see by what manoeuvre, countermarch or other, Xenophon would have dealt with that problem, particularly in the heat of battle. In theorising within the manouvres of this fictional battle Xenophon gives us the semblance of the kind of battle plan which worked so successfully for Hannibal at Cannae.

Reference has been made to the passing of orders and, as a codicil to this section, a brief discussion of the means by which this was done seems appropriate. These could be by word of mouth and by visual and aural signals,[33] and the choice depended on the mode of warfare, prevailing conditions, the need for concealment of intention and the distance between the sender and the recipient. In the *Kyropaideia* Xenophon was dealing with armies the numbers of which far exceed those of the average Greek hoplite battle. Obviously his Asiatic service with Agesilaos and Kyros the Younger gave him experience on which to base his account in an amalgam of Greek and near Asiatic practice. Prior to the opening of the battle, Kyros gives his commanders their orders by word of mouth, and these are presumably passed down the command chain through the files much in the same manner as was customary in a Spartan army. Croesus, with an army of a third of a million men, the extremities of the two wings of which are separated from the centre by a considerable distance, must have relied on visual signals, presumably in relay, because of the distances involved. Even so, passage of orders, though quick, cannot have been immediate given the reaction time required. Two such orders are given to the wings, one to halt and face about, the other to begin the inward advance on the Persians (*Kyr.* VII.i.23). Kyros combines his verbal order to Arsamas and Chrysantas to lead the centre forward slowly with one which relies on the use of the paean as a signal for them to increase immediately the pace of the advance. The lack of further detail is regrettable and there is no indication as to what method Kyros employed for his wings to left and right face (*Kyr.* VII.i.25). He had, earlier in the initial advance, given orders that his ensign should be watched, and this may well have been a means implied by Xenophon, by which an agreed set of signals could be passed, as well as being a marker for an even advance (*Kyr.* VII.i.4). The signal to charge is clearly the battle cry to Enyalos. It is interesting that Xenophon's near contemporary Sun Tzu, who occasionally commanded armies of near similar size to that of Croesus, declared that 'fighting with a large army under your command is nowise different from fighting with a small one: it is merely a question of instituting signs and signals' (Sun Tzu V.2). He adds, 'The Book of Army Management says; On the field of battle, the spoken word does not carry far enough: hence the institution of gongs and drums. Nor can ordinary objects be seen clearly enough: hence the institution of banners and flags' (Sun Tzu VII.23); 'Gongs and drums, banners and flags, are means whereby the ears and eyes of the host may be focused on one particular point' (Sun Tzu VII.24)[34]; 'In night fighting, then make much use of signal fires and drums, and in fighting by day, of flags and banners as a means of influencing the ears and eyes of your army' (Sun Tzu. VII.26).

Although Xenophon is uniform in his mention of the *salpinx*, in the *Anabasis* (*Anab.* I.ii.17; III.iv.4; IV.ii.1; IV.ii.8–9; V.ii.14; VII.iv.16) as the instrument to signal attack, he refers to the *keras* (κέρας) (*Kyr.* V.iii.52) as the instrument used for the arousal call for Kyros' midnight march. This is a repetition of the use of this word in conjunction with the night march (*Kyr.* V.iii.44). *Keras* is also the instrument used to signal 'turning in' (*Anab.* II.ii.4). To understand the distinction fully is to recognise the two forms of signalling instrument available (not made clear in[33]): the *salpinx* made from metal and the *keras* from animal horn. Both required mouthpieces and the *keras*, probably with a wider bore, would have had a less piercing and more mellow sound than the *salpinx*. Less carrying power and strident tone would be needed more for a camp than in a field of battle where helmets and the inevitable noises of movement and equipment would stifle all but the most penetrating of sounds and implies a wider choice of instruments for such use than is implied by Krentz (also[33]). Both instruments are reputed to be of Etruscan origin (*Athen.* IV.184).

In the description of the ideal commander Xenophon has given a standard against which commanders, including himself, can be measured.

End Notes

1. The first reference to the raising of a Spartan cavalry arm of 400 men, *Thuc.* IV.55, was in 424 BC, along with a force of archers. This was in response to the need to counter the danger of coastal raids by the Athenians.

2. For the likelihood that Xenophon also served under the Thirty Tyrants, see Anderson, *Xenophon*, pp.18, 47ff.

3. The issue of right or left handedness is never addressed. It is obvious that training from an early age was dictated in terms of the right hand and it would be essential for this to be the case for the individuals within a phalanx. An interesting scenario would have been for a right handed phalanx to have, unknowingly, faced a left handed one and to have been matched in their sideways edging to the shield side.

4. A suggestion is made that this should be viewed in the tradition of moral instruction and advice, ὑποθῆκαι, in Gera, *Xenophon's 'Cyropaedia' Style, Genre and Literary Technique*, p. 50.

5. For further discussion of sacrifice see Hanson (ed.), *Hoplites*, Chapters 8 (M.H. Jameson) and 9 (A.H. Jackson).

6. For the all-pervading religious observances of the ancient Greek world see Zaidman & Pantel, *Religion in the Ancient Greek City*.

7. During the Persian invasion only thirty-nine Greek cities fought the enemy and only thirty-one are mentioned on the 'serpent column' set up originally in Delphi but now in Istanbul.

8. Heavy cavalry in the strict sense did not come into being until the Sarmatian example led to a complementary establishment of the cataphract.

9. The battle of Sepeia, 494 BC, saw Kleomenes I recognising that the Argives opposing him were reacting to all Spartan orders. He then gave the verbal order that an attack should be made when the herald gave the order to take breakfast (*Herod*. VI.77.3–VI.78). For other uses of signals or orders to mislead an enemy see Xenophon, *Anab*. IV.iii.28–34.

10. 'At its simplest there are two fundamental elements for operation. Fix and strike.' Sun Tzu coined the terms Ordinary Force for the function of fixing the enemy or denying him the freedom to achieve his purpose, and the Extra-ordinary Force for the function of manoeuvring into a position of decisive advantage from which he can be struck.

See also: 'To fix is to deny the enemy his goals, distract him and thus deprive him of freedom of action in order for us to gain freedom of action.'

'To strike is to use that freedom of action to: manoeuvre and hit the enemy.' (Edited version of 0229, reprinted in Army Doctrine Publication Vol 1: *Operations* (June 1994).)

11. *Herod*. VII.89.3 describes the Egyptians as having 'hollow shields with broad rims'. At *Kyr*. VIII.v.11, Xenophon, although describing the shields as large, uses the word γέρρα, denoting that it was made of wicker. The word is also used of the Persian oblong wicker shield.

12. See 0432, Army Doctrine Publication Vol. 1: *Operations*: 'Tactical commanders are, however, most unlikely to have direct access to all sources and thus cannot be self-reliant. The operational commander needs an intelligence focal point in theatre which is able to coordinate the collection effort of all systems committed to the operation: analyse, assess and disseminate the intelligence product to those requiring it . . .'. Kyros is his own focal point.

13. Sun Tzu VIII. 7. There are five types of spies:

a. Local spies – using the local inhabitants of a district. VIII.9
b. Inward spies – disaffected and aggrieved persons 'should be secretly approached and bound to one's interest by means of rich presents. In this way you will be able to find out the state of affairs in the enemy's country, ascertain the plans that are being formed against you, and moreover disturb the harmony and create a breach between the sovereign and his ministers'. The list includes criminals who have been

punished; concubines who seek wealth; men who are aggrieved by being placed in a subordinate position; those who wish to have a ' foot in both camps' (VIII. 10).

c. Converted spies – detatching enemy spies from their original masters by bribes and using them for dissimulation (VIII.11).

d. Doomed spies – 'We ostentatiously do things calculated to deceive our own spies who must be led to believe that they have been unwittingly disclosed. Then when these spies are captured in the enemy's lines they will make an entirely false report and the enemy will take measures accordingly, only to find that we do something quite different. The spies will thereupon be put to death' (VIII. 12).

e. Surviving spies – those who bring back news from the enemy's camp. 'This is the ordinary class of spies ... a man of keen intellect, though in outward appearance a fool ...' (VIII.13).

14. 0301, Army Doctrine Vol. 1, *Operations*.

15. It is highly likely that Xenophon served in the Athenian cavalry, possibly under Alkibiades or Thrasyllos in Asia Minor in 408 BC, and under the Thirty Tyrants, see Anderson, *Xenophon*, pp.18, 47ff.

16. Anderson makes the telling point that puncture wounds are less traumatic to the observer than those made by slashing weapons such as the arms used by the Romans with their more open infantry order, which led to the total severance of limbs and decapitation. He supports his point that this had a significant effect on Macedonian morale at the beginning of the Second Macedonian War (Livy 31.34.3) in Hanson (ed.), *Hoplites*, pp.26–7.

17. Spartan commanders such as Agesilaos, in Asia Minor, and his brother Teleutias, near Olynthos, saw to it that their forces had reliable and competent cavalry present and used this arm effectively. See Part Two of this volume.

18. Sun Tzu's observations on garnering provisions (II.15) – previously illustrated in Part One, endnote 14 – are also relevant here: 'A wise general makes a point of foraging on the enemy. One cartload of the enemy's provisions is equivalent of twenty of one's own, and likewise a single picul of his provender is equivalent to twenty from one's own store.'

19. The stories of Gobryas' son and of Panthea and Abradatas give a Persian flavour to Xenophon's novella but do not prove by their presence in his writing

that there was a Persian epic in circulation from which they sprang. See Gera, *Cyropaedia*, pp.21–2.

20. The account of the fall of Sardis in *Herodotos* (I.84) differs only in detail from Xenophon, e.g., in *Herodotos* the capture is the result of an accidental observation by Hyroiades the Mardian. The entry and capture of the ramparts at the most precipitous point of the defences is common to both.

21. The *anastrophe* was the about-turn of files on one or both wings of a phalanx followed by a march to the rear, where by wheeling and coming behind the phalanx the depth of that phalanx could be strengthened and the length of its line shortened. The *anastrophe* was obviously an effective drill but needed time and a sufficiency of distance from an enemy to be secure in its outcome. Mnasippos was much too close to an eager enemy for his men to carry it out successfully (*Hell.* VI.ii.20–22), whereas Agesilaos had 'room to manoeuvre' (*Hell.* VI.v.18–19), although exactly what the manouvre was in his case is still conjectural. A possible, but by no means confident, suggestion is made in Part Two.

22. 'Deception seeks to manipulate perceptions and expectations in order to mislead the enemy into acting in a way prejudicial to his interests. The main effort must therefore be concealed until it is too late for him to react effectively.' 0448, Army Doctrine Vol. 1.

23. Sun Tzu (IX.23) goes further than Xenophon. 'When there is dust rising in a high column, it is the sign of chariots advancing; when the dust is low, but spread over a wide area, it betokens the approach of infantry. When it widens out in different directions, it shows that parties have been sent out to collect firewood. A few clouds of dust moving to and fro signify that an army is encamping.'

24. 'Tempo is the rate or rhythm of activity relative to the enemy, within tactical engagements and battles and between major operations. It incorporates the capacity of the force to transition from one operation of war to another.' 0352, Army Doctrine Vol. 1.

25. 'Because operations cannot be conducted continuously, there may be a need for periodic pauses, while retaining the initiative in other ways. Operational pauses may be needed when an operation has temporarily reached the end of its sustainability; this could be because the troops involved are exhausted; terrain and climate compel a halt; the character of the campaign has

changed (for instance a pursuit meets a hardening defence) or due to a combination of these factors. The initiative is retained by ensuring that when an operational pause is imposed on one line of operations, activity on another must be stepped up.' 0357, Army Doctrine Vol. 1.

26. 'An operation reaches its culminating point when the current operation can just be maintained but not developed to any great advantage ... the culminating point is therefore an involuntary operational pause, but one that a commander must anticipate.' 0358, Army Doctrine Vol. 1.

27. Tatum, *Xenophon's Imperial Fiction*, Chapter 5, pp.115–33 explicitly shows the strategy employed by Kyros to achieve ascendancy and containment of Kyaxares.

28. Sun Tzu III.8: 'It is the rule in war, if our forces are ten to the enemy's one, to surround him; if five to one, to attack him, if twice as numerous, to divide our army into two'. III.9: 'If equally matched, we can offer battle; if slightly inferior in numbers, we can avoid the enemy; if quite unequal in every way, we can flee from him.' VI.24: 'Carefully compare the opposing army with your own, so that you may know where strength is superabundant and where it is deficient.'

29. 'The Centre of Gravity is that aspect of the enemy's overall capability which, if attacked and eliminated, will lead to the enemy's inevitable defeat or his wish to sue for peace through negotiations.' 0328, Army Doctrine Vol. 1.

30. 'Decisive Points are those events, the successful outcome of which is a precondition of the successful elimination of the enemy's centre of gravity. Decisive points are the key to unlocking the enemy's centre of gravity ... defeat of the centre of gravity is made possible by successfully attacking the decisive points which allow access to it.' 0335, Army Doctrine Vol. 1. This is a development from Clausewitz's idea of a decisive point being a geographical one.

31. Croesus' original line was to have a depth of thirty. However the Egyptians insisted on deploying at a depth of a hundred men (VI.iii.20) thus shortening Croesus' original design and reducing the overlap on the flanks. James Tatum hints that this might have worked, *Xenophon's Imperial Fiction*, p.152.

32. For a good diagrammatic representation of the 'tiles' see Anderson, *Military Theory*, fig.VII, p.400.

33. See also Krentz, 'The Salpinx in Greek Battle', in Hanson (ed.), *Hoplites*, p.117. The comment here implies a 'catch all' for camp calls for the *salpinx* and is not proven. The camp calls seem to have been shared between the *salpinx* and the *keras*, with the latter being associated in Xenophon with those made at night. An ivory *keras* is presently part of the collection in the Boston Museum of Fine Arts.

34. See Plutarch *Crassus* 23 for the use of drums and bells by Parthians.

CONCLUDING COMMENTS

Taking each of the sections of the three main parts of the text an attempt is made here to draw together the main points in a brief commentary. One interpolation is made covering mercenaries before the summaries on 'Intelligence' and 'Tactics'. Thereafter, comment is made on areas related to, but not directly concerned with, the main text. Source references are only given here for those which would not duplicate references already in the main text.

Cavalry

In terms of the ability to raise a strong and efficient cavalry arm it is evident in Xenophon's writings that much depended on the nature of the terrain surrounding a City State. So it is that it comes as no surprise that Thessaly, Thebes and Olynthos are deemed as the three significant areas where good cavalry were present in his history. Areas where fodder was plentiful alongside those needed for agrarian purposes were not so common in regions of this mountainous country. Later, of course, the Macedonian cavalry was to become preeminent and for the same reasons. They had a sufficiency of arable land on which to raise horses without impairing the ability to produce enough foodstuff for the population. A further factor was that the terrain was advantageous to the deployment of this more mobile military arm which in social terms was an elite led by the aristocracy. It has been noted that Athens, controlling a less fertile area than others but relying on maritime trade for some essential resources such as grain, established a useful cavalry arm in the fifth century but this was initially from the propertied class who could afford to maintain and train the animal. What appears surprising is that Sparta was virtually forced into the creation of a cavalry arm to defend its coastal regions from Athenian attacks during the Peloponnesian War. Controlling Messenia as it did and relying for much of its agricultural produce on that area, one would have thought that Sparta would have found it easier than most states to find space on the Lakonian plain for serious horse-raising activity. That it did not, and relied within the period of our study on others such as the Phleiasions and Syracusans to supply this arm, is indicative of a social conservatism within the Spartan miltary where the citizen continued to be a heavy infantryman.

The first half of the fourth century proved to be a period of experimentation. Those who continued to use cavalry in terms only of screening the flanks of the infantry, skirmishing and pursuit eventually failed. Reconnaissance, scouting, making contact and attacking foraging parties became the norm. More importantly, the development of cavalry into an arm of attack against infantry in some semblance of formation, albeit supported and interspersed by peltasts, was successfully attempted by Epameinondas at Second Mantineia. This heralded the later tactical developments of the Hellenistic period when the cavalry arm was of the greatest importance to the battle plan.

It was essential to have cavalry when operating against Persians. Good commanders such as Agesilaos and Xenophon himself learned quickly that to be without this arm against an enemy strong in this resource would be to operate under a handicap. It took a good commander to realise and use the potential available to him in a body of horsemen. Agesilaos learned this quickly and this is proven by his summary defeat of the Thessalian cavalry, a force which by its experience and enviable record should have worsted Agesilaos' force. What is significant is that it was he who ordered the particular antidote to the Thessalian annoyance and not the *hipparch*, the commander of the cavalry. It is interesting to note that thereafter his brother, Teleutias, saw to it that he was supported by the excellent cavalry commanded by the very able Derdas and one cannot avoid coming to the conclusion that in the course of the many conversations the two brothers would have had, the subject of cavalry tactics was thoroughly pursued. This makes it all the more surprising that such a poor showing was made with this arm at Leuktra. It suggests that one of the royal families was of a more conservative cast than the other.

Xenophon devotes considerable space to the matter of selecting and looking after a suitable mount and in the training and tactical use of cavalry. His significant recommendations are to intersperse infantry among the cavalrymen and to disguise the size of the force at the commander's disposal. Common sense suggestions for resting the mounts and for the care of their feet are still valid today. Xenophon is suitably caustic about poor command of cavalry in his comments about the Lechaion and for the inappropriate size of a force selected by Iphikrates, but praises those who recognise good ground over which cavalry can be effective.

The various formations available, the wedge, the rhomboid and the rectangular, all have their virtues depending on circumstances. The Scythian wedge was adopted by Epameinondas but was bolstered by intersupportive peltasts in his *emvolon* at Second Mantineia. The rhomboid was the preferred formation of the Thessalians offering a wedge to the front and rear, although the reason for the rear wedge remains unclear unless it allowed the formation to maintain its integrity if obliged to retire or face about. The rectangular formation was the most conservative and mirrors the phalanx formation adopted by Kleombrotos at Leuktra.

What is significant in this period is the move from exploiting gaps in the enemy formation to that of creating gaps in the enemy line. The length of pursuit was extended and the frontal attack by cavalry supported by light infantry on an enemy's line was a new tactic.

In Xenophon's theoretical writings we see a suggestion of two forms of cavalry, light and heavy. He is not clear whether the latter should be used in the directly confrontational manner but the fact that he distinguishes between the two suggests differing roles. The differences between the armaments of the two suggest that the heavy cavalry is of a more offensive nature. Indeed, at the fictional Battle of Thymbrara, Kyros the Great opens his action with simultaneous attacks by cavalry on the enclosing wings of the enemy albeit supported by infantry in a follow-up formation. Xenophon is ambivalent at this point and we are not wholly secure in our minds that these horsemen are heavy cavalry but the implication is that they must have been to achieve the success that they did. Perhaps this was the mid-fourth century question later resolved by Phillip of Macedon after the exploits of Pelopidas at Tegyra and Epameinondas at Second Mantineia showed him the way. Frontal attacks by cavalry were highly unusual within this period.

What is most significant is that a small force of cavalry adeptly used could make the difference between the survival of a force of infantry and its annihilation. In the *Anabasis* we see how a newly-formed force of fifty horsemen and the firepower of Rhodian slingers transformed the fortunes of the Greek army in their hour of desperation and how the lack of cavalry led to the desperate plight of those of the Greek forces who had decided to raid the Thracian villages without such support. They were only rescued from their plight by Xenophon coming with a balanced force including cavalry. It therefore comes as a surprise that one who extolled the necessity for cavalry support should make one of his last actions as supreme commander one which found no place for cavalry. It is ironic that he was only extricated from his predicament by the cavalry force of a friend.

In the 'theoretical' third part of this book, while the reform and training of infantry are given much space, we are constantly presented with Kyros the Great's efforts to build an ever-increasing cavalry force well beyond the proportions of a mid-fourth century army. This reflects Xenophon's views on the importance of this arm and, in view of later developments, shows him to be very much in the van of tactical thinking in his time.

Piety

With all its contributions to civilisation it is sometimes difficult to realise that hardly a year passed within the Classical period without some outbreak of hostilities between city states. Warfare was part and parcel of life's pattern and, like much else, the Greeks established an agreed code of conduct upon it.

The retention of traditional practices into the fourth century when all else in the military sphere was undergoing change was not an aspect of conservatism but rather of piety. Almost all practices had their roots in religion. The visits to the oracles to seek approval for the opening of hostilities, the ceremonies at the crossing of the border in the case of Sparta and other states, the taking of daily omens, the on-field sacrifice, the reverence for the battle dead by both victor and vanquished, the setting up of trophies in recognition of victory, the dedications at places such as Delphi, the gift of part of any booty to Panhellenic shrines, were all retained in the period under consideration However, the number of reported abuses rose and points to a weakening of the underlying moral climate. Nonetheless, the chosen commander was expected by his men to observe the traditional rites and set an example.

Morale, Training and Discipline

Not surprisingly Xenophon is clear that these three elements are interdependent. Often the absence of one is cited as being the cause for failure. A commander had to know his men, their needs and lead by example. These are the maxims of Xenophon. The commander had to establish himself in the good opinion of the men who followed him and therefore the personal conduct of the commander was always under scrutiny. The commander's attitude to religious observance and his punctilious observance of rites could be critical to the maintenance of morale and discipline. The moral aspect of command was very much a supportive issue to sustaining morale.

With the exception of the Spartan army much depended on the supply of provisions for the soldiers, the organisation of which was the responsibility of the commander. While the arrangements of the Spartan commissariat were firmly established for campaigns in Greece the same is not quite so securely known for those taken abroad. Therefore we must assume that Agesilaos took responsibility for, or delegated, this aspect, when undertaking his activities in Asia Minor. Provisioning is perhaps the most important aspect for an army in any age. A shortage of food could lead to a loss of physical condition which is a sure prelude to a loss in morale leading, thereafter, in some cases, to indiscipline.

There are examples of what appears to be insubordination in modern terms, particularly in Parts One and Two, but perhaps our understanding of the ancient world is deficient in terms of attitude. The fact that the commanders often accepted such occasions as commonplace should alert us to a difference. It may well be that orders were strictly followed during occasions of direct combat, but on matters pertaining to foraging, looting and the fate of a conquered opponent, control of the forces under a commander seems to have been more lax. Citizen soldiers called up from their normal occupations from time to time, serving in differing capacities ranging from commander to ordinary hoplite on separate occasions, may well have taken the battlefield order as sacrosanct. However, with the battle over, individualism re-emerged. This was patently true of the more democratic societies. Sparta, although having its own form of democratic principles, is set apart from other city states in that it was the only one which had the nearest thing to a professional army.

Trust between men and commander was an imperative. Initially a well loved commander, Kyros the Younger nearly lost the support of the Greeks in his expedition against his brother by keeping the true purpose of his mission a secret. He only regained it by throwing more money at the problem in terms of increasing the payment of the hoplites, not the best solution to his self-made problem. His was not the best way to sustain morale, but suppressing the truth when it meant concealing bad news could be useful. Such was the case when, immediately prior to the Battle of Koroneia, Agesilaos pretended that Sparta had achieved a notable victory at sea rather than a damaging defeat. It would not have been helpful to have his mens' concerns for friends and relatives raised prior to their own action.

Training is seen to be the key to successful command. Though we see little of it in the first part of this book for fairly obvious reasons, it is present in the second, particularly in relation to Agesilaos and Iphikrates, and it is of paramount importance in the third. Xenophon's first hand experience of serving with Agesilaos gives us an insight into this general's methods. Agesilaos' training schedules while in Asia Minor deserve attention and it is highly likely that these are given more detailed treatment in Xenophon's novella concerning Kyros the Great, modelled as they are on Spartan methodology. Thanks to the survival of the *Hellenika* his knowledge of Iphikrates' training methods have meant that later generations could appreciate the preparations made by Iphikrates in terms of training his men prior to action and of his care for their security.

Security could only be assured if a commander kept his men in good physical and mental condition, with a readiness for action and competitive spirit when in enemy territory. Their alertness as a consequence of his care for their well-being would be an asset. Unfortunately not all commanders could achieve such standards.

On the March and in Camp

Here we must turn to Xenophon's novella on Kyros the Great in which the writer carefully prescribes the preparations and dispositions which a commander must make for marches with differing pupuses. As we have seen in the other sections of this book, Xenophon is drawing together the threads of good practice from his own and others' experience and particularly that of the Spartan army in his fictional tale. So it is that we find Seuthes' method of having fires lit some distance in front of his camp guards, as a precaution against a surprise attack, is given as Kyros' methodology. We know that Xenophon was surprised when he first encountered this arrangement towards the end of the *Anabasis*. We can therefore take the Kyropaedeia as a handbook of good practice, albeit with differing weaponry.

Most marches were tactical and there is an obvious overlap with the content of the section on 'Tactics'. Xenophon rightly believed that topography was the key element in determining the speed and safety of an operation. It affected the formations adopted by the marchers and depended on whether the way was narrow or broad and whether forward positions should be secured prior to the passage of the main body. It also promoted the need for intelligence, reconnaisance and preparation. The place of the baggage train and the identification of individual's possessions assumed an importance together with the need to take repair materials and spares. Orders given by file leaders or leaders of half files were the norm and a difference between marches by day and night is made. Those positioned at the van of a daytime march were those best suited to fight within the terrain encountered. A safe advance at night was made with light infantry in front of the main body with advance and reconnaisance units of cavalry ahead of these. The slowest led the way of the main body. The Spartan army always had the Skiritae ahead of their van on any march.

Obviously, by pointing out examples of bad practice Xenophon is implying good practice as an alternative. The case of the laxity in preparedness during the final stages of Kyros the Younger's march into Persia is significant, as is that of Anaxibios, when he knew that Iphikrates might be in his vicinity.

Choices had to be made and night marches could augment the distance between opposing forces if they were achieved with a concealment of purpose. Indeed, timing became an issue within the period in question as the overnight march over the Oneion pass by the Thebans attests. Someone with local knowledge had calculated that the attackers would reach their advantageous position at the time that they did, suggesting a refinement in practice. Similarly, Epameinondas himself led his forces to a surprise attack on Sparta following a successful overnight march.

Celerity of march proved to be of great tactical importance. The surprising distances covered by the forces of Agesilaos through Thrace on his return from Asia Minor and those on his invasion of Akarnania proved that speed of movement often disrupted the organisation of the opposition.

Recipes for making a force seem larger than it was are given in the last section when Kyros keeps halting his van in order that the passage of his forces takes longer to pass an opposing force. The obverse of this is Xenophon's recommendation to cavalry forces to conceal their true stength by adopting a formation which indicates a smaller force by hiding the additional strength behind a narrow front.

Timing of orders was important and those of both Kyros and Agesilaos when they used the *anastrophe* were important to the safety of the men under their command. Great detail is given concerning the position and layout of a camp, in which the central position of the circular design is that of the commander. For defensive reasons those with shields are placed on the perimeter with those requiring greater preparation time, such as cavalry, being placed near the command position. The use of cut trees as impedimenta is noted in the case of the approach to Epameinondas' camps and on the routes to the rear of Teleutias' withdrawals form the territory of Olynthos.

Mercenaries

With the duty of the citizen to fight for his city being paramount there was limited call for mercenaries on mainland Greece prior to the Peloponnesian War. But the protracted nature of that conflict led to greater and greater reliance on such forces, particularly those of a specialist nature. As was noted in the Introduction, it became economically unsound for a citizen to be on duty all year round. He had obligations at home which were necessary to his city. At the end of that war states had come to the realisation that, in future conflict, it was not enough to rely on the citizen body particularly in relation to specialist troops. Hoplites could be engaged from the poorer parts of Greece such as Achaea and Arkadia, Crete supplied bowmen and Aetolia light armed troops similar to peltasts. Thrace was the recruitment area for true peltasts, Rhodes for slingers and Syracuse was a supplier of quality cavalry which helped Sparta after the Leuktra debacle. It was cheaper to hire than to train citizens in specialist skills.

Mercenaries had been used with regularity much earlier in the time of the tyrants but by the beginning of the Classical period the notion of citizen duties had taken root with the onset of democratic and oligarchic governments. However, it has been noted that the Peloponnesian War saw a growth in the need for the paid services of specialists. In Athens the constant requirement of oarsmen for their fleet was later to be matched by the naval needs of Sparta. The end of the war did not bring about a lessening in the number of mercenaries but rather the reverse.

Many combatants found that they were unable to return successfully to the land. Many had no skills other than those of warfare, such had been the duration of the conflict. The known world at large increased its requirement for specialists and found a ready market. Syracuse and other cities in the Western Mediterranean sustained their power base on the back of mercenary armies. Through much of the period under review Persia had a requirement of several thousand heavy infantrymen, satisfied by Greek hoplites. The fact that Kyros the Younger at the beginning of the century was able to raise over twelve thousand mercenaries with little trouble is an indication of the availability of such forces.

This soon became the preferred route to raising an army for the wealthier city states. By the end of the 380s Sparta allowed its allies to give money for a campaign in place of men. Payment for the services of citizens came into vogue as a natural consequence. The balance between supply and demand was such that rates of pay were relatively low. The underlying hope of any mercenary lay in the opportunities for plunder.

Secrecy, Spies, non-combative Deception and Intelligence

The first two parts of this book deal with historical events, the third with an amalgam of good practice insofar as Xenophon viewed it. What emerges is a picture wherein strong hints of collection procedures are made, but none of a clear intelligence evaluation structure for the information received. The last seems to rest with the commander-in-chief or, in the case of the *Anabasis*, the leader of the van and rearguard. The sifting of evidence rests with an individual or a limited few. A case in point is Agesilaos' suppression of the news of the Spartan naval defeat immediately prior to Koroneia. How many people knew the truth within the Spartan army one will never know. It may well have been only Agesilaos himself, but his concern at that time was to sustain morale which shows there are differing needs for intelligence receipt or gathering.

Obviously there was a clear difference between operating in areas familiar to a commander on matters of topography, distances for marches and the attitude of the local population, e.g., mainland Greece and the Aegean littoral, and the march of the Ten Thousand through unknown terrain. The difficulties of the latter account for the more extreme measures taken by the commanders in eliciting information even to the point of killing one man in front of his companion in the search for veracity. Desperation bred desperate measures.

Tissaphernes' report to Artaxerxes of the probable intent of Kyros the Younger was an example of correct intelligence evaluation. However, his later evaluations of Agesilaos' intentions in the field were well wide of the mark and eventually were the cause of his own loss of life.

Intelligence gathering came in a variety of forms. These can be divided into two areas: those which were derived from sources outside the forces under command and those directly organised by the commander from within his forces to collect information. Arguably the latter would be the more reliable. It is interesting that Xenophon has Kyros the Great cross-checking information received, rarely relying on a singular point of view. He used all the expected routes to intelligence gathering from reconnaissance, the populace of the locale, spies, prisoners and deserters, to sending his own 'plant', Araspas, to the enemy camp posing as a turncoat to bring him news of the enemy numbers, their likely disposition in the coming battle, aspects of the battle plan itself and the fighting methods and armament of the opposing side. Kyros received the information but was his own analyst.

In the *Anabasis* the lack of anything other than short term information was a handicap. The main sources of intelligence for Xenophon and his colleagues were local villagers, hostages and prisoners. It is clear however that they had set up a very reliable scouting unit as mention of Demokrates being one of the *best* attests. The main problem for the Ten Thousand was the limited knowledge they had of the land ahead of them on their march. This deficit allowed the forces of Spithridates and Rathines to escape from the Greeks following their engagement. Had the Greeks been aware of the further ravine ahead they would have pressed their pursuit. Xenophon kept an 'open door' policy so that he could receive any new information from his men at any time.

It was as important then as it is now to keep secret the size of forces if only for the surprise element it affords a commander. Part Two contains several suggestions as to how this could be done particularly when cavalry are involved. Alkibiades' operations around Sestos and Kysikos sought to conceal his true naval strength from the Spartans. We are lucky to have the description of the lengths he went to, to deceive his enemy. Similarly, by deception, Lysander lulled his opposition into a false sense of security which brought about a laxness in their conduct by his refusal to come to battle. When that point had been reached and had been ascertained through intelligence gathering he made his attack on an unprepared enemy. As alluded to earlier, Agesilaos so foxed Tissaphernes as to his intentions of operation that he made the latter appear tactically inept. For sheer brinkmanship the deception of Epameinondas' opening attack at the Second battle of Mantineia showed brilliance. A ploy well thought out and possibly even rehearsed with his men beforehand so that its success could be assured in matters of timing.

Some scholars may disagree, but it is hoped that the argument set out in Part Two is sufficiently convincing to suggest that the capture of Thebes by the Spartans was not one of opportunism but rather of well laid plans with collaborators, which matches that of the planning concerned with its recapture.

Possibly the best use of intelligence was made by Agesilaos on his invasion of Asia Minor, relying as he must have done on the information supplied about personalities and topography by Xenophon himself.

Tactics

In battle the Spartans enhanced the natural drift of the phalanx to the right into a manoeuvre which led to an outflanking movement of the enemy left. This enabled them to roll up the opposing line by a purposeful turn inwards followed by a massive attack on the unshielded side of each segment of the enemy line in turn. What had been successful as the product of an accident at First Mantineia (418 BC) was refined at both the Nemea and Koroneia. It is clear that it had been adopted by Sparta as a battle winning tactic, for the evidence indicates that it was Kleombrotos' intention to attempt the same at Leuktra. That he was unsuccessful was because the Theban commanders Epameinondas and Pelopidas had devised a manoeuvre to nullify its success.

This was the product of observable experience and was based on the pre-dilection over many years for the Theban phalanx to be arranged in greater depth. They had seen that they could break through a Spartan phalanx by their sheer weight at Koroneia and also had the experience of Tegyra. There, instead of passing through the avenue made for them by the Spartan formation in response to their charge in considerable depth, they had turned to attack the sides of that avenue with great success.

Leuktra then became the developed model for Theban tactics. Its components need to be listed. The positioning of the strongest part of the army opposite the command position of the enemy with the new command position on the left; a trailing centre and right, uncommitted but threatening the opposition troops with a flank or rear attack should they make the first move; the natural edging to the right of the phalanx converted into a purposeful edging to the left to counter the anticipated attempt at an outflanking movement by the Spartans; the driving back into their own lines of the Spartan cavalry by those of Thebes to cause disruption; the pinning down of the Spartan lead to the right by the Sacred band with an attack at the double; the oblique onslaught of the main phalanx to the depth of fifty ranks on the command position; and lastly, the most important component of all, *surprise*.

What is common to all the Theban successes is surprise. From Tegyra – where the surprise lay in the use the Thebans made of the corridor created in their ranks by the Spartans – to Leuktra and Second Mantineia where the timing of the Theban onslaught caught their enemy in mid-manoeuvre in the first and unprepared in the second. Thus a commander can be evaluated by the advantage he gains from the use of surprise. In the case of Epameinondas it is clear that his surprises were planned and timed well. In Xenophon's imaginary scenario for Thymbrara Kyros also planned his surprise attack on the enemy flanks while just managing to hold the centre long enough for the operation to be successful. However, a commander must also be given credit for his quickness to turn surprise to his own advantage in an unplanned situation as was the case with both Tegyra and the Tearless Battle when both sides shared the surprise of unexpected confrontation.

The switch of command position from the right to left wing was repeated at Second Mantineia. Here, the massive depth of the Theban phalanx was achieved by the continuity of the march in column towards the foot of the highest point of the mountains near modern Skopi. There the column had stopped and right faced, seemingly in preparation for encampment. Concealed behind a cavalry screen the phalanx was built to the required depth and the remainder of the column also right faced, the cavalry reformed in wedge formation intermingled with peltasts and made their charge on the unprepared Mantineian and Spartan right followed closely by the phalanx. Again Epameinondas did not offer his centre or his right but maintained them in a position to threaten any attempt to help their right wing by the Athenians and allies on the left of the opposing line. Similar tactics to Leuktra but with the positive element of deception. An opposing commander of experience would not have stood his men down until he was absolutely clear of the enemy's intentions, nor would Epameinondas have attempted this ploy had he not been reasonably sure that it would work. Thus, on the evidence of his care for the security of his men, we have a further reason to be sure that Agesilaos was not present at Second Mantineia.

In using his cavalry as part of a strike force it is debatable if Epameinondas would have done so against a fully prepared battle line of heavy infantry but the lesson of the action is there to be assessed. To achieve such a result required careful planning, backed by opportunism and could only be done with troops of high morale, good training and clear signalling procedures. Here there is the example of Epameinondas using interdependent forces, cavalry, heavy and light infantry.

Longer periods under the same commander allowed men such as Iphikrates to adapt and lighten the equipment of peltast and hoplite thereby increasing the mobility of both. The shedding of greaves, the wearing of laced leather bootlets protecting the lower shin, the replacement of the cuirass by quilted linen, the introduction of a smaller leather covered shield in place of the heavier *hoplon*, must have made a startling difference to the speed at which this new 'hybrid' phalangite could operate. Needless to say the lessening of protective armour led to a lengthening of the heavy spear to about three and a half metres. Important in terms of the length of command with the same body of men was the opportunity for progressive training. Such training is evidenced in terms of peltasts within the main text in Part Two with such successes as that at the Lechaion. It should be noted that it was achieved in conjunction with the support, if not direct engagement, of a threatening hoplite phalanx.

Throughout Parts One and Two the actions of light armed troops (peltasts) have been shown to have been highly successful when in conjunction with other units and much less so when acting alone without the advantage of surprise. Similarly, Part One demonstrates the dire straits in which unsupported heavy infantry (hoplites) could find itself.

By and large the 'quick fix' of a set battle was a last resort. As the time span for an operation lengthened, the interplay of manoeuvre between near equals became more complex. The Corinthian War set the pattern for much of the period and actions increase in complexity.

An army on the move, whether in line of battle or in column, needed protection on flanks, van and rear. This was achieved by the light armed and particularly by cavalry. The former was most useful in mountainous areas commanding the high points through which an army had to move and the latter in open country. In the *Anabasis* both hoplite and peltast were employed in securing successive forward high positions to achieve safe passage for the main body. The more mobile cavalry could be directed to points where its effectiveness would be at its greatest. Agesilaos' use of cavalry in Thessaly is a prime example. As a cavalryman at heart Xenophon gives numerous references to the successful use of cavalry in the *Hellenika* (Part Two). His admiration of the several actions of the Phleiasions and those of Derdas against the Olynthians demonstrate his approval of the growing importance of this arm. Similarly, it is clear that without the fifty cavalry raised by the Greeks from their own ranks after the Battle of Kounaxa (Part One) the outward march would have held more perils. No matter how few, cavalry was essential. Indeed at the fictional Battle of Thymbrara Xenophon has Kyros' infantry line holding, but only just, the opposing line of heavy infantry while his cavalry did its work. Thus we must ask if he is recommending a practice which was the kernel of Phillip's and Alexander's later successes.

The use of *reserves* should be noted. The *Anabasis* (Part One) is clear in the reason for their use and deployment. Those selected to ensure the integrity of the line or column when on the march, and those units held back in support of and behind the main battle line in the action against Spithridates and Rathines, show analytical sophistication.

As a long postscipt to this section we turn to the phalanx which was at its most flexible in manoeuvre at this time. What needs to be examined is the relative effectiveness of a deepening of the formation as was the Theban habit. At p.169, Chapter 2 of du Picq's *Battle Studies* comes the statement:

> Suppose your first rank stops at the instant of shock: the twelve ranks of the battalion, coming up successively, would come in contact with it, pushing it forward ... Experiments made have shown that beyond the sixteenth (rank) the impulsion of the ranks in rear has no effect on the front, it is completely taken up by the fifteen ranks already massed behind the first.

There can be little doubt in the substance of the argument. It is difficult to see an advantage being garnered in terms of weight beyond a particular number, whatever that may be, and perhaps the Thebans had even passed that point in Epameinondas' arrangements. Therefore we must ask why the arrangement was made to one of fifty shields. Possibly an additional reason for the increased depth lay in the planning for possible action to be taken after an achieved breakthrough of the enemy line. Unfortunately, there is little or no evidence to support the following. What we do have is the opportunist action of the Thebans at Tegyra where, as has been noted earlier, instead of passing through the gap made by the Spartans in their line as was to be expected, the close order of the Thebans was directed to attack both sides of the corridor. Obviously, the unshielded side of the Spartans would suffer the most casualties from the bigger target area afforded the Thebans when their flank attack was in progress. From this one example we can extrapolate, and it is stressed that this is pure speculation, that the arrangements made at Leuktra and Second Mantineia were designed for what would happen *after* a breakthrough of the enemy line. Such a breakthrough had also been made at Koroneia but the purpose of that had been mere survival and it is to be noted that the Theban formation also increased its density by closing ranks, i.e., with locked shields. Nonetheless the lesson that a breakthrough could be achieved was a significant issue on which Pelopidas and Epameinnondas, as good commanders, would obviously have spent much time in discussion, debating what could follow such an event.

Our only contemporary evidence comes from Xenophon who was a likely participant at Koroneia. He was not present at Tegyra, Leuktra or Second Mantineia, making no comment on the first and relying on information garnered from participants in the second and third. What happened at Tegyra remains a mystery insofar as detail is concerned. Was the action ordered or was it opportunist? Plutarch's *Life of Pelopidas* is the only concrete evidence of any substance available and that considerably later than the event, but no less reflecting the Theban tradition. What is a truism is that a concerted action can only be the outcome of planning, albeit in the short term in the case of Tegyra. Men were ordered to do something, even on the spur of the moment.

Moving from the opportunist order to the planned event is to take us from Tegyra to Leuktra. The initial attack made by Epameinondas on the Spartans, already disrupted by their own cavalry being driven back into their formation, begs the question as to how many of the Spartans were in line or column at the point when the king ordered the lead to the right. The broad hint given by Xenophon is that those on the right were in column and were already in motion while the greater remainder did not know what their commander, Kleombrotos, was doing and presumably were still in line of battle. They could only look on as their comrades and king were anihilated. We must ask ourselves what it was that dissuaded them from coming to the rescue of their comrades. It could not only be the threatening trailing centre and right of Epameinondas' army. There must have been some additional reason, for it would have been easy for the uncommitted Spartans, with their famous quick wheeling and countermarching, to have reformed and taken the Thebans on their unshielded side or in rear if they, the Thebans, had already surrounded the king's position. In turn the Spartan allies could have remained to pose a counter threat to the Boeotian centre and right. Some form of formidable obstacle was in their way threatening just such a reforming maneouvre and we can only guess that Epameinondas had arranged a subdivision of his phalanx for this purpose. He would have had the numerical capacity to do so, for only that part of the Spartan section of their army who had heard the king's order would have followed and they would be much inferior in number to the Theban phalanx. If this was the case, and it must again be stressed that this is highly conjectural and totally unsupported by evidence, then the Theban formation would still have had a greater front than the Spartans adjacent to the action had the latter turned to column prior to attempting a secondary maneouvre.

The Spartans did not initially concede defeat. To them, disastrous as it had been, the action had been a sub-battle. Their casualties had been disastrously high in terms of full Spartan citizens but not so great that full battle could not have been rejoined. The later news that another Spartan army was on its way must have further bolstered the Spartan spirit and it is this point which may have led the Thebans first to call on Athens and then Jason of Pherae to come to their assistance to share in the destruction of the Spartan army before relief arrived. This suggests that successful as they had been in the action, the Thebans were still concerned that, in the long term, they required additional support to finish the job for they too had reluctant allies. Both requests were rejected and we gather from Xenophon that the concession of defeat by the remaining Spartans arose from the general reluctance of their allies to continue rather than the initial success of the Thebans.

Having seen the disorder caused by cavalry being driven into its own line at Leuktra and the advantage derived therefrom, we can turn to Epameinondas' likely planning for Second Mantineia. Here surprise was essential. The unprepared line of the opposing forces was subjected to an attack by a mixed force of cavalry and peltasts with the phalanx, again in considerable depth, following for the exploitation of the possible breakthough. It goes without saying that at this time cavalry would not have been sent against a fully formed line of heavy infantry. However, it should be noted that the peltasts interspersed among the cavalry were the most suited to fight in open order, particularly against a disordered line of heavy infantry. The following phalanx of heavy infantry would complete the rout at the command position. There can be no doubt that it was these peltasts who were significant to the success at Second Mantineia for it was they who were confronted and destroyed by the Athenians in the secondary stage of the battle following their over-zealous pursuit from left to right over the battlefield.

Finally, in this postscript the reader should be reminded of Xenophon's personal view of a deepened phalanx. In the fictional battle of Thymbrara he notes the depth of a hundred shields of the Egyptian phalanx, an exaggerated oblique reference to the Theban practice. He makes it clear through Kyros that it is better to have more men in active terms of engagement and therefore to a lesser depth than to have inactive members of a fighting formation. Given that the length of the spear allowed only perhaps the first three ranks to have an offensive role this seems to make sense. Obviously any fallen front-line man would be replaced by his follower in line but there are physical limitations to the individual's capacity to sustain an attack over a prolonged period. Men tire and need to be replaced if they are not initially successful. This is where the few references and hints to forms of reserves which we find in Xenophon's writings are so important. It may well be that these were commonplace for the resolution of problems and seemingly undeserving of mention towards the middle of the fourth century. However, the particular detail he gives of the arrangements made for such forces in the *Anabasis* suggest that at the turn of the century these were still quite novel.

After Xenophon

Much of the period Xenophon covered was one in which the hegemony of Greece was never capably sustained or exercised. The city states required strong leadership and a common policy. It could not be achieved in a short time span because of the differing constitutional arrangements. Voluntary agreement was out of the question, each city had its own agenda. It was inevitable that strong leadership would have to be imposed. That imposition came from without in the person of Phillip, a king of a centralised state who had continued the work of one of his predecessors, Archelaos, and built a national standing army of professional quality. He had learned well from Epameinondas and Pelopidas when a hostage in Thebes. Many of the trends noted in Xenophon's pages were further developed, e.g., the lightening in weight of body armour, the further improvement in mobility of both heavy and light infantry as a consequence, the further lengthening of the spear to become the *sarissa*, the notion of attacking the enemy's command position, the heightened importance of the cavalry, its use as a shock force, the eventual self-sufficiency of the phalangite who carried his own kit and supplies which allowed baggage trains to be dispensed with, permitting the achievement of lightening tactical marches.

Had Jason of Pherae lived he may well have achieved some form of control over the Greeks. He may well have pre-empted Phillip in much that he achieved. Certainly for the time, it had to be some form of despot who forced a semblance of unity on the Greeks and if that meant vassalage in all but name the city states had only themselves to blame.

The passing on and adoption of tactical ideas is not difficult to discern from the examples in the main text. Their progressive effects can be seen in successive centuries through arms such as cavalry and spear or pike men. All successful generals learned from the experiences of their forerunners. Indeed, part of Hannibal's conduct of the Battle of Cannae bears an uncanny resemblance to the theoretical Battle of Thymbrara. Only the Romans, in obtuse fashion after the Punic wars, neglected to raise the kind of battle-winning cavalry which had served the hellenistic monarchies so well and themselves in the latter stages of the war against Hannibal. They relied thereafter on adequate forces from their allies, some of whom proved to be of dubious quality and allegiance. Scipio Africanus was the last Republican Roman to recognise the need for high quality cavalry to achieve success. His detachment of the Numidian cavalry from their employ under Hannibal proved to be the deciding factor in the Second Punic War. Even then, deprived as he was of one of his most efficient arms, Hannibal's battle plan almost brought him success had not the Numidians returned early from their pursuit of Hannibal's substitute cavalry to attack him in rear.

Almost two centuries later we see the much lauded Julius Caesar relying on cavalry forces which, at best, could only serve for screening and pursuit. It may well be that his reputation was safeguarded by his assassination. Had he lived, his intended expedition against the Parthians would have brought his ability to counter an enemy incredibly strong in cavalry, and mounted archers, under severe scrutiny.

Throughout the main text frequent reference has been made to the writings of Sun Tzu. What has yet to be given thorough investigation is the reciprocal transmission of ideas between East and West. As a tantalising example, the action of the Chinese general Tian Dan gives us pause for thought. Besieged within the city of Jimo he devised an unusual idea to achieve a breakout. Gathering together 1,000 oxen he had his men tie blades to the horns of the animals and wrap their tails with oil-soaked reeds. At nightfall, the torches on the tails were lit and the oxen were driven into the enemy's camp followed by 5,000 picked men. The resulting chaos saw the opposing Yen army suffer tremendous casualties and Tian Dan wholly regain the initiative. This happened in 279 BC, yet sixty years later (217/216 BC) we find Hannibal using 2,000 cattle with burning torches attached to their horns, accompanied by spearmen, capturing the saddle of a mountain and, in so doing, diverting the Romans away from the pass they were guarding (*Pol.* III.93–94). The result was that Hannibal's army passed unscathed through the pass and on the following day was able to relieve those of their men still at the saddle.

The reader must decide whether this idea was the product of coincidence or study.

APPENDIX 1

JASON OF PHERAE

Mention needs to be made of this personality, who only appears briefly within the main text. At *Hell*. VI.i.4–19 Polydamas of Pharsalus comes to Sparta as a supplicant ally to ask for help against Jason's threat to take control of the city and thereby complete his control over all Thessaly. The Spartans, embroiled on several fronts against Thebes and Athens, did not have the specific qualitative manpower available to offer help against a man who had a highly trained mercenary army as the core of his power together with the available forces from the cities under his control. At a review of his available strength it is stated that he could put into the field more than 8,000 cavalry; 20,000 hoplites and innumerable peltasts. He is described as being an honourable man and an extremely capable general. He annexed part of Macedonia and was reputed to have Epirus as a client state. He was in the process of bringing further neighbouring states under his control when he was assassinated in 370 BC.

Jason was reputed to have had as his goal the subjugation of Persia but this may have been an echo of the writer's desire and that of others of his time, for a Panhellenic expedition of revenge against Persia. The more likely scenario can be seen from Jason's acts following Leuktra. At the close of the immediate hostilities it was far from clear that all was at an end. The remainder of the unengaged Spartan army was intact and the knowledge that a further relieving army from Sparta would soon be on its way led the Thebans to send first to the Athenians and then to Jason who was campaigning in neighbouring Phokis. Theban desires to destroy the remainder of the Spartan army were disappointed by Athens. The Theban plan for Jason with his mercenaries to attack the Spartan army from high positions while they made the frontal assault, was rejected by Jason. He negotiated the truce and the Spartans withdrew. Both sides were then obligated to him and he maintained for a time the need for Thebes to be concerned with matters to the south rather than to the north. On his return to Thessaly he captured and destroyed Herakleia which controlled the pass of Thermopylae and the route south. This could have been the prelude to a planned expansion of Jason's direct power through Lokris to Boeotia and perhaps to the establishment of control over most Greek states. What his intentions were will never be known for he was dead within the year.

APPENDIX 2

SIEGE WARFARE
AND FORTIFICATIONS

It was preferable to Greeks to take a city by deception rather than to invest it with a siege. A city could fall because its antagonist held control over the surrounding territory, thereby depriving its population of a sustainable food supply. This did not work in the case of Athens in the Peloponnesian War because of its maritime ascendancy for much of the conflict. It was only when Sparta cut off its corn supply by control of the Hellespont and effected a naval and land blockade that Athens was starved into submission. Sieges were expensive in resources and in manpower.

A hoplite, whose role was designed for close order fighting, was unsuited to an assault of a fortification. Such an action would have called for more open order arrangements. The hoplite defence as an individual combatant was alarmingly diminished from that which he had as a member of a phalanx. Ravaging the enemy's countryside could sometimes provoke a battle, a preferable state of affairs to the conduct of a siege.

Fifth century fortifications reflect this and rely on a simple city wall which would act as an impediment to hoplites. Walls protecting a city's connection with its port were built at Corinth and notably between Athens and the Piraeus. Early in the fourth century square towers were built at intervals along walls which now encompassed those areas of the city which had hitherto been undefended. These towers allowed missile attacks to be made on the flank of any attacker. Sparta was the notable exception in that the city had no physical defences whatsoever. Even on the occasions of Theban assault they relied on the bravery of their limited manpower.

Siege technology was known as is demonstrated by the siege which Sparta conducted against Plataea between 429 and 427 BC and the unsuccessful Athenian siege of Syracuse in 416 BC. The latter failed because Nikias did not complete the northern, containing wall foolishly believing that the Syracusans would capitulate. This allowed the relieving general sent by Sparta to enter

Syracuse without problem and organise the building of a wall out to Labdalum over the plateau of Epipolae thereby threatening the Athenian flank.

Plataea proved to be a protracted affair. The Spartan attackers built an earth ramp and the defenders built their wall higher in response. Further, they sapped the ramp withdrawing earth from underneath so that the Spartans were constantly having to bring up new materials to sustain its height. Another wall was built by the Plataeans facing that section of their wall which was under threat. Battering rams had their tips broken by timbers dropped from above. Finally an attempt to burn the city was foiled by an unexpected storm. At that point the Spartans desisted from attempts to take the city by storm and settled to the waiting game of starving the inmates into submission. To do this they constructed double fortifications around the city. These had turrets and were crenellated and the Spartans took their position between so that they would have a defence against any possible relief force from Athens. Some Plataeans were successful in capturing and holding a section of this double wall long enough for almost two hundred to escape. However, hunger took its toll and the remaining defenders surrendered. The fact that they were killed to a man rather than enslaved was at Theban insistence in reprisal for an earlier massacre of a Theban force which, having infiltrated the city with the intent of capture, were tricked on discovery by the Plataeans with the promise of safe conduct.

So it is that within the first half of the fourth century sieges were rare and preference was given to ravaging the enemies' territory as a less expensive and possibly more profitable means of prosecuting a war.

Not that fortified places were ignored, rather, a simpler solution to one of siege was sought. A typical example was the investiture of Mantineia by the Spartans not wholly covered in the main text. This followed a period of ill-feeling between the cities, hitherto allies. Sparta called for the demolition of Mantineia's walls and when refused, laid waste the neighbouring countryside, dug a ditch and built a wall around the city (385 BC). Becoming aware that the city was well provisioned and fearful that a long siege would ensue, Agesipolis dammed the river which flowed through the city at the point at which it had its outflow. This resulted in a flood which covered the lower courses of the housing and the city walls. As the lower courses disintegrated the closest section of the wall achieved a state of collapse and the Mantineians agreed to take down their walls and disperse their population into villages.

APPENDIX 3

ECONOMIC WARFARE

P rior to the Peloponnesian War the threat of depredation to an enemy's territory usually led to battle. The meeting of heralds, the agreement on the locality for the coming conflict, the clear-cut nature and acceptance of its outcome and the limited loss in manpower are all classic features of hoplite warfare.

In the prolonged attrition of that war the economic issue eventually became the deciding factor. From the irritations of the yearly plundering carried out by the Spartans in Attica and the Athenian raids on the coastline of Lakonia, the strategy of Lysander eventually brought an end to the war. By control of the sea against a city dependent on its maritime power, food supplies were denied to Athens.

To enlarge on Endnote 11 of Part Two, where issue is taken with a conclusion in Hanson's *Warfare and Agriculture In Classical Greece*. On the depredation of crops, the matter comes down to a question of degree. Was the action one of provocation or of serious intent to cause lasting economic damage? That there was a difference is beyond doubt. The former, in terms of minor spoilation was sometimes enough to provoke a state to come to armed conflict following an initial reluctance to do so, and such provocation can be termed tactical. The latter had more serious intent at both tactical and strategic level. That intent was often not merely to defeat an enemy in the field but also to bring him firmly under control.

Taking a practical approach to the matter one has only to look to the lesson of the changes in agricultural methods in Greece in recent times. It was only some years after entry into the Common Market that tractors became commonplace in the country, much to the regret of archaeologists concerned with the damage done by the increased depth of tilling to, as yet, uncovered evidence. It was a common practice for Greeks to buy second-hand tractors from England and Germany well into the early 1990s and the habit is still not unusual. Indeed, a mere ten years ago it was not uncommon to see families tending their *stremata* with what can only be described as short-handled mattocks. This form of 'hand' tilling and weeding was little changed from the methods used at the time of our present concern. The activity had to be constant in the growing season to prevent weeds from encroaching and smothering growing crops. Therefore regular visits had to be made to the growing area to keep the land weed-free and to ensure adequate irrigation of spring water where necessary. Denial of access to the growing area could lead to a reduction or failure in grain and vegetable crops. Such denial could be achieved by an army in the area. An army of a few hundred, let alone thousands, could destroy great areas of produce merely by marching over the terrain. With long term crops such as those fruits gown on trees, it has already been pointed out in the endnote that the felling of trees was totally unnecessary. An army on the move could, with successive ranks, denude a tree of blossom, of partly-formed or of fully-formed fruit, depending on the season. Such an army need only to have moved through an area once in the growing season to ruin annual crops such as fruit and olives, and at intervals for those ground crops which could be resown. Having seen areas of agricultural land in Greece subject to neglect for other reasons than war over the course of a season it is clear to me that denial of access and depredation of growing crops on a large scale could lead to economic hardship if extended beyond one season. In the retrieval of an area neglected for a season there is the additional problem that the prevalent weeds have seeded. This sets back the 'cleanliness' of the area. It takes more than two seasons of attention to bring it back to the standard it held prior to the period of neglect. Any surplus which had been built up would soon be used. The reliance thereafter on supplies from neighbouring friendly states would have had its own limitations, not least that of the common treasury and the fear of reprisals from the agressor felt by the donor states.

In terms of animal husbandry, the capture of herds of cattle which was an additional problem for Akarnania, would have led to a breeding problem and loss of standard if prolonged beyond one season. Agesilaos was astute in his comments on the matter to the Achaeans when they expressed their initial dissatisfaction with his first season's activities on their behalf.

Raiding, which had hitherto only been an annoyance, was therefore developed as a tactic by which an enemy could be brought to heel. These raids, however, were conducted often with relatively large forces. The period under review calls several such events to our attention, those of Agesilaos against the Akarnanians and the Thebans in particular proved highly effective. The latter probably gave Epameinondas the idea for his overall strategy against Sparta following Leuktra. His great achievement was not the mere winning of battles, but the prolonged use of the initiative he had won over the Spartans as a result of Leuktra.

With Sparta on the defensive he detached her former allies and in successive invasions brought fear to the heart of the city itself. By freeing Messenia he further deprived Spartan society of its economic base. The establishment of the cities of Messene and Megalopolis and the refortification of Mantineia led to the encirclement of Sparta so that the economic stranglehold could be sustained.

MAIN CHARACTERS

Agesilaos	King of Sparta of the Europontidai from 398 to 350 BC. A highly successful general, campaigning against Tissaphernes in Asia Minor, defeating the Thebans, Athenians and their allies at Koroneia and sustaining the Spartan Hegemony until his royal colleague's defeat at Leuktra. Thereafter he tried to revive his country's fortunes, even serving as a mercenary general in Egypt where he died in his early eighties.
Agesipolis (1)	King of Sparta of the senior house, the Agiadai, from 394 to 380 BC.
Agesipolis (2)	King of Sparta of the Agiadai from 371 to 370 BC.
Alkibiades	Gifted Athenian general during the Peloponnesian War whose astonishing career saw him avoiding a trial in Athens for impiety by fleeing to Sparta, where he gave military advice to his one-time enemies. Eventually he fell under suspicion there and this, together with the personal animosity of King Agis, led him to be sentenced to death. He fled to the Persian Tissaphernes from where he was given amnesty and recalled to the service of Athens once more.
Anaxibios	Spartan general who was killed in an ambush set for his forces by Iphikrates.
Archidamos	Son of Agesilaos. King of Sparta from 360 to 338 BC. He succeeded his father Agesilaos. Commanded the relieving army after Leuktra and played a vital role in the defence of Sparta. Victor of the Tearless Battle. Later went to fight in support of Lyctos in Crete, thereafter to Italy to fight for Sparta's ex-colony Taras against the Lucanians.
Ariaios	Commander of Kyros the Younger's Asiatic troops.
Artaxerxes	King of Persia and elder brother of Kyros the Younger.
Brasidas	Gifted Spartan general of the Peloponnesian War.

Cheirisophos	General of the vanguard for much of the *Anabasis*.
Derdas	Ruler of Elimia and excellent cavalry commander who served in the Olynthian campaigns under Teleutias.
Derkilidas	Spartan general who served in Asia Minor.
Epameinondas	Boeotarch of Thebes on several occasions. The victor at Leuktra. A great general and tactical innovator. His successive campaigns brought about the reduction of Sparta from the position of a great power. His death at Second Mantineia saw the end of Theban Hegemony.
Eteonikos	One of the garrison officers at Byzantion.
Iphikrates	Athenian general responsible for the defeat of the Spartans at Lechaion. He revolutionised the training and deployment of peltasts.
Jason of Pherae	Tagus of Thessaly. Mediated after Leuktra. One of the most powerful men in Greece whose career was cut short by assassination.
Klearchos	An exiled Spartan who served as commander-in-chief of the Greeks in Kyros the Younger's attempt to gain the throne of Persia. A very able commander who was treacherously done to death by Tissaphernes.
Kleombrotos	King of Sparta of the Agiadai House from 380 to 371 BC. Killed in the Battle of Leuktra.
Konon	Athenian naval commander. Lost his fleet at Aegospotami. Victor of the Battle of Knidos. Rebuilt the Long Walls at Athens.
Lysander	Spartan land and naval commander. Victor at the battle of Notium and captor of the Athenian fleet at Aegospotami. With the blockade of Athens he effectively ended the Peloponnesian War. He accompanied Agesilaos on the expedition to Asia Minor. Displaying uncharacteristic bravado he lost his life in action at Haliartos.
Marcellus	A Roman Consul and general reputedly admired by Hannibal. A competent commander who sought to limit the movements of his Carthaginian opponent. In charge of the fleet at the siege of Syracuse. He later lost his life when ambushed on reconnaissance.
Mnasippos	Spartan naval commander who conducted an expedition against Kerkyra in which he was killed.

Neon	Deputy commander to Cheirisophos (*Anabasis*).
Orontas (1)	A Persian in the army of Kyros the Younger who was executed for treachery.
Orontas (2)	Subordinate satrap or governor of the province of Armenia. Married to one of the Great King's daughters.
Pausanias (1)	Spartan Regent who commanded the Greek land forces who had not medised at the Battle of Plataea in 479 BC.
Pausanias (2)	Spartan king of the Agiadai who ruled from 408 to 394 BC before being exiled on two counts: for not arriving at Haliartos at the same time as Lysander as agreed, and for virtually admitting defeat for the Spartans by claiming the bodies of the fallen under truce.
Pelopidas	Another great Theban general and a direct contemporary and friend of Epameinondas. Instrumental in the defeat of the Spartans at Leuktra. His campaigns were mainly to the north of Thebes and are not covered by Xenophon's history. The lesson learned from his victory at Tegyra laid the foundation for future Theban tactics.
Pharnabazos	Persian satrap of the Hellespontine area who gave support to the Spartans during the Peloponnesian war.
Phoibidas	Spartan general who captured Thebes by a ruse. Killed in pursuit of Theban forces after their abortive attack on Thespiae.
Rhathines	One of Pharnabazos' generals.
Scipio Africanus	Eventual Roman victor at Zama over Hannibal.
Seuthes	King of Thrace who enagaged the services of the mercenary Ten Thousand to prosecute his wars.
Sokrates	Greek philosopher. Teacher of Plato and Xenophon. Forced to take his own life by hemlock by the Oligarchy in Athens.
Sphodrias	Spartan governor of Thespiae who made the infamous and impossible attempt to march overland during the night to capture Piraeus. The originator of the scheme is still a matter of conjecture.
Spithridates	One of Pharnabazos' generals.
Teleutias	Brother of Agesilaos. A well loved commander of both land and sea forces. Conducted a very successful sea campaign against the Athenians in which he gained control of the seas

	around Attica. He was killed in one of his northerly land campaigns against Olynthos.
Thibron	Spartan commander to whom Xenophon passed over his men at the end of their journey. Thibron was conducting a restricted war against the Persians.
Tiribazos	Persian satrap of western Armenia.
Tissaphernes	Persian satrap and one of the senior generals in the Great King's army.

CHRONOLOGY

411	Athenian sea victory over Spartans at Kynossema
410	Athenian naval victory at Kyzicos
408	Cyrus the Younger appointed to rule Persia's western provinces
	Lysander takes command of the Spartan fleet
407	Alkibiades is welcomed back to Athens
406	Alkibiades appointed admiral of Athenian fleet
	Spartans win the sea battle of Notion while Alkibiades is absent
	Athenian sea victory over Spartans at Arginousai
	Athenian commanders tried and executed for neglect in picking up survivors at Arginousai
405	Lysander defeats Konon at sea battle of Aigospotamoi
404	Death of Darius II and the succession of Artaxerxes II
	Blockade and surrender of Athens to Lysander
	Destruction of Long Walls
	Pro-Spartan oligarchy set up in Athens
	Thrasyboulos leading Athenian exiles overthrows the Oligarchy
401–400	Kyros the Younger makes his attempt on the Persian throne. The Anabasis
400	Thibron prepares for operations against the Persians in support of the Ionian cities. He enrolls the survivors of the 'Ten Thousand'. Succeeded by Derkylidas
399	Trial and death of Sokrates
396	Agesilaos takes command with additional forces of the Persian campaign
	Persian monies given to Sparta's enemies resulting in the Corinthian War 395–386
395	Lysander killed at Haliartos
	Timokrates continues to disburse Persian subsidies to those opposing Sparta
394	Spartan victory at the Nemea. Recall of Agesilaos to Greece

253

364   Pelopidas dies in his successful action against Alexander of Pherae
        at Kynoskephalai
        Slaughter by Thebans of all male citizens in Orchomenos
        Establishment of navy by Thebans

363   A schism appears in the Arkadian Federation
        Tegea and the recently founded Megalopolis remained in alliance
        with Thebes. Mantineia and her surrounding settlements appeal to
        Sparta and Athens

362   Second battle of Mantineia. Epameinondas is killed

BATTLE OF KOUNAXA

Phase 1

Note the Greeks' position with the river on their right flank

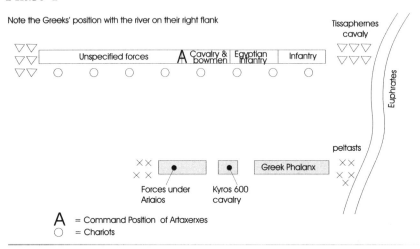

A = Command Position of Artaxerxes
○ = Chariots

Phase 2

[Chariots were ineffectual]

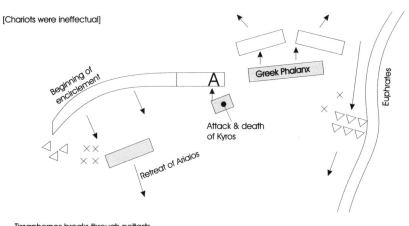

Tissaphernes breaks through peltasts.
The Greek phalanx was victorious on its wing.
Ariaios is forced to retire as the attempted encirclement begins.

Phase 3

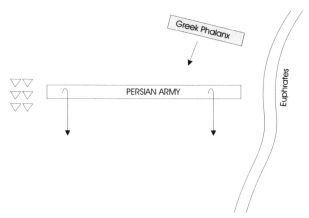

After pursuing Ariaios, capturing the Greek camp, and being rejoined by the successful Tissaphernes, Artaxerxes turns to meet the returning Greek phalanx. Both armies faced each other in a direction opposite to that in which the battle began. The Persians took to flight before contact.

BATTLE OF NEMEA

Phase 1

Possibly 25 deep

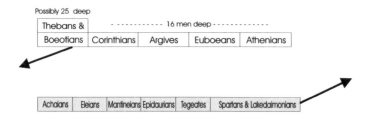

Thebans & Boeotians	Corinthians	Argives	Euboeans	Athenians

- - - - - - - - - - - 16 men deep - - - - - - - - - - - -

Achaians	Eleians	Mantineians	Epidaurians	Tegeates	Spartans & Lakedaimonians

Both right wings make purposeful moves to the right to achieve an outflanking of the opposition.

Phase 2

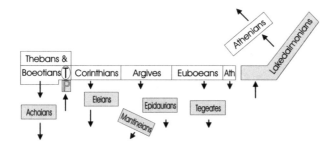

P = Men from Pellene who fought valiantly and slowed the advance of the Thespian contingent.
T = Thespians

Phase 3

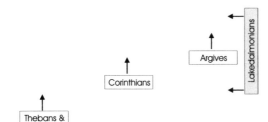

Destroyed forces of returning
Euboeans & Athenians although
total fatalities were few.

The sweep from right to left over the battlefield gave the Spartans the
opportunity to take the enemy contingents in flank as they returned from
the pursuit of the Spartan allies.

Most casualties were sustained by Argives, Corinthinians and Boeotians.

BATTLE OF KORONEIA

Phase 1

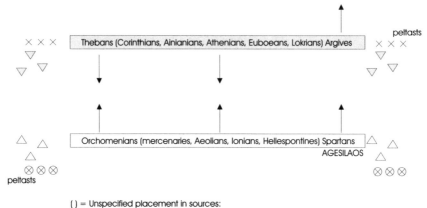

peltasts

Thebans (Corinthians, Ainianians, Athenians, Euboeans, Lokrians) Argives

Orchomenians (mercenaries, Aeolians, Ionians, Hellespontines) Spartans
AGESILAOS

peltasts

( ) = Unspecified placement in sources:
only wing dispositions are given

Phase 2

a) The Thebans defeat the Orchomenians and go on to plunder Agesilaos' camp.

b) Elsewhere all the forces in Agesilaos' phalanx are victorious.

c) The Argives flee before contact.

Phase 3

A countermarch brings Agesilaos' phalanx into line

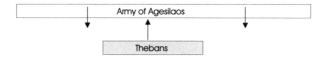

Army of Agesilaos

Thebans

Both sides now face each other in the opposite direction.

Phase 4

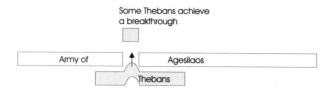

Significant carnage in this phase. Agesilaos is wounded.

It is noted that the Thebans adopted an unusually compact formation for their phalanx, the depth of which is unknown.

BATTLE OF LEUKTRA

Phase 1

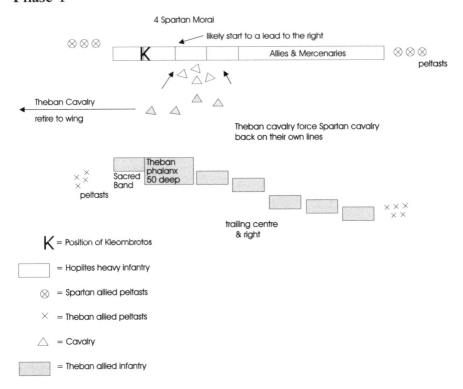

4 Spartan Morai

likely start to a lead to the right

K   Allies & Mercenaries

peltasts

Theban Cavalry
retire to wing

Theban cavalry force Spartan cavalry
back on their own lines

peltasts

Sacred
Band

Theban
phalanx
50 deep

trailing centre
& right

K = Position of Kleombrotos

= Hoplites heavy infantry

⊗ = Spartan allied peltasts

✕ = Theban allied peltasts

△ = Cavalry

= Theban allied infantry

Phase 2

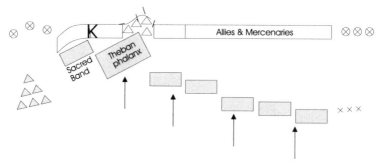

At the double, the Sacred Band pins down the Spartan lead to right.
Theban phalanx smashes into Spartan line already in disorder from its own cavalry.
Kleombrotos' initial order to lead to the right was not known to the line and indecision occurred.

Phase 3

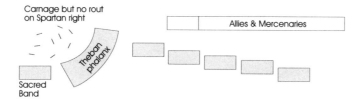

Death of Kleombrotos but Spartan resistance permits his body to be taken
from the field.
Spartan centre & left unable to assist their right wing threatened as they are by the Boiotian
centre and trailing right.

Battle of Second Mantineia 362 BC

Phase 1

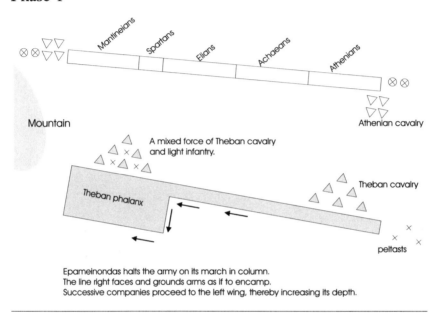

Mountain

Athenian cavalry

Theban cavalry

peltasts

A mixed force of Theban cavalry and light infantry.

Epameinondas halts the army on its march in column.
The line right faces and grounds arms as if to encamp.
Successive companies proceed to the left wing, thereby increasing its depth.

Phase 2

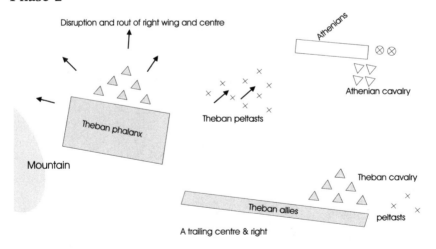

Disruption and rout of right wing and centre

Athenians

Athenian cavalry

Theban peltasts

Mountain

Theban cavalry

peltasts

A trailing centre & right

Phase 3

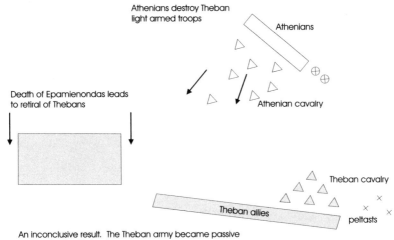

Athenians destroy Theban
light armed troops

Athenians

Death of Epamienondas leads
to retiral of Thebans

Athenian cavalry

Theban cavalry

Theban allies

peltasts

An inconclusive result. The Theban army became passive
on the death of its leader.
The Athenians were victorious in their sector.

Battle of Thymbrara (Fictional)

Phase 1

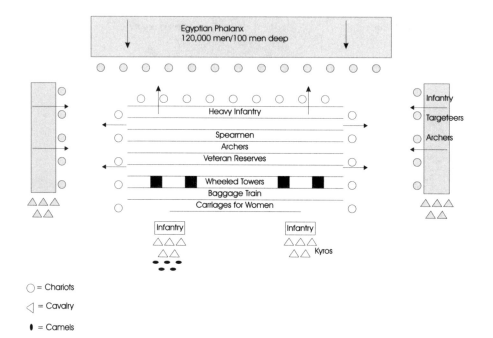

= Chariots

= Cavalry

= Camels

The dense 'tile' shape of Kyros' army is encircled by the open 'tile' formation of the wings and centre of his opposition.

Phase 2

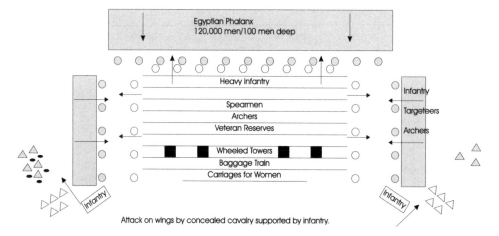

Attack on wings by concealed cavalry supported by infantry.

Phase 3

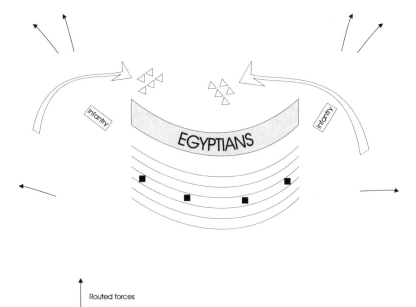

Routed forces

Dispersal of wings after attack in flank.
Kyros' centre buckles under weight of Egyptian phalanx.
Beginning of encirclement.

Phase 4

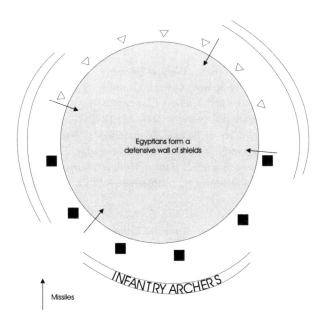

Egyptians form a
defensive wall of shields

INFANTRY ARCHERS

Missiles

SELECT BIBLIOGRAPHY

Anderson, J.K., *Military Theory and Practice in the Age of Xenophon* (University of California Press, Berkeley, 1970).

Anderson, J.K., *Xenophon* (Duckworth, London, 1974).

Andrewes, A.A., 'The Generals of the Hellespont', *Journal of Hellenic Studies*, 73 (1953).

Barry, W.D., 'Roof Tiles and Urban Violence in the Ancient World', *Greek, Roman and Byzantine Studies*, 37(1) (1996) pp. 55–74.

Bodil, D., *The Cyropaedia: Xenophon's Aims and Methods* (Aarhus University Press, Aarhus, 1989).

British Army Doctrine publications ((restricted), Ministry of Defence, 1994).

Bruce, I.A.F., *An Historical Commentary on the Hellenica Oxyrhynchia* (CUP, Cambridge, 1967).

Buck, R., *Boiotia and the Boiotian League 432–371* (University of Alberta, Edmonton, Alberta, 1994).

Buckler, J., *The Theban Hegemony 371–362* (Harvard University Press, Cambridge, MA, 1980).

Buckler, J., 'Epameinondas and the *Embolon*', *Phoenix* 39 (1985).

Cartledge, P., *Agesilaos and the Crisis of Sparta* (Duckworth, London, 1987).

Cartledge, P., 'Hoplites and heroes', *Journal of Hellenic Studies*, 97 (1977).

Cawkwell, G.L., Introduction to *The Persian Expedition*, translated by R. Warner, (Penguin, London, 1972).

Cawkwell, G.L., 'Agesilaos and Sparta', *Classical Quarterly* 31 (1981) pp. 69–83.

Cawkwell, G.L. 'The Decline of Sparta', *Classical Quarterly* 33 (1983) pp. 385–400.

Cawkwell, G.L., 'Epameinondas and Thebes', *Classical Quarterly* 22 (1972).

David, E., *Sparta between Empire and Revolution 404–243 BC* (Ayer, Salem, NH, 1981).

Devine, A.M., 'Embolon: a Study in Tactical Terminology', *Phoenix* 37 (1983).

Dillon, M., *Pilgrims and Pilgrimage in Ancient Greece* (Routledge, London, 1997).

du Picq, Col. A., *Battle Studies* (Stackpole Books, Mechanicsburg, PA, 1987).

Ehrhardt, C., 'Xenophon and Diodoros on Aegospotami', *Phoenix* 24 (1970) pp. 225–8.

Forrest, W.G., *A History of Sparta 950–192 B.C.* (Norton, New York, 1968).

Gera, D.L., *Xenophon's 'Cyropaedia' Style, Genre and Literary Technique* (Clarendon Press, Oxford, 1993).

Goodman, M.G. & Holladay, A.J., 'Religious Scruples in Ancient Warfare', *Classical Quarterly* 36 (1986).

Gray, V.J., *The Character of Xenophon's Hellenica* (Duckworth, London, 1989).

Gray, V.J., 'Dialogue in Xenophon's Hellenica', *Classical Quarterly* 31 (1981) pp. 321–34.

Gray, V.J., 'The years 375–371 BC: a Case Study in the Reliability of Diodorus Siculus and Xenophon', *Classical Quarterly* 30 (1980) pp. 306–26.

Hamilton, C.D., *Agesilaos and the Failure of Spartan Hegemony* (Cornell University Press, Ithaca, NY, 1991).

Hanson, V. (ed.), *Hoplites: The Classical Greek Battle Experience* (Routledge, New York & London, 1991).

Hanson, V., *Warfare and Agriculture in Classical Greece* (Giardini, Pisa, 1983; University of California Press, Berkeley, CA, 1998).

Hanson, V., *The Western Way of War. Infantry Battle in Classical Greece* (Hodder & Stoughton, London, 1989. Reprinted in paperback by University of California Press, Berkeley, 2000).

Hindley, C., 'Eros and Military Command in Xenophon', *Classical Quarterly* 44 (1994) p. 347ff.

Holladay, A.J., 'Hoplites and heresies', *Journal of Hellenic Studies* 102 (1982) pp. 94–103.

Hornblower, S., *The Greek World 479–323 BC* (Methuen, London, 1983).

Kagan, D., *On the Origins of War And The Preservation of Peace* (Doubleday, New York, 1995).

Keegan, J., *A History of Modern Warfare* (Hutchinson, London, 1993).

Keegan, J., *The Mask of Command* (Viking, NY, 1987; Penguin, London, 1988).

Kelly, D.H., 'Agesilaos' strategy in Asia Minor 396–395 BC', *Liverpool Classical Monthly* 3 (1978) pp. 97–8.

Krentz, P., *Hellenika I–II.3.10 and II.3.11–IV.2.8* (Aris & Philips Ltd., Warminster, 1989 & 1995).

Krentz, P., 'The Salpinx in Greek Battle', in V. Hanson (ed.), *Hoplites: The Classical Greek Battle Experience* (Routledge, London, 1994).

Lazenby, J.F., *The Spartan Army* (Aris and Philips Ltd., Warminster, 1985).

Lazenby, J.F., 'Logistics in Classical Greek Warfare', in *War in History* (eds. H. Strachan and D. Showalter, 1(1) (Edward Arnold, London, 1994), pp. 3–18.

Lengauer, W., *Greek Commanders in the Fifth and Fourth Centuries BC* (Study Antiqua, Warsaw, 1979).

Marsden, E.W., *The Campaign of Gaugamela* (University of Liverpool Press, Liverpool, 1964).

Nussbaum, G.B., 'The Ten Thousand' in E.J. Jonkers (ed.), *Social and Economic Commentaries on Classical Texts* (E.J. Brill, Leiden, 1967).

Perlman, S., 'The Causes and Outbreak of the Corinthian War', *Classical Quarterly* 14 (1964).

Pritchett, W.K., *The Greek State at War I–V* (University of California Press, Berkeley, 1971–1991).

Pritchett, W.K., *Studies in Ancient Greek Topography* (University of California Press, Berkeley, 1965 (ongoing, but particularly part IV, 'Passes')).

Rice, D.G., 'Agesilaus, Agesipolis, and Spartan politics, 386–379 BC', *Historia* 23 (1974) pp. 164–82.

Sage, M.M., *Warfare in Ancient Greece* (Routledge, London, 1996).

Seager, R., 'Thrasybulus, Conon and Athenian Imperialism 396–386 BC', *Journal of Hellenic Studies* 87 (1967).

Sealey, R. *A History of the Greek City-States 700–338 BC* (University of California Press, Berkeley, 1976).

Shipley, D.R., *A Commentary on Plutarch's Life of Agesilaos* (OUP, Oxford, 1997).

Snodgrass, A.M., *Arms and Armour of the Greeks* (Cornell University Press, Ithaca, NY, 1967).

Spence, I.G., *The Cavalry of Classical Greece* (Clarendon Press, Oxford, 1995).

Stronk, J.P., 'The Ten Thousand in Thrace: An Archaeological and Historical Commentary on Xenophon's Anabasis', in *Classical Monographs, Vol. II* (Gieben, Amsterdam, 1995).

Sun Tzu, 'The Art of War' (foreword by Prof. Norman Stone) (Wordsworth Editions, London, 1993).

Sun Tzu, 'The Art of War' (foreword by J. Clavell) (Hodder & Stoughton, London, 1981).

Tatum, J., *Xenophon's Imperial Fiction* (Princeton University Press, Princeton, 1989).

Tritle, L.A., (ed.) *The Greek World in the Fourth Century* (Routledge, London, 1997).

Tuplin, C.J., *The Failings of Empire: a reading of Xenophon's Hellenica 2.3.11–7.5.27* (Franz Steiner, Stuttgart, 1993).

Tuplin, C.J., 'Education and Fiction in Xenophon's Cyropaedia' in A.H. Sommerstein & C. Atherton (eds), *Education in Greek Fiction* (Levante, Bari, 1997).

Tuplin, C.J., 'Xenophon, Sparta and Cyropaedia,' in A. Powell & S. Hodkinson (eds), *The Shadow of Sparta* (Routledge, London, for the Classical Press of Wales, 1994).

Underhill, G.E., *A Commentary on the Hellenica of Xenophon* (Clarendon Press, Oxford, 1900).

Vaughn, P., 'The Identification and Retrieval of the Hoplite Dead,' in V. Hanson (ed.), *Hoplites: The Classical Greek Battle Experience* (Routledge, London, 1991).

Wheeler, E.L., 'The Origins of Military Theory in Ancient Greece and China', in *Acta 5* (Bucharest, 1980).

Zaidman, I.B. & Pantel, P.S., *Religion in the Ancient Greek City*, translated by P. Cartledge, (CUP, Cambridge, 1992).

INDEX

Historical Names in the Text

271